ADD VALUE · INSPIRE OTHERS · CHANGE THE WORLD

THE FIVE INSIGHTS
OF ENDURING LEADERS

Bristlecone Learning Press
135 Country Center Drive
Suite B5, PMB 225
Pagosa Springs, CO 81147

FIRST EDITION

"The Enduring Leader" is a trademark of Bristlecone Learning, LLC.

Grateful acknowledgement for the following copyrighted material:

"Further Along the Road Less Traveled," ©1993 by M. Scott Peck reprinted with permission of Simon and Schuster Adult Publishing Group.

Quote from "The Passion Plan at Work: Building a Passion-Driven Organization," ©2001 by Richard Y. Chang reprinted with permission of John Wiley & Sons, Inc.

"Show the Way," words and lyrics by David Wilcox, ©1994, used by permission, Irving Music Inc. and Midnight Ocean Bonfire Music. All Rights Administered by Irving Music, Inc. All Rights Reserved.

Edited by Cristina Opdahl
Cover, interior design and chapter graphics by Shan Wells
The text was set in Minon Pro
Graphics by Al Lewis
Outward Bound graphics, courtesy Outward Bound, USA

Library of Congress Cataloging-in-Publication Data
Library of Congress Control Number: 2006909907
Morris, Jim, 1958-
The Five Insights of Enduring Leaders — Add Value • Inspire Others • Change the World / by Jim Morris
Includes bibliographical notes and index.
158'.4
p. 325   cm. 23.49
ISBN 0-9790257-0-2

1. Psychology 2. Leadership 3. Self-Improvement 3. Business 4. Management 5. Morris, Jim

For T – Thanks, mean it.
For Jess – Tomorrow is yours. On belay.

CONTENTS

FOREWORD

Good people:

Read this book as if your future depends on it. It very well might. After all, you're either growing or you're stagnating. Wouldn't you rather grow? *The Five Insights* provides interesting perspective and is a helpful book. There's only one problem: it's a book.

Nothing against Jim or anything, but I really haven't seen a lot of good personal growth or leadership coming from just reading a book. That is, unless the reading is accompanied by some genuine action: deep personal introspection and experimentation with new behaviors out in the real world.

A good time to start experimenting with new approaches to leadership would be right now. Immediately. I hope you will. All of us in the various groups we find ourselves—in the private sector, the public sector, schools, non-profits—we're all in great need of authentic, enduring leadership—now. O.K., so it's a book, but it can help if…

…if you are willing to go to work—on yourself. Real leadership starts with amazing self-awareness.

You'll gather value from *The Five Insights* most when you're ready to lace up your boots and take an extended journey into yourself. This book provides a mirror to see yourself more clearly along the way. To make the most of the journey, share your discoveries and create a dialogue (about you) with some close friends and family members.

The best leaders I've met, in more than two decades of leadership development work, are those who are constantly checking in with, and learning from, a range of people. They have a refined ability to neatly adapt to nearly any situation and to create an impact that inspires people to come along and add their own unique contributions.

And why do we really need better leaders? Because, fundamentally our survival depends on it… it always has! The ability to identify new opportunities, socially, politically and economically AND to inspire others to create new outcomes based on those opportunities is one of the most important and fundamental differences between the human species and all other forms of life.

We are custom built to solve problems and manage sophisticated social interaction because of our rather large brains and our exceptional communication skills. Those individuals who can combine these two advantages are the best leaders.

In this paradigm, leadership is about capitalizing on the abundance of possibility. It's about combining diverse perspectives and generating unique solutions from an endless sea of opportunity, not competing to be first to get the best of a scarce set of options.

Leadership today and in the future requires a generative mindset, not a reactive impulse.

I have worked with Jim Morris in a variety of settings, most recently at IDEO where we are exploring the value of truth as an essential component of problem solving. When I call him, I always pack a lunch. Nothing as big as the topic of leadership can be handled in a short conversation or codified in a simple model.

Leadership development is intensely personal and requires a coach who provides a combination of clarity, grounding, empathy, and a swift kick in the pants. Jim is the best of that kind of coach. Jim knows that learning to lead is a journey, not an event.

The writing in this book is based on Jim's experience making that journey possible and taking the trip—along with scores of people.

Jim is serious about helping people dig deeply into themselves. He's had countless one-on-one interactions with powerful, effective leaders and those who aspire to be better in this challenge. With *The Five Insights*, he's created a simple reflection tool and straightforward way to help you in your own self-assessment and personal development.

Simplicity aside, change is always challenging. Still, I know you're up to the task. As my favorite professor Charles F. Luna liked to say, "Things that matter are messy." How true. And sometimes getting messy matters. Like right now.

To take full advantage of *The Five Insights* you will eventually have to move from reflection to action and get messy with it. Think about it. What's the best way to discover and practice new ways of becoming your best self? Through experience. And experience is usually unpredictable because it involves other people and situations that are out of our control. Messy.

At IDEO, where we help people and organizations find innovative solutions to difficult problems, we depend on people who have the courage to ask difficult questions and to accept unique, creative, solutions. Yet these same people are humble enough to realize that the best solutions come from many people… not one superstar. They have the courage to try things out and see them fail so they can learn, move on, and try again with an improved approach… quickly. And they have the humility to approach each new problem with a naïve mind, not an expert's swagger. Courageous humility—an interesting paradox of leadership.

Learning about leading is an active process and a deeply personal endeavor that involves personal risk and courageous humility. It also promises to occasionally make you feel inadequate and uncomfortable along the way. If you fail to take the risk, fail to step up and try to help take care of the world, I think you actually face a much bigger danger—letting the world take care of you.

I challenge you to take the trip. Then, find a way to make your own difference in the world.

So get messy with it. We need you.

John Foster,
IDEO Head of Talent and Organization Development

INTRODUCTION

The Five Insights of Enduring Leaders began when I noticed that companies around the world consistently used different words but the same essential characteristics to describe their vision of a great leader. Diverse companies from biotech manufacturers to professional service firms were all looking for the same kinds of people to lead them—people who possess character traits that are as essential as they are tough to find.

Ask an executive or senior leader in most organizations to describe what the characteristics of a great leader are and you'll get your answer in an instant. Most lists include the universal qualities of any competent leader like "great business sense," "an excellent understanding of people" or "expertise in our markets." It is likely the list would also include "great motivator," "charismatic," or "the kind of person others are willing to follow"—characteristics often thought to be innate. These crucial qualities, it is believed, can't be taught. But do you really have to be born with them?

No. Just because something cannot be taught does not mean it cannot be learned. If you want to learn to lead, learn how to become a better leader, or help others to learn leadership, *The Five Insights of Enduring Leaders* is for all of you: active, interested learners and teachers alike.

Learning is an active process that may or may not involve a teacher. But learning does require a student who has to be actively interested in enriching, advancing or deepening him- or herself.

Most companies list a lot more than just five competencies when describing their picture of an ideal leader. It's a lengthy, diverse set of skills that is tough to categorize. But when I distilled the list, I found that the skills all fit into five key traits—innate gifts, hard to get, but absolutely vital characteristics of leaders. These unique gifts were so innate and so absolutely essential,

I began to call them insights. And when a leader has these five insights, in spite of other deficits or strengths, she is able to add significant value to her business. These leaders inspire and bring out the very best in those around them, and they have the means to change the world—at least their part of it—for the better. So I began to call this group of highly talented people enduring leaders. Their innate, overarching ability to lead is effective not just in a flash or in a moment, but over the long term.

This book is about these five insights, and how one may begin to acquire them. It is also about enduring leaders—how they act and behave, how they think and feel—and ultimately, how you too can become one.

My colleagues and I have used the five insights to help aspiring leaders develop the talents they need to move to the next level in their careers. We have successfully used the five insights again and again with senior executive teams in both the public and private sectors, with project leaders, and with high school football coaches who learned better ways to motivate players and strategize winning seasons. The program has been successfully applied to non-profit board leadership and to develop internal coaching models for organizational development departments, talent searches, leadership due diligence, and leadership interviewing.

Not too long ago, influential thought leaders in the field of leadership argued over who was right and who was wrong about how to develop a leader. Which approach works? Can leadership be learned or is it innate? Is it more reliant on education or personality? Is it more about business acumen or the ability to communicate? What I have learned is this: The magic of leadership lies not in whether someone is charismatic or a whiz at shrinking costs, but in his ability to connect these five essential insights in his own way.

Discovering the attributes that make leaders effective is straightforward. Finding ways to help people learn to embody them is daunting, but we are untangling new threads of understanding and discovering new pieces of the puzzle all the time.

The Five Insights of Enduring Leaders takes those tangled threads of leadership and weaves them into a tapestry that is simple, possible and usable for aspiring leaders and for those who want them to be successful. I believe enough research has been done on the subject of leadership to make sense of it. The problem with developing leaders isn't a lack of data, but a lack of perspective. *The Five Insights* brings that perspective into sharp focus so we can start growing leaders who can and will tackle the tough issues. These leaders will also add value, inspire others and ultimately change the world.

So let's get to work. We have lots to learn. And then, we have a world to change.

SECTION ONE
THE FIVE INSIGHTS

PART ONE
THE INSIGHTS OF ENDURING LEADERS

One of my favorite bosses and mentors of all time, irascible, saavy, and poignantly blunt Mike Muley, taught me a lot about leadership. As one of Mike's Program Directors for Outward Bound, I was struggling with a difficult political and personnel decision and was looking to Mike for advice, as I often did. I can still hear Mike in his immutable style holding forth on the secret of great leadership, something he took great joy in talking about:

> *James, just because you have lots of leadership experience doesn't amount to jack if you don't have character. Half of what I do, I do based on experience, just like you. The other half of what I do is what can't be seen, or read about or predicted. I have to—**you** have to—learn to make decisions when there is no right answer, when there is no good solution and when every option seems like the wrong option. That's when character enters the game. You got character, son?*

I figured if I didn't, I'd better develop some fast. I took Mike's challenge to heart more than he knew and, sadly, more than I could tell him before he died several short years later. And as my career progressed, I eventually took it a step further. I began an in-depth study of the hundreds of skills that most corporate chiefs believe their leaders need to have to be successful in business. When combined, these skills comprise what companies typically call their "Leadership Competency Model." Competency models are the backbone of the company's leadership development plan.

When a company decides to outsource leadership training, they hire firms like our firm, Bristlecone Learning, and we dutifully set about customizing a training based on their competency model. After about the fifth of our customized designs, my business partner, Betsey Upchurch, and I started to notice a pattern. Almost everyone was talking about the same set of competencies, but they were using different words to describe them.

We also noticed that each client had what we referred to as an "easy list" of competencies leaders needed to possess and a "hard list." The "easy list" consisted of skills such as business acumen and time management. These skills are vital to effective leadership but they aren't particularly hard to learn if one is motivated. The hard list, however, was different. It consisted of leadership traits like "inspires and motivates others" and "makes quick and conclusive decisions." The hard list included such elusive characteristics as "able to cope with and lead through ambiguity" and "expects excellence from self and others." "How do you teach this stuff?" I remember thinking. This is the stuff that we knew, and our clients knew, was impossible to learn in the context of a three or four day course or even in a year long course. But we also knew that learning the skills on the hard list was what really separated the wheat from the chaff when it came to being a great leader.

I set about analyzing these models and working to truly understand what made the hard list hard. I realized that what great and enduring leaders have can be distilled down to five essential components. I call these components the Five Insights.

An insight is more than a simple feature of personality or a trait or an innate ability. Insights are traits plus character plus how we show up to work every day, a state of mind, or "beingness." Affecting our beingness happens at a deep level inside our conscious and unconscious selves that is hard to access, but when we do, the results we produce can be profound.

Here is another way to think about it: Each of us is driven by a need to produce results. Whether we are trying to improve our skiing ability by executing a series of perfect turns or making an effort to change the way we are viewed by others, we tend to take action in the hope of achieving a result. Typically, we work to achieve that result by modifying our behavior. Yet our behaviors are more complicated than they seem on the surface. Our behaviors are the result of how we feel and think. If we feel anxious or afraid of losing control on a challenging ski run, that feeling will undoubtedly show up in our behavior. If we work to change the way we are viewed by others because we think we have to be popular to be successful, our thinking will also show up in our behavior, even if we try to mask it.

In other words, changing your behavior requires changing how you think. It requires becoming conscious of your unconscious. The five insights represent ways of thinking—of becoming conscious of your unconscious—that will revolutionize your leadership ability and your ability to mentor other leaders.

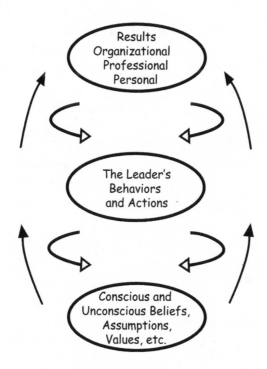

The Connection Between Results and Our Conscious
and Unconscious Thinking

THE LEADERSHIP CRISIS

There are more than five million aspiring leaders working for corporations and organizations in the United States today, yet virtually every industry from the high tech sector to the construction industry reports that the single greatest threat is a scarcity of qualified, capable leaders.

Corporations are spending more money than ever on leadership development, yet the failure rate of leaders— from middle managers to CEO's—is at an all-time high. The Five Insights proposes that the problem isn't the people, but how we prepare them.

A 2004 survey by the Corporate Leadership Council of 276 large companies revealed that less than 20% felt they had an effective leadership succession process. Most organizations report that the greatest long term threat to their success is a lack of successors to senior leadership positions. And the higher up the ladder the hire, the less effective we seem to be. According to the National Association of Corporate Directors, almost half of all American companies with revenues of $500 million or more have CEO succession practices that don't work.

Why is it so hard to find good people? Why do so many promotions or succession plans fail? Are we producing fewer qualified future leaders? Has there been a shift in how societies raise and educate children that results in fewer children who are capable of leading? Is it that existing leaders have become less competent at training and mentoring their replacements? Or is the problem due to how corporations and organizations operate?

The quest for finding, growing and promoting leaders is part of what is fueling the boom in executive level leadership training. To counter lagging results and increasingly competitive markets, corporations are investing huge amounts of money and time into the acquisition and development of effective leaders. By some estimates, U.S. businesses are spending upwards of $23 billion a year on formal leadership development. This number reflects leadership and executive level training for *existing* leaders, managers and executives, not students. The investment in dollars is probably minor compared to the lost opportunity cost that comes from CEO and senior executive turnover or from the time lost from productivity that comes from sending employees to training.[1] In spite of the billions they are spending on coaching, teambuilding, and other performance enhancing activities, organizations and businesses are still getting mixed results in terms of their ultimate goal: to help middle and senior level managers move up, do more, and do better.

Many companies send employees to expensive, pedigreed trainings for four or five days and hope that they gain skills that they can immediately begin to apply when they get back to work. Better still (usually) are internal corporate universities and training programs. These programs do a great job of delivering trainings that address current business issues tied to the overall strategy of the business and developing the technical skills of the employees, but the focus of these leadership development programs is only different, not better, than most of the off-site options available. All of these approaches are predicated on the notion that if we spend enough money and energy and send employees to the right kinds of trainings, prospective leaders will be more ready and more likely to lead. There are at least two problems with this thinking:

Instead of teaching what needs to be learned about leadership, businesses are teaching what they know how to teach. Managers and leaders are expecting people to learn and apply what is needed to be successful without much support and; aspiring leaders are looking for answers that work *now!*

Being successful in business is harder today than ever. Purchasing decisions by customers have become more complex. Cost competition has become more intense and the use of technology instead of people to solve business problems has led to a job market that favors specialization over well roundedness. Improvements in business processes have far outpaced increases in the number of people required to manage these increases resulting in a higher work load on everyone, particularly senior managers. The performance of most businesses is measured over an unrealistically short time period. The expectations for return on investment are particularly intense for publicly traded businesses that are beholden to shareholders and investors who expect steady quarterly improvement—sometimes at the expense of true, sustainable growth. For leaders and managers in these organizations who fear for their job security, the choice becomes clear: manage the processes, produce short term results, and take care of the people later.

We have created a spiral of diminished results managed and led by increasingly exhausted and frustrated people. We have more willing and motivated leaders than ever, but we aren't attracting them and we have too little time or energy to prepare them. We are working hard, but business conditions require us to focus on the wrong work. We are *doing* instead of *leading* and all we can hope to produce when we work like this is people who are prepared to do the same.

Overwhelmingly, the body of literature and research on leadership says it can be taught and developed *if* we work on developing the essential characteristics and competencies leaders need to possess. So if leadership *can be* taught and if so much time, attention and money has been focused on what makes a leader and how to develop it, what's the problem? Why is there a leadership crisis in businesses and organizations? Why are so few newly appointed or hired leaders effective? Why do so many middle managers fail? Why is it harder and harder to find qualified leaders the farther up the ladder we climb?

We have been teaching the right group of people, more or less, but we've been teaching them the wrong skills.

THE FIVE INSIGHTS

> *Insight (n): an innate ability that becomes effective*
> *when it is guided by character.*

We are more likely to change something when the change is easy to make than when it involves hard work, of course. But often in life it is the worthwhile changes that are the most difficult. So it is with the five insights. They are not easy, but through practice and time, they can be developed. When they are, you will notice a difference in the frequency and duration of the results you seek.

My research on competency models revealed that there are five universal requirements of leaders, without exception:

The Ability to See and Influence Systems:

The ability to see and understand the complex interactions of many components in a system and predict how they will interact as situations change. Competencies frequently connected with Seeing Systems include:

- Seeing the whole picture and prioritizing accordingly
- Utilizing good problem solving skills
- Utilizing existing capabilities and systems
- Developing systemic solutions to local problems
- Identifying when and where change is needed

Seeing and influencing systems takes the ability to tap into our intuition about the big picture and find workable, creative answers, so I also refer to this insight as *Perspective.*

The Confidence to Make a Difference:

Having the will and the confidence to see what needs doing and then do it. Confidence is important, but only when it is directed at a task or a need, hence the combination of "confidence" with "making a difference." Competencies frequently connected with the Confidence to Make a Difference include:

- Visualizing Success
- Creating and working towards a positive future
- Providing a clear vision for others
- Understanding current capabilities versus future needs
- Prioritizing accordingly
- Possessing vision
- Planning for the future
- Inspiring and motivating others
- Appropriately challenging others

At the heart of this insight is courage, and as you will see, I believe courage is best built through an orientation of service to others, so I also refer to this insight as *Courage through Service.*

Comfort with Complexity and Change:

The ability to lead while embracing complexity, ambiguity, and conflict. Life, people, and business are non-linear systems. Solutions to leadership problems are rarely absolute and frequently involve risk. Leaders who possess this trait address problems directly when necessary and don't shy away from discomfort and conflict. Competencies frequently connected with Comfort with Complexity and Change include:

- Makes quick and conclusive decisions
- Evaluates progress towards goals

- Prepares for and leads through change
- Understands change
- Manages complexity
- Comfortable with ambiguity
- Organizes complex tasks, projects or systems in a manner that leads to productive action

Learning to thrive in a changing world that is becoming increasingly complex takes both an understanding that everything changes always, and the ability to wrap ourselves around change when it occurs, so I also refer to this insight as *Faith and Agility.*

Self-Awareness and Personal Mastery:

The constellation of personality traits that allow leaders to consistently connect with people and themselves. Competencies frequently connected with Self-Awareness and Personal Mastery include:

- Holds self and others accountable
- Coaches and develops others
- Sees and promotes talents in self and others
- Embraces diversity
- Demonstrates credibility and integrity
- Builds consensus when needed
- Develops people networks
- Confronts and works through conflict

Self-Awareness and Personal Mastery begin with being awake and sensitive to what is going on around and inside us. This knowledge of self leads to better relationships with others, so I also refer to this insight as *Connection.*

Passion and Timing:

The love of achievement, service, success, and winning and the commitment to do whatever is necessary to go get it defines Passion. The ability to know when the time is right and, equally important, to know when it's not right to act, defines Timing. As we shall see, Passion and Timing by themselves are important skills, but combining them in how a leader works makes them an insight. Competencies frequently connected with Passion and Timing include:

- Taking responsibility for personal and team actions and results
- Recognizing the efforts and effectiveness of others
- Setting ambitious goals for the business
- Continuously seeking self-improvement
- Fostering a sense of urgency
- Expecting excellence from self and others

I refer to this insight the way I have it listed: *Passion and Timing.*

The Five Insights

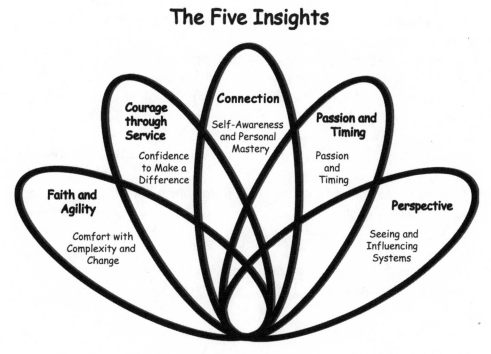

The Five Insights

There is no right place to begin in your study of the five insights, except that you should begin where you feel you need the most information or help. Some insights more naturally dove tail with others, but ultimately they all join in a singularity of sorts, and that's where you fit in. The insights of

Faith and Agility and *Courage Through Service* are synergistic, or mutually beneficial. Faith builds courage and vice versa. Service builds agility, and vice versa. The insight of *Perspective* requires a willingness to tirelessly study a system to understand all of its intricacies and once studied, a leader's sense of timing becomes critical in where and how they intervene. Connection is the keystone of the five insights and perhaps the most important of them all, for it is a leader's ability to connect with others that helps them bring the other insights to life.

Insights, like traits, are significantly different from skills. Insights are those desirable characteristics of behavior, attitudes, and personality features that assist leaders in being effective. Skills are methods and proficiencies that should improve both individual and organizational performance through tangible actions. Skills can be learned and applied regardless of an individual's core personality features, beliefs, or attitudes. Understanding and applying leadership insight requires first understanding enough about ourselves—the literal definition of insight—and our core personality features. Once we've got a handle on ourselves, so to speak, our effectiveness in seeing the world more objectively improves and with it, our ability to act as an effective leader in it. Understanding and applying a skill requires accessing a piece of knowledge, becoming proficient at using it, and then applying it to the task at hand. Understanding and applying an insight is not nearly as easy, but learning to work with insights is as important—if not more so—than working with a skill.

Consider this: Pretend you are called in to your boss's office one day and you are given a choice between these two directives. Choose the easiest one:

- Whenever meeting or greeting a new customer, employee, or colleague, you *must* make eye contact with them.

Or...

- You must commit to only speaking positively and in an upbeat way at work every day, all day, in all situations.

Which one did you choose? Chances are, you chose the first option—making eye contact with each new person you greet—over being positive at work every day, all day. Why? Because one involves a relatively simple action (a skill) that may eventually become a habit while the other behavior—committing to only speaking positively and in an upbeat way at work—requires a shift or alteration in how you may think and feel about work (an insight). Changing where we look is a lot easier than changing how we feel.

There are two key differences between skillfulness and insightfulness—the time required to learn it and the difficulty involved in learning it. Insight is intrinsic, meaning it is a natural quality of a leader's personality. Changing natural behaviors and core attitudes requires significant internal motivation and a high degree of self-awareness. Since insight is part of our habitual selves, improving it takes time. Skills, on the other hand, can be learned and applied easily because they do not involve changes in the leader's personality or core beliefs. But as we've seen, producing lasting results requires working at a deeper level.

Our personalities and behaviors are our insights manifested in the world.

THE SHOULDER TRAITS

Athletes who excel at a single sport combine several different but related skills to perfect their sport. Skiers must combine strength, balance, timing and judgment to get the most out of a ski run. Musicians must have a sense of rhythm and vocal skills to create different tones and pitch dynamics to get the most out of a piece of music. While in action it's hard to notice these separate skills, in practice it helps to separate them out and work on them individually, as a singer might focus on rhythm or hitting the correct note.

Similarly, each insight requires different forms of practice to develop. *Perspective* is an insight that is built over time by being able to translate our intuition about systems into sustainable improvements in them. *Passion and Timing* require searching for, and committing to, that which brings us joy. Learning to have *Faith and Agility* requires developing our ability to be quick, flexible and effective in how we respond to change. *Connection* begins with learning to notice when we are awake and alert and when we are not. *Courage through Service* requires working on one's imaginative vision—the ability to see a future the way we want to create it—and the courage to go after that vision.

The leadership competency research we studied revealed a separate set of important traits that were similar to, but distinct from the insights. These were competencies that we definitely felt were more than skills, but were not so deep as the insights themselves, otherwise I would have called this book The Nine Insights. They are referred to as the shoulder traits, because they seem to bridge gaps between the insights. In fact, they are an element of both of the insights they bridge. Shoulder traits are important for leaders, but they aren't developed through a direct approach. Instead (and coaching with clients bears this out) they are a fringe benefit of practicing the Five Insights.

INSIGHTS:
FAITH AND AGILITY & COURAGE THROUGH SERVICE
Shoulder Trait: Compassion

INSIGHTS:
COURAGE THROUGH SERVICE AND CONNECTION
Shoulder Trait: Vision

INSIGHTS:
CONNECTION AND PASSION AND TIMING
Shoulder Trait: Purpose

INSIGHTS:
PASSION AND TIMING AND PERSPECTIVE
Shoulder Trait: Innovation

Shoulder traits will be explained in the sections related to them; important as they are, don't get stuck on them, because they are primarily developed by focusing on the insights. If you do the work on the insights, the shoulder traits become more readily accessible.

When watching an athlete in action or a singer perform, it's difficult to isolate the individual skills that make them brilliant. Similarly, the insights of enduring leaders overlap and complement to create a whole leader. The specifics of how each insight complements the others will be discussed in depth in the chapter dedicated to that insight. Models such as the one on the following page are frequently used to visually represent an intellectual or emotional idea. A good model helps us remember and ties everything together in what would otherwise be a complicated concept.

The Five Insights

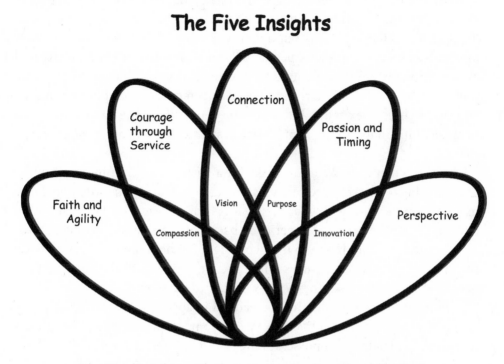

The Five Insights with their Corresponding Shoulder Traits

The danger of models is that, in the hands of someone who doesn't know better, the interpretation of them can either become overly complicated or overly simplified. Everything about being a leader, for example, doesn't fit inside the model for enduring leaders, just the five insights and how they connect to one another. And just because I present a model that shows how they connect doesn't mean that the model is static, perfect, or complete.

ONE SONG, INTERCHANGEABLE WORDS

Once the five insights had been identified, we started testing them against every leader we knew or learned about. We also started using the five insights in our teaching, coaching, and consulting with clients. Assessing their strengths or areas of improvement consistently fell well within the definitions we developed. One CEO was a master at innovating based on his ability to intervene in systems—what I call Perspective—and had tremendous passion and timing, but was unable to build lasting connections with people nor could he successfully manage change. As a result, he was perceived as intelligent and hard working but unapproachable and rigid. Another senior project leader was a fabulous people person and dealt with complexity and change brilliantly. When it came to finding effective solutions to systemic problems, he faltered. As a result, he was spectacular in keeping up morale and maintaining flexibility, but his team kept hitting the same dead ends because of his inability to intuit global, systemic barriers and find solutions to them.

Now when a client calls us and asks for a customized training, we explain the enduring leadership model as a starting point for discussion. This helps us and them determine if what they want is truly customized—meaning we have to create the learning experience based on entirely new concepts—or just a customized approach to the five insights to help their leaders embody the insights of enduring leaders. Time and time again, the five insights have been at the heart of what they were working to develop.

In short, the insights of enduring leadership appear to be universal.

And because they are universal, when the necessary recipe of insights is balanced, the leader who possesses them is able to be effective in just about any business situation or environment. If you develop these skills as the owner of a whitewater rafting company and you really get them, you can go work for a newspaper publishing company and, once you learn the industry, be just as effective. The "music" of enduring leadership is universal, meaning that core ingredients for enduring leaders are needed just about everywhere. The "words" of enduring leadership, or how we manifest and exhibit the insights, are interchangeable.

Leaders who possess the insights are like very talented musicians; it doesn't matter if they were trained in classical music or in bluegrass, they can apply their skills to just about any musical genre.

Hopefully a few fiddle players will become classical musicians as a result of what they learn here, and maybe a few opera singers will learn to rap. Being a leader has as much to do with versatility as it does with mastery.

REMOVING THAT WHICH IS NOT DAVID

If after reading the last section you are saying to yourself, "Great, another book with a list to memorize and practice!", you are missing the point. The insights of enduring leaders aren't something to be mastered or memorized, they are a journey. Effective leaders continually work on them. And my next point is just as important: developing the insights in yourself has as much to do with what you shed as what you gain.

Someone once asked Michelangelo where he found the inspiration and vision to sculpt and create the statue David. The 17 foot statue today resides in the Vatican and was completed by Michelangelo in 1504 after 3 years of work. The fruit of Michelangelo's efforts was a sculpture of unparalleled beauty and remarkable accuracy, a masterpiece of the Renaissance. The sculpture depicts the biblical David, rock sling draped over his shoulder, at the moment he decides to engage Goliath in their famous fight. David was carved from a huge block of granite that weighed somewhere in the neighborhood of 10 tons. When he was asked how he created David, so the story goes, Michelangelo replied, "I simply removed everything that was *not* David." Michelangelo removed 8,000 pounds of granite to reveal David.

Beingness does not require doing or being more; it requires doing and being less. By removing all that is nonessential to reveal our true selves, we become more human and more accessible to other humans. By letting go of the need to maintain a persona, by being our true selves, we have more energy to focus on what really matters: using who we are to do the best we can in the world.

The idea that less is more is certainly not new, and it shows up all the time in people who have developed mastery of a skill or discipline. Watch a beginning skier or ice skater compared to one who has mastered the skill. The master spends little or no energy keeping their balance, which allows them to apply all of their energy to skiing or skating better, faster, and more gracefully. Watch someone who knows how to think through difficult problems well. They may chase down unnecessary information, but they have a singular focus on the task at hand and are not distractible. As we master any skill, we do less of what is unnecessary and more of what improves our performance. Likewise, becoming a better leader happens as much because of what we stop doing as what we start doing.

Leading is not just about acquiring new skills or abilities, it is also about tapping into ourselves, removing all that is not us. It's no wonder that in virtually every study on the characteristics of their leaders that employees admire and are motivated by, telling the truth regardless of what the truth is makes the top of the list. People want to know what we really think so they can better understand who we are if they are to follow us. The point is, learning to make any behavioral change involves as much *unlearning* as it does learning

ENDURING LEADERSHIP

The power and influence that leaders have as a result of their positions may be enough of a motivator for the people they lead over the short term. But a leader who uses his or her power and position as a primary motivator with employees will eventually erode and lose their trust and respect.

Enduring leadership builds on itself and expands outward and upward through the organization. Enduring leaders are those who embody the insights that help them improve themselves and in turn help others. By embodying the insights, they produce sustainable results. Through years of working as a leader and coaching, training, and consulting for other leaders, I've seen the results that this type of leadership produces. My colleagues and I have also helped countless leaders work to develop the insights of an enduring leader and we have seen marked differences in the results they achieve both personally and professionally when they develop the awareness that lasting leadership, sustainable leadership, comes from the inside out. Enduring leaders share the following benefits:

People who work for enduring leaders stay, or when they leave, they leave better for the experience and remain loyal to the people who were their leaders. They become walking advertisements for the leaders and organizations they worked for.

People who work for enduring leaders are committed and more likely to produce results. They understand how their jobs fit into the overall value of the company and they work to produce value.

People who work for enduring leaders are more likely to contribute to the betterment of the work environment, their friends and families and their communities. They apply the same insights of passion and self-awareness their leaders possess to more aspects of their lives, which in turn impacts the people around them at work and in life.

People who work for enduring leaders know they are cared for and valued. How? Their leaders consistently tell them and show them.

Enduring leaders use their skills to win the respect and trust of those who work for them, relying on their position or power only when appropriate or unavoidable.

PRACTICE MAKES PERFECT...SORT OF.

Blaine Lee, author of *The Power Principle*, wrote, "The leader who exercises power with honor will work from the inside out, starting with himself." Leadership is an art developed over a lifetime. It comes from the inside out, not from the outside in. Leadership is about being—that is, it is about who we are much more than it is about what we know. Beingness has little to do with public speaking, charisma or advanced degrees. Unlike business acumen or the host of learnable, acquirable skills associated with business or organizational leadership, the competencies discussed in this book are those that must be embodied in order to be effective. In other words, they must become part of who you are, not just how you act.

As we learn something new, the simple act of having learned it changes our perspective about ourselves or about the world and people around us. This in turn affects our way of interacting with them. Now that our way of interacting with things has changed, the things that happen around us also change, which in turn requires us to again change our perspective. In this way, leadership as a practice is an endless loop of growth and learning. It is a practice to pursue and a journey to embark on versus a skill to master or a destination. When we are not practicing leadership, but instead viewing it as something we have to acquire or can master, our mindset undermines any hope of becoming a better leader. Thinking we know something sometimes limits our ability to learn something else. Unless, of course, if what we believe we know is that we have a lot to learn.

Leaders who think they have leadership mastered are a liability to their companies, their employees, their families and themselves. You've met them. They may have a lot of charisma with just a touch of arrogance. Or they show up to meetings with an air of detachment and aloofness. More insidious is the leader who has the appearance of being interested and caring. They ask questions about important problems as if they want your input. They seek other ideas as if they value a divergent opinion when they don't. Unfortunately, leaders who know how to look like they are practicing leadership when they are not usually have a good act, and the cost of that act is astronomical. Not only do they eventually cost everyone around them—stakeholders, shareholders, suppliers, and customers—they influence aspiring leaders who watch and try to emulate them. Even after they have left or been fired from a position, they leave a legacy of observant and aspiring admirers who may or may not get the leadership lesson they were really teaching: that genuineness and learning are more important and will ultimately benefit us more than façade and subterfuge.

Leadership is a practice. A practice, like a marvelous painting or sculpture, can be hard to describe. Explaining your own progress in a given practice—where you are in any given moment of the process—is difficult. The immediacy of our culture rebels against the notion of practice. In an age where information is a click away and technology speeds the learning curve for so many things, the notion that something cannot be mastered, ever, is not a popular one. We have adapted to crave immediate gratification. Waiting and being patient with a process is difficult, not to mention when the process is a lifelong one. But, take heart: when one practices any skill having to do with personal mastery, his or her life ultimately improves. This may happen in work, it may happen in life, and maybe in both, but when we focus our attention on our beingness, relationships change, our responses to events change, and our understanding of ourselves change. It is this change—this adventure—that makes the pursuit of a practice so gratifying. Even the smallest new discovery or most minute incremental improvement creates a sense of enormous accomplishment.

When a leader practices the skills of being, their power and ability to influence everything expands exponentially. Being does not have to be some mysterious process or mystical mindset. There are no secret handshakes, special mantras, or easy to memorize acronyms to help someone learn how to be. You can't watch an infomercial to better learn how to be; nor can you learn about it from self-improvement books. But you have all the tools you need at your disposal and you only have to invest the most precious commodity you possess to become a better leader—time.

Effective leaders are not superhuman, Buddha like characters who spend all day seeking enlightenment. In fact, some of the world's best leaders have the art of beingness down cold and they don't even know it. Great leaders frequently don't even match our personal models of what an "ideal" leader is. They take all forms: some are popular with their employees, some are unpopular, even feared. Some act like Mother Teresa while others use a style more akin to Attila the Hun. Some are introverted and shy while others are outgoing. Some are grounded and uncomplicated, others are mysterious and complex. Some leaders are driven by high standards of integrity and honesty; others have no problem bending the truth to achieve their vision or to save their hides. Regardless of their approach, effective leaders all do one thing very well: they produce lasting results.

Getting employees excited about work for a short period of time isn't hard. Getting them to find their own excitement in the day-to-day tasks of their job is. Satisfying a customer's needs for a period of months or even a few years is a nice achievement, but it is not the same as the achievement of turning a customer into a lifelong business partner. Improving profitability is a great feather in the cap of any leader, but creating a culture where everyone is thinking about how to improve profitability is much harder. Each of these alternatives represents a "sustainable" solution—one that will stand the test of time. Enduring leaders produce sustainable results.

It will take time to put the insights of an enduring leader to practice, of course, but not as much as you might think. My experience teaching, coaching, and facilitating learning for leaders is that the amount of time it takes to identify, learn, and put into action leadership skills is no shorter than the amount of time it takes to put the practice of insight development to work. The difference is in the sustainability of the results. Good leaders practice being good leaders every day, especially when they are getting a lot of feedback that they are doing a good job. They don't read a book, put the skills to work, and—in an instant—voilá! They've changed! You can attend all the seminars, read all the books, and spend tens of thousands of dollars on coaching, but if all you ever focus on is skills, you will simply not be able to sustain the results. Again, and at the risk of being redundant, leadership is a practice.

APPLYING THE INSIGHTS TO WORK AND LIFE

The insights of effective leaders are not exclusively applicable to work. In reality, if I were to presume to understand enough about life to define the insights shared by individuals who live fulfilled lives (which I absolutely don't) in the same way that I have defined the insights of a leader, some of the leadership insights would probably make this list. Passion certainly would make the list, and because timing addresses when and how to apply our passion, timing might stand a chance of making the list as well, although we might call it "restraint" or "patience." The ability to roll with the punches as the cosmic tumblers of life spin is certainly important to living a healthy, happy life, so comfort with complexity and change might make it as well—except we might call that insight "faith."

Seeing systems sounds awfully academic and cerebral. But actually, seeing systems is also involved in observing the natural world at work. There are certain constants that explain how the natural world works. Gravity is one. And the first law of thermodynamics (for every action there is an equal and opposite reaction). There's also the second law of thermodynamics (entropy, or the tendency of matter to go from order to disorder), and so on. Seeing systems is to notice the principles that govern the interaction of things and learn to appreciate those principles and work with them. These principles include human behavior as well. The name for the inimitable insights of human behavior—human nature—is an accidental reference to the fact that we humans are subject to the same laws of nature as everything else.

Finally, most of us would agree that the abilities of being aware of who we are individually, what we think, and how we act are important life skills. So is learning to relate well to others. Both of these abilities help us maintain that which we covet above all else—human connection, love, acceptance, and feelings of belonging and purpose. So self-awareness and personal mastery would make the fulfilled life list as well.

Depending on how comfortable you are with this sort of thing, enduring leadership is as much a spiritual practice as it is a professional one. If that statement is a stretch for you, reject it and move on. If it fits, work with it.

Regardless, the insights of enduring leaders have as much application in life as they do in work, perhaps more so. For example, the ability to see things systemically can be just as useful to parents raising children as it can be for a leader planning corporate strategy. The insights effective parents bring to bear on how and when to guide their children are in many ways influenced by their ability to predict and link cause and effect, an aspect of perspective. The ability to determine what to teach a child—who should teach it and when—is derived by what I am calling self-awareness, passion and timing, and faith and agility. Every parent confronts situations where they have to confront behavior or problems with their children in ways that can be painful and uncomfortable, and choosing the right time to do so are skills related to the insights of faith and agility as well as passion and timing. The same comparisons can be made to the development of personal relationships, or decision making about a career or life path, or coaxing better performance out of an employee, or resolving impasses with customers. The most usable insights are those that can be applied to both work and life.

The term "work/life balance" gets a lot of press these days in corporations, but I am not sure it is relevant given the ability of technology to seamlessly connect us anywhere, any time. The concept sounds nice, but it rarely proves to be a reality in practice. I have developed relationships and friendships with literally hundreds of senior executives, and I have yet to see one who balances work and life as much as I've seen them integrate work and life. Some executives involve their life partners and families in their work-a-day worlds while others come home and focus solely on personal and family issues with little or no conversation about what is happening at work. In either case, leaders who have learned to integrate work and life have developed the skill of seamlessly moving from one to the other with little or no disruption to the people around them. They attend parent-teacher conferences with equal focus and attention as they do in meetings with key customers. They don't separate work and life, but they know how to prioritize both in a way that does not cause disruption to either. Knowing and using the insights of enduring leaders helps leaders learn to integrate who they are with what they do.

As I mentioned earlier, enduring leadership is a practice—not a catchy acronym or a system of behaviors that one chooses to adopt when necessary and discard when it's not applicable. It's not something you switch off when you jump in your car to go home. The practice of leadership is a lifestyle. If you already embody the insights of an enduring leader, you know what I am talking about. If you don't, but you want to embody these insights, commit yourself to a change of lifestyle, because that's what it takes.

The leaders who embody the insights of enduring leaders are—above all else—grounded. Without exception, they have full personal lives marked by reasonably healthy relationships and dear life-long friends. They each have their own version of love that is different, but similar, and love is important to them. Within normal limits, they are happy people, and when they are not happy, they take it upon themselves to correct the situation instead of waiting for someone else to come change it for them. They each have a relief valve that helps them maintain perspective and stay grounded. In some cases, the relief valve is their family. In other cases, it's a hobby or vocation they pursue outside of work like dancing or flying or sailing or carpentry. In still other cases it's a lifestyle or health style they pursue and practice, such as yoga, rock climbing, physical conditioning, maintaining an organic diet, etc. Whatever the specific relief is, they each have at least one and they work to maintain it. It is much a part of their practice as leading.

Embodying the insights of an enduring leader at home does not mean you need to go home and "lead" your friends, family, and children like you may be required to do at work. On the contrary, if we spend all of our time leading others, we miss out on the opportunity to learn from others who are leading—or following. Since their awareness of what is happening within systems, that is, their ability to see the big picture, is heightened, enduring leaders see the connections within systems and insert themselves on an "as needed" basis. The enduring leader's understanding of complexity helps them be patient when a solution is needed; they know that sometimes it is better to watch and observe what is happening for a while rather than to jump into the middle of a problem and solve it before all of the conditions are right to create a sustainable solution. And when it is time to start working towards solutions, they are comfortable with the changes that will be the natural result of solving a problem or changing the way a process or a business is run. Finally, enduring leaders are effective because of their ability to be both self-aware and to connect with diverse personalities. An enduring leader's ability to monitor themselves—to notice their own emotional and human reactions to various situations before acting on their feelings—requires remarkable self-awareness. They practice noticing how they feel during their whole day and they deal with their feelings before acting, intervening, or leading.

BALANCING THE INSIGHTS

As we've seen, the insights of leadership are a system unto themselves, meaning that they are interdependent and mutually reinforcing. Therefore, applying them effectively requires leaders to advance their knowledge and practice all of the insights, not some of them. In this way, insights need to be in balance for leaders to be effective. By including the need for the insights to be in balance, I realize I have complicated matters considerably. Learning to embody insights is a lifetime of work. However, as we practice and improve upon our ability to sense and respond to events at the right time, we also improve our ability to see the various components of the system and their connectedness.

Focusing on one insight to the exclusion of all others is harmful, even detrimental. Being passionate about a project, issue, or situation is a key insight for effective leaders. But imagine a leader who allows their passion to rule their behavior with little awareness of timing their comments or understanding the value of patience in the process. If a leader has the ability to see cause and effect in systems but lacks the self-awareness necessary to know when and how to intervene in the system, their efforts won't be as effective.

Learning to balance how we apply our insights is as critical as developing them at all. There is one insight included in the list of essential insights that helps us learn to balance them: connection. If you are self aware, you are better able to understand your place in the world and you are more able to see systems and your place in those systems. Self-aware leaders learn how and when to apply their other insights to any situation.

INSIGHTS VARY— ## JUST LIKE PEOPLE AND PERSONALITY

Each of us has insights that we come by naturally. Other insights, once we identify them, must be developed or improved upon.

The insights we possess are a curious coincidence of a number of factors— a customized recipe of experience, genetics, morphology, events, education, and upbringing. To complicate matters further, the blueprint of the design of our brains is one of a kind. Our brains are each wired differently, which means that how we extrapolate meaning and store the information gleaned from that meaning is as individualized as the street layout in any city. As a result, each of us has strengths and abilities attached to each insight that are uniquely ours, and each of us has areas in which we are less strong.

Research shows that much more is accomplished with people in the areas of personal performance when they focus on what their strengths are, not on what their weaknesses are.[2] Therefore, as you learn about each insight and the characteristics associated with it, find those areas where you are strongest and work on developing them while making note of those areas where you feel less strong.

As you learn about the insights and your own brilliance in them, pay close attention to the strengths you possess in each insight and consider how you can use them even more in your work and life. Don't ignore areas you identify as weaknesses, but don't focus too much on them, either. Knowing where one's weaknesses are can be very helpful in both working around them and in improving upon them. The first step is to see that which is directly in front of us, but not obvious. It is the foundation on which enduring leaders build their practice: themselves.

PART TWO
A CALL TO ACTION

Why Now? Why Us?

Ultimately, the solution to the world's most important and compelling problems isn't science. It's people. What is keeping us from solving the enormous problems that face the world today is not a lack of scientific knowledge. It is an inability to create significant change in the manmade institutions of government, industry, culture and economy. What could create that change? People could. Leaders could. The quality of their thinking, behaviors, actions and plans is critical, more so now than ever.

Medical and scientific breakthroughs change the world on a daily basis. HIV is no longer a guaranteed death penalty. Technology exists that could make affordable, potable drinking water available to everyone, everywhere. Agricultural science and seed genetics have made great strides so that no one on the planet needs to suffer from malnutrition or starvation.

Yet in spite of these advances, the world's problems continue to mount.

Proportionally, more people are starving or without drinking water now than in 1906. One child dies every five seconds from hunger, and 852 million people die from starvation and malnutrition every year.[3] In 2002, an estimated 4.2 million people died from preventable diseases worldwide, and the World Health Organization predicts that number will continue to increase. In this age of unparalleled prosperity, over 1 billion people worldwide live below the international poverty line and earn less than $1 dollar per day.[4]

Virtually every reputable scientist with an opinion on the subject agrees that the planet is warming quickly as a result of human activity. Predictions about what will happen as a result of global warming vary, but none of the scenarios bode well for humankind. In the United States, we are spending more and more money attacking each other through the legal system. In 2002, we spent $180 billion (1.8 percent of the Gross Domestic Product of the United States) suing each other through tort claims, twice as high as the rates of any other developed country.[5] Forty-Five million Americans are without health care, and that number is predicted to increase by about 800,000 people per year.[6]

The most troubling aspect of these depressing statistics is that we are largely to blame for them. As the global population increases, so seems to increase our ability to inflict suffering and horror on each other and the rest of earth's creatures. In the grand scheme, is it possible that humankind was an experiment of nature that *almost* worked? Did nature *almost* get the genetic recipe right and now she is just waiting for us to die off so she can start over again? If so, maybe next time, she will create a human brain that has more capacity for compassion, is less prone to violence and has a stronger instinct to see each individual as a critical link to the survival of the entire tribe. Until nature runs her course, we are obliged to follow our own survival instincts and continue to try and make it. Giving up isn't an option.

Those of us who were born into the privilege of the developed world like to talk about the instability and ills afflicting developing and third world countries, but the truth is we, the governments, economies and institutions of the developed world, are the biggest problem. Our privilege is the world's liability. In 1998 the Worldwatch Institute, armed with data assembled by the Global Policy Forum, estimated that if every country on planet Earth lived to the level of consumption and expenditure of resources that the United States currently enjoys, it would take three planets to sustain all of us. On a planet with 6.6 billion people, Americans account for less than 5% of the population, but we consume over 40% of the resources. If we add the rate of consumption of all developed nations together, we account for 80% of consumed resources and slightly over 10% of the global population.

How remarkable. How tragic. How overwhelming. And ultimately, how preventable.

I believe our privilege comes with an important responsibility. I learned to think that way by working with and watching a number of businesses and organizations who are working to make a profit *on behalf* of humankind, not at our expense. There are businesses and investment models that view the services provided by Planet Earth as finite. They work to reinvest in the preservation and restoration of those services as they would in any other source of capital. These businesses are examples of a growing trend called social responsibility. Social responsibility is a philosophy that holds we are all connected and that we benefit from the betterment of all humankind, not just those of us that was lucky enough to be born in New York or L.A. or Dallas or Rotterdam or Munich or Tokyo. Socially responsible businesses see the world like nature does, as an endless loop of growth—adaptation—nourishment—birth and once again, growth. They attempt to operate as if what they do really does matter in the world, and they use that belief to make a positive difference.

If I have done my job satisfactorily in this book, at a minimum, you will be better equipped to be an effective leader or the mentor of an aspiring leader. If I have done my job really well, you'll understand a lot more about what social responsibility is and how you can build it into your work.

We need more and better leaders, and we need them now. We need them working and volunteering in villages, schools, churches, synagogues and ashrams. We need them building consensus in government, crafting intelligent policies and laws. We need them to think outside of the box to relentlessly pursue solutions to our toughest problems. We need them to be capable of—and passionate about—truly developing people. We need leaders who see the environment as a critical element of our collective survival and who treat it as the source of all capital and health. We need leaders whose priority is humankind, and who have the skill to make responsible decisions in the midst of paradox. More, better, now.

NOT "HOW-TO" BUT "WHAT-TO"

This is a "What-To" book for two groups of people working in the world of business:

1. Aspiring leaders who are struggling to find a better way to add value to their organizations or businesses and see themselves as having the potential to do more than they are currently doing.

2. CEO's, senior executives, directors, bureau chiefs, and presidents who want to do a better job developing and nurturing the leaders underneath and around them.

It is my fervent belief that the future of business—and therefore the future of society—is in the hands of these two groups. "How-To" books build skills and skills are important. However, developing skills such as time management, delegation, giving performance feedback, or business acumen will only make a bad leader more tolerable or a good leader more effective. Skills are just the tip of the iceberg. If learning skills was all it took to be a better leader, we would have a lot more great, competent leaders than what we currently have.

I can't imagine a more difficult audience to write a book for than this book's audience:

Aspiring leaders who are working their tails off to get ahead and have little time (or use) for another book and the senior leaders who are working *their* tails off to actually *run* the businesses the aspiring leaders work for who have little enough time to spend mentoring leaders, much less reading another book on how to do it.

Fear not, I have taken your lifestyles and attention spans into account in how *The Five Insights of Enduring Leaders* is structured. The body of the book has been designed in a *read what you need* format. This introduction and the first section explain the premise of the book and foundational research that led to the five insights. You will need to read them to understand the context for the other sections, but other than that, you're on your own. The remaining sections are written to stand alone so that readers can go to the section they are most interested in and read it without needing to refer to previous sections.

I structured the book this way because, frankly, I know you. You squeeze your reading in between responding to an endless stream of emails, going to meetings, actually leading, and occasionally even taking time away from work to recharge. Or you cram in a few pages on the airplane before it reaches that magic number, 10 minutes after take-off, when you can fire up your computer and get back to work. Or you read material like this late at night after the kids have gone to bed. Likely, you've also discovered by now that this stuff takes work, and you've chosen to read *The Five Insights of Enduring Leaders* in small doses. Good for you. Your time and attention span is limited and setting boundaries around how you manage your time is important. So important in fact, that boundary setting is a subject that is addressed as an important element of one of the insights. Jump in wherever you like and read what you need, but jump in—we've got a lot of work to do.

Each section of this book begins with a story about a leader who I feel exemplifies the insight being described and how they bring that insight to bear on the problems and business issues they face every day. The leaders I chose are not national celebrities or widely known gurus on the subject of leadership. In fact and without exception, the leaders I use as exemplars of each insight had a hard time understanding why I thought they embodied the insight I ascribed to them. They are so busy just "being" that they don't see the point in describing something that to them comes instinctually. Since this is a "what-to" book for aspiring leaders and the people who can help coach them to achieve more of their potential, I thought it was important to use mere mortals who get up every morning, put on their socks (or hose), drive or take the train to work (as opposed to being driven to work by a chauffer), roll up their sleeves, and get down to it just like the rest of us. I made it a point to use leaders who come from a wide range of businesses—from the CEO of a regional construction company to the leader of an international educational movement. I also made it a point to use people who have very, very different styles to achieve the results they produce. I did my best to use leaders who are both male and female, but sadly, American business still has a long way to go to equalize the playing field for women, so far more of the exemplars I used are male. In spite of their diversity, all of them have at least three things in common:

1. They are all successful—very successful—at what they do.
I think their success is substantially tied to their practice of the insight I connect them with.

2. They all lead businesses or organizations that are trying hard to make a difference in the world for their employees, their customers, their constituents or stakeholders, for their suppliers, and for the greater good of society.

3. They have been successful over the long term, hence the term enduring leaders. We all know leaders who lead well in the moment or when fate and circumstances collide. The leaders described in this book lead well regardless of circumstances in their worlds.

The second part of each of the main sections is devoted to fully understanding each one of the five insights. I use mini case studies of how the insights play out in work and life when an example is needed, but I also wrote this book on the assumption that the readers, you, have similar experiences to draw from to anchor your understanding. To add credibility to my point of view, I also tap into the wisdom of other, better thinkers on the subject who happen to agree with me.

Third and finally, each of the main sections has a section called "The Practice" that describes What to Do to put a specific insight into action. The most important exercise in each of these sections is the exercise of dialogue between the aspiring leader and their coaches, mentors or bosses. If this book fosters constructive dialogue, I will have accomplished at least one of my two goals, the other being a call to action to start, run and sustain businesses that are socially responsible.

COURAGEOUS EVALUATION

If you are a CEO, senior leader, president, bureau chief, etc., next to managing and leading your business, department or group, your top priority needs to be developing the people around you. There are elegant, effective ways to identify and prepare the next generation of leaders in your company, but doing so has to begin with you making it a priority. Your job has to be the development of people who can lead when you're gone.

Leaders need mentors and coaches to help them find their way. If you are a senior leader, like it or not, you are a mentor to people who want to have more of what you have and do more of what you do. They may look to you as a role model. Knowing how to help them, to really help them, requires cutting through the extraneous details and focusing on what's really important—who they are, how they think, what they believe and how they behave. The ideas laid out in this book and the methods used to develop the insights that will be discussed are tools for mentors. Use them.

As each insight of enduring leadership is discussed throughout this book, evaluate your competence in each, and ask colleagues who know you to do the same for you. Compare the two, then courageously evaluate yourself.

If you are an aspiring future leader hoping to advance, you may be as perplexed about how to get promoted as many businesses' senior leaders are about how to find you. Do you have to play politics and suck up to get ahead? The reality of the business world is that, yes, sometimes you do have to play politics. But much more important to your success as a leader are your talents and ability. People who play politics to get ahead eventually let down themselves or the group they are leading, unless they can back up their political maneuvers with talent, ability and a thirst for getting better. Life is a series of choices. Time and energy are finite. If I were you—and I have been—I would focus on improving your ability and learning. Leave politics to everyone else.

For you, reading this book may take a little courage. You will be asked to take an honest look at your own aptitudes compared to the five insights of enduring leaders. The good news is, if you *do* take an honest look and you find yourself coming up short in one or more of the insights, you will be clearer about what you need to do to develop them.

Whether you are an aspiring future leader or a senior leader, you know that there is no single formula to leadership, no magic recipe for becoming a better or more effective leader. There is also no single type of leader, and what it takes to be successful as a leader varies significantly. One thing is certain. Leadership—enduring leadership—begins with understanding the most complex, intangible, mysterious organism on the planet.

You.

Section Two
Faith and Agility

THIS SECTION IN BRIEF:

As nature shows us time and again, change isn't optional, but it is natural. Enduring leaders understand that things change; as a matter of fact, they rely on that knowledge. They have faith that things will change, and they lead based on that premise. Faith is a deep understanding and a trust that everything changes, always. Enduring leaders also recognize that it is hard to predict, so they rely on their ability to be agile and responsive in the face of it.

What's more, change isn't linear, so our response to it can't be, either. At times, change requires us to reduce a complicated problem into core elements that can be solved. Other times, change cannot be reduced—it's too complex to be simplified—and we have to learn to accept its complexity. *Faith and Agility* describes the ability to lead through change while being comfortable with complexity, chaos and non-linear processes.

Perhaps more than any other insight, *Faith and Agility* tests our emotional stability. Change and the chaos it brings trigger emotional responses in us that make it even harder for us to respond optimally. Among these triggers, our own, primal need to feel in control of our environment, our destiny and our work exerts itself most strongly. Change can be resisted, but it can't be avoided. Enduring leaders thrive in change instead of avoiding it or trying to plan around it. They are able to do so because they have faith that change is natural, needed and ordinary.

The practices that help leaders develop this insight don't involve analytical genius, improved problem solving ability, or an intimate knowledge of chaos theory, although these skills help. Instead, the practices that assist leaders in developing this insight involve learning to understand the universal processes of change, dealing with our own need for control (and the lack thereof) and learning to lead people through change instead of denying it.

To learn more about the practices of this insight, go to page 81.

PART ONE
BETWEEN A ROCK AND A HARD PLACE

Mining, the extraction of minerals and rocks from the earth's crust, has been a tremendous agent of change in the American West. The mentality of the rugged individualists who struck out from the east across the untamed Rockies 200 years ago is the same as the mentality of many, if not most, westerners to this day: Stake your claim and work the land as you please. Distrust government and the regulations it tries to impose. Protect your independence at all costs. Throughout the westward expansion, scratching out an existence wasn't easy, but for those who were lucky, or hard working, or both, mining held the promise of a better life.

But the earth has never given up her bounty willingly. In its early years, the burgeoning mining industry had to develop powerfully destructive technologies to make mining cost effective. The irresponsible use of that technology has decimated some of the earth's most beautiful and fragile natural habitats. Early mining companies saw no problem in scaling off the entire tops of mountains, mesas and hills in search of profit. Mining has been the justification for some of the most onerous, irresponsible, shortsighted and damaging environmental problems on the planet. Nowhere is it more visible than in the American West. Near Silverton, Colorado, the scars from surface mining activities over 100 years ago appear as new and fresh today as they did 100 years ago. The beauty of the area is permanently tarnished by poisoned, discolored, dead streams and naked, eroding stubs of mountains, their bounty of minerals and coal excised with a precision that is best likened to performing surgery with a soup spoon. The effects will be felt and seen for generations.

And yet humankind has benefited in hundreds of ways from mining. Coal generated electricity is still the United States' primary energy source, and technology is improving the cleanliness of coal fired electrical generating facilities all the time. Molybdenum acts as a hardener for steel and is used in everything from airframes and engines to improving the conductivity of alloys. Our reliance on fossil fuels and the utility of hundreds of types of ores and minerals has become an integral element of America's technological prowess.

For mine operators and owners, mining can be a hugely profitable business. The cost of extractive technologies is high, but so is the profitability of a well run mine. Even with the cost of clean-up, fines for environmental violations and fighting community and environmental lobbies, mining makes money. The mindset of the industry overall is one of opportunism and Manifest Destiny: if man has dominion over the land, what's wrong with stripping a few acres for the greater good? Or, as one popular pro-mining bumper sticker reads:

"Earth First...We'll Mine All the Other Planets Later"

The Surface Mining Control and Reclamation Act, or SMCRA, was enacted by Congress to insure that when a mine—specifically a coal mine—was tapped out, the mine operators were responsible for returning the land to a "beneficial use" instead of leaving mine sites a wasteland of leftover rocks and polluted retention ponds. Obviously, it was impossible for a mine operator to rebuild mountaintops, so returning the land to some form of "beneficial use" was about as good as it was going to get. Congress left the interpretation of the law to each state involved in mining activities. And to be sure, determining what level of "reclamation" was acceptable was a matter of wide interpretation. To interpret the law, states began creating their own bureaucracies in an ever-increasing spiral of complexity and administration.

In the State of New Mexico, which sits atop some of the richest coal, natural gas, petroleum, mineral and ore deposits in the country, coal mining alone produced over 600 million dollars in revenue in 2004. Not bad for the 5th largest—and one of the most unpopulated—states in the Union. Combined with mineral or "hard rock" mining, mining activities for New Mexico today account for $1.2 billion in revenue or annual tax revenue of over $30 million dollars. Like any successful industry, the coal mining industry hopes to pay as little as possible for the cost of doing business. The more efficiently mining operations can be conducted—and the less mine operators have to pay for cleaning up the mess once the party's over—the more profitable the business. In the face of SMCRA regulations, the posture of mining companies towards reclamation has been to do the bare minimum required and to do it as slowly as possible. But the work of the mining companies is under constant scrutiny and pressure from numerous environmental organizations whose only concern is the natural environment that was destroyed or disturbed by the mine. Taking the middle ground in the debate are most private citizens—you and I—who either don't know a problem exists or have no idea of its scope and magnitude. In New Mexico this human dynamic is further complicated by the presence of three cultures—Indian, Hispanic and Anglo—all with very different views of environmentalism and the definition of "wealth." To top it off, New Mexico is an archeological jewel with more sites of ancient Indian culture within its borders that any other state in the union.

In response to the SMCRA legislation and to settle the issue of "How good is good enough?" with regard to clean up, or "reclamation" as it is officially known, the State created the Division of Mining and Minerals, or "MMD." Initially, MMD's function was only to protect archeological sites and enforce SMCRA. Then the State expanded the Division's charter to include both hard rock (mineral) mining and coal mining activities. In 1987, the state's Natural Resources Department and the Energy and Minerals Department merged to create the Energy, Minerals and Natural Resources Department, or EM-NRD. The Department's mission: "To position New Mexico as a national leader in the energy and natural resource areas for which the Department is responsible." Today MMD's objective is to regulate mining, issue mine permits and enforce the laws that are designed to protect our environment and assure responsible utilization of New Mexico's resources.

EMNRD is a large bureaucracy composed of 5 Divisions and roughly 500 employees. The Divisions are Oil Conservation (OCD), State Parks (SPD), Forestry (SFD), Energy Conservation and Management (ECMD) and Mining and Minerals (MMD). Each Division has a Director and each Director manages Bureau Chiefs who in turn manage the staffs and programs within each division. Typical of all state bureaucracies, New Mexico's is full of departments, secretaries, divisions, and offices just like MMD, each with its own acronym and hierarchy

Karen Garcia is the Bureau Chief of the Mine Reclamation Bureau for New Mexico's Mining Act Reclamation Program and the Coal Mine Reclamation Program (we'll just call them the "Coal" and the "Hard Rock" programs from now on) among other programs in the division. Her job is to balance the competing, often conflicting, interests of the various groups and policies related to mining including:

- The mining industry, which contributes to the state's coffers through taxes, fines, and mining permit fees;
- The citizens of the state of New Mexico;
- The regulations and policies she is paid to uphold and enforce;
- The environmental groups that serve as watch dogs to the mining companies and protect the larger environmental issues facing the state.

Karen reports to a gubernatorial appointee, the Division Director for Mining and Minerals, so her boss may change every 4 to 8 years. She answers to three distinct external constituencies in a state that has three distinct cultures. She is charged with upholding and interpreting the federal mandate of the coal program and for oversight and implementation of permitting and compliance with the Hard Rock program. While the Coal program's regulations and guidelines were established over a 30-year period, the Hard Rock program's regulations are not clearly defined, and are comparatively new (only 13 years old). Answerable to both the Division Director and the Department Secretary, Karen has to balance internal politics with the passionate opinions of colleagues who are in similar positions, all the while providing clear and credible direction to her staff, despite knowing that every 4 to 8 years, the political climate and agenda from the Governor could change.

Karen's staff is comprised of top-notch scientists, geologists, chemists, archeologists and engineers who share a common passion to protect and preserve the natural environment of their state. Like Karen, they have a pragmatic understanding that, while the environment would be better off without any mining whatsoever, mining is an important element of the state's economy and is there to stay.

To add to the complexity, the programs Karen oversees must be self-sustaining, meaning they need to collect enough permits and fees to pay for themselves. While the relationship between the mining companies and her bureaus is civil, they represent very different sides of the issue. In some cases, the cost of legal defense by mining companies approaches the cost of mine operations themselves. Permits, rulings on violations, penalties and the reclamation projects move at a glacial pace. Karen works with other agencies, which also have strong opinions about what position the state should take to move forward. It is important for the state to have a consistent and unified approach so Karen and her colleagues spend a lot of time and energy coming to a consensus, no easy task in the complicated bureaucracy of state government.

Karen Garcia is a great example of a leader who possesses the insight of *Faith and Agility*. She has to balance the need for action—in this case reclamation of mined lands—with inaction, the relentless ability of mining companies to tie up reclamation activities in a tangle of scientific and legal dead ends. Were Karen to engage in obstructionist tactics with the mining industry, she would not gain their cooperation when pushing for better reclamation than they originally proposed. Mining companies would simply bog down the system with legal arguments about why more costly reclamation activities are not necessary. So instead, Karen and her staff must constantly distinguish between which battle is necessary to fight and which is not worth the expenditure of time and resources for little gain. As Karen put it, "If both environmental groups and mining companies are equally unhappy with you, you've probably handled the situation correctly."

Making complex decisions and picking battles are ever present challenges of Karen's position and those who work in her department. There was a case in which her bureau had to decide whether to label a mining site that had been previously used as "new" or "existing." New unit requirements are more strict than existing unit requirements under the New Mexico Mining Act. But the circumstances of this case were unique because of the location of the unit, which was near a large pit that was generating acid. The waste piles in this pit were not going to be reclaimed. Instead, water contaminated by them would be treated for as many years as necessary. This pit capture zone was essentially a sacrifice area. The plan was to discourage wildlife from going to the area by using fences and bird netting.

If the bureau chose a strict interpretation of the law to label the island of land in this contaminated area a "new" unit, it would be covered with soil and seeded to create an area with grasses and shrubs that would probably attract wildlife. The wildlife would have been exposed to hazardous chemicals. Karen and her staff negotiated with the company to meet new unit requirements in other areas away from the contaminated zone, but did not require the company to meet the more strict new unit requirements near the pit. The company reluctantly agreed. A strict interpretation of the law would not have resulted in a decision that was good for wildlife, and the company would have engaged in a protracted legal battle. Instead, the mine reclamation plan was improved for other areas and the sacrifice zone was left alone. An environmental group considered appealing the decision, but later also decided this was not a battle worth fighting.

Connected Competencies

The competencies associated with Faith and Agility all have to do with the ability to lead through change while being comfortable with complexity, chaos and non-linear processes. These competencies include:

- Able to manage and prepare for change
- Able to cope with and lead through ambiguity
- Flexible/adaptable to new plans, ideas or processes
- Capable of non-linear, complex thinking
- Makes quick and conclusive decisions
- Able to visualize the whole and lead accordingly
- Evaluates progress towards goals
- Prioritizes accordingly
- Finds workable solutions to complex problems
- Prepares for and leads through change
- Understands change
- Multi-tasks
- Embraces diversity

Some of the competencies associated with this insight overlap with the other insights of enduring leaders. For example, every competency listed above works better in the hands of a self-aware leader who has the insight of *Connection* because change is an emotional process. Enduring leaders understand their emotional reactions to change, which allows them to respond to change objectively instead of resisting it based on their emotions. Likewise, the connected competencies of "Managing in chaotic environments" and "Non-linear, complex thinking" are related to, but different than, the insight of *Perspective*. Both insights involve seeing things differently than we are accustomed to. *Faith and Agility* enables leaders to sort, compartmentalize and respond to information while the insight of perspective helps them see the connections between discrete pieces of information. For example, Karen Garcia's understanding of how acids, water and wildlife interact in mining environments shows her understanding of systems. But it is the insight of *Faith and Agility* that helps her work around and through regulations and procedures.

The shoulder trait between *Faith and Agility* and *Courage Through Service* is *Compassion*. Managing change and serving others requires being empathetic to the feelings of distress people who won't like going through change feel. Exercises to lead people through change and to perfect your own insights, with Compassion, are covered in this section under The Practice.

Like all of the insights, this one requires us to challenge our traditional view of the world and see things in a new way. *"Faith"* as an insight isn't a religious belief. It is a deep understanding and a trust that everything changes, always. People change, even though we sometimes complain that they are not changing in ways we like. The status quo changes, even when we work to preserve it. Governments and political systems of entire countries change—some overnight and some over the course of decades. Laws and legislation like the kind Karen Garcia is expected to enforce change. Our understanding of the physical and even metaphysical world is evolving, and as we understand more, our perspective changes about science and history and the unknown. The weather changes and there is nothing we can do about it except prepare for it. Globally, and for the first time in human history, our climate is changing in ways that are irrefutably caused by man. *Faith* is an innate belief that things will change and we better learn to adjust to them when they do, which means we need to be agile.

Change isn't linear or sequential, so our response to it can't be, either. At times, change requires us to reduce a complicated problem into core elements that can be solved. Other times, change cannot be reduced—it's too complex to be simplified—and we have to learn to accept its complexity. Agility is having the emotional, intellectual and even physical ability to wrap ourselves around change as it occurs. By wrapping ourselves around change, we become part of it, not separate from it, which allows us to respond faster and more fully to the next change, whatever it is.

WHY FAITH AND AGILITY MATTERS

In his book *Future Shock*, futurist and author Alvin Toffler provides readers with an interesting prediction about the essential skills for dealing with the changes in the future. Toffler suggested that, in response to complex and increasingly rapid change, the nature of what we knew and what we needed to know would change as well. Toffler suggested that some new skills would be required from all of us to be successful in the future. These skills included:

- **The skill of learning how to learn**
- **The skill of knowing how to choose**
- **The skill of learning how to relate**

Learning to learn: Toffler's point was that how we learn is changing and will continue to change in the future. Being comfortable with complexity and change requires us to learn whatever is needed in the moment. Leaders who are comfortable with complexity don't get hung up on knowing all the answers. They know that they can learn what they need to know to respond appropriately, just in time. Put a 12-year-old at a computer with an internet connection and ask them to research any topic about which they have at least rudimentary knowledge. They have at their fingertips an unlimited virtual library of information from around the world on that topic, and they know how to access it. Twenty years ago, our research was limited to what we could find at our local library. Information can be so easily accessed—and there is so much information in the collective wisdom of civilization now—that educational fundamentals already include teaching students how to direct their own learning. Making this change will be a critical shift if our educational system is to remain relevant.

Learning to choose: Toffler predicted that the problem would not be access to information, but knowing which information is important to know. Because the internet has created an unlimited virtual library, today the question is not how to learn, but rather choosing what is important to learn. And with so much information available and only a limited amount of time to review it to make decisions, the ability to choose the right direction in the face of change and complexity is a critical skill for enduring leaders.

Learning to relate: The amount, quality and timeliness of the information we have access to has come with some costs—among them is the loss of person-to-person contact. It is somehow reassuring to know Toffler predicted that no matter how abundant information and technology became, how we relate to one another would always be important, and finding new ways to relate effectively without actual face-to-face contact would be an emerging skill.

Toffler's predictions were poignant and accurate. The insight of Faith and Agility is a state of mind, a mindset, a mentality. It enables enduring leaders to embrace these new skills: learning, choosing, relating. Life is speeding up; technology is both the solution and the culprit. We have created a world in which just about everything touched by human intellect has been optimized, enhanced, sped up or hyperlinked. Human connection, for example, cannot be rushed; it takes time. Yet, we continue to take technologies whose primary purpose is to enable us to save time and try to convert them to tools that will enhance our connection with people. We send text messages over our phones instead of calling the person we are texting. We structure work so we can do more and more of it alone, because working alone is faster, even though it may not be better. We carry hand held devices that allow us to respond quickly to emails that don't matter under the assumption that doing so will free up more time for us to focus on what DOES matter. We are victims of our own success, and we have no choice but to respond. As we develop new, accelerated skills, there is a growing awareness that not all acceleration is beneficial. As we learn to keep pace with the urgent world we have created, perhaps we will also learn where, how and when to apply the brakes.

Until we learn to slow things down, we rely on leaders to keep pace and manage the chaos. Around the world, leaders who can manage and thrive in complexity and lead through change are in high demand. They know how to lead through change because they have an understanding that all things change; that is, they have faith. They rarely feel victimized by changes. They know that as soon as a new process is running smoothly, there is a strong likelihood that the process will need to be changed. Since they wrap themselves around change, facing it doesn't frustrate them; they are part of it.

One of Karen Garcia's greatest attributes as a leader is her unflappable response to change. Her calmness and flexibility have resulted in ongoing increases in her job responsibilities and supervisory scope. She takes on new challenges, builds support for them with her staff, and produces results.

THE PROCESS OF CHANGE

If we look carefully at the lessons nature has to teach, we find that change has some predictable patterns that apply to all living organisms and systems. The better able we are at seeing these patterns emerge, the better equipped we are to respond to them. Change is one of nature's imperatives. If you don't believe it, look around at all living things and at all systems, manmade or otherwise. They are all either growing or dying. All of them. Always. Change is not a likelihood, it is a certainty, and enduring leaders need to understand everything they can about it.

George Land wrote a book in 1973 that explained the phenomenon of transformation and change called *Grow or Die—The Unifying Principle of Transformation.*[1] Land was a systems theorist and ecologist who eloquently described the obvious: all things in nature go through the same process. Understanding that process, Land believed, could help us unlock the secrets of change.

Land's work was originally geared towards the scientific community. As it gained exposure it was adopted by several organizational development pioneers who superimposed his model onto the growth patterns of organizations. Among its other distinctions, Land's work may have been the first intentional effort to integrate and overlap the disciplines of organizational development and natural science.

Phase One is the birthing or formative phase. Everything is new, routines have not been established, patterns have not formed and the organism, whether it is a person or an organization, is working to meet one survival imperative: find replicable patterns of behavior that will allow life to continue. Land eventually relabeled this phase the Entrepreneurial Phase based on feedback from organizational development practitioners who were experimenting with his model.

Leaders of Phase One organizations help by clarifying the vision and priorities of the organization in the face of so much uncertainty. Since experimentation is a critical process to discovery, successful Phase One leaders also work to bring out the creativity and innovation of the employees. What does a Phase One company need? Customers, users, or purchasers of their services. Therefore, a lot of emphasis in successful Phase One organizations is placed on listening to the needs of the customer and trying to find creative solutions to their needs.

A Phase One organization is a start-up organization or a new business unit or department. Phase One can also describe a phase of human behavior, as in a new relationship or the formation of a new work team or group, or someone who is in a new position. Teams in Phase One organizations focus on results, not on hierarchy, so the organizational structure tends to be flat.

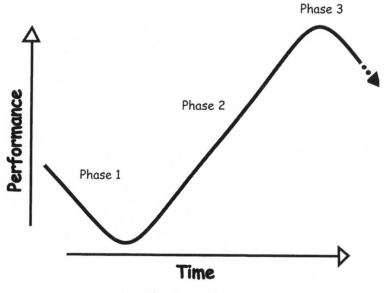

The Growth Curve

Phase Two, or what Land refers to as the Improvement Phase is marked by the establishment of a replicable pattern. In Phase One, the imperative was to experiment until successful survival strategies were discovered. In Phase Two priorities have changed from finding a replicable survival strategy to learning how to efficiently and accurately reproduce that strategy with as little expended energy as possible. Early Phase Two is the industrial equivalent of mass-producing a product or service that helped the business survive. As a group starts to work together and become more organized, group members take on roles to help increase efficiency and production.

Leaders in Phase Two organizations provide focus. Now that the organization has achieved success in surviving, it has to make a shift from being innovation-driven to being production-driven. Systems and procedures based on optimal production methods are required during Phase Two, so Phase Two leaders have to help transition the culture to a more systematic approach. This shift is a difficult one for many organizations, perhaps because the chaos and creativity of Phase One is often more appealing than the structure and focus of Phase Two. Employees who during Phase One were allowed and even encouraged to do whatever it took to be successful suddenly find themselves in roles that focus on one specific discipline or function with fairly rigid boundaries.

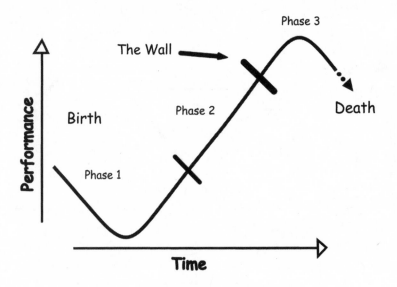

The Wall

As individuals within the group begin to take on fixed roles within the organization, lines of communication become more hierarchical and rigid. In a solidly Phase Two organization, everyone has very specific work assignments. Departments form. Groups organize. Competition between groups spur on improvements, at least for a while. In Phase Two, the focus is on efficiency. In a highly efficient production environment, there is little room for new or provocative ideas (unless the ideas increase efficiency and productivity). Chaos is seen as the enemy. The more the elements of the culture become rigid, the harder it is for the organization to change. Meanwhile, the customer's needs evolve and change, meaning that the organization has to change to keep pace with the customer.

Leaders in Phase Two know how to manage conflicting priorities, how to delegate and follow up on delegated tasks and how to monitor compliance with procedures and systems. They have gone from being unconsciously incompetent to consciously incompetent; from not knowing what they don't know to knowing what they don't know. As one emerging leader once said, "I've gone from doing things wrong about 100% of the time to doing things about 50% wrong and 50% right. The trouble is, I don't know which half is which yet."

Whereas Phase One organizations focus on listening to the customer and doing anything necessary to win business, Phase Two organizations focus on the product or service. Their attention shifts from being purely customer focused to what they sell and how to make it better, faster or cheaper.

Eventually, Phase Two organizations begin to experience declining results. The reasons for this vary:

- The customer's needs may have changed.
- More time and energy-efficient methods for delivering the service or making the product may have been developed by the competition.
- What was a novel service or product has now become mainstream and is being replaced by new product types.
- The competition may have gotten stiffer.

Regardless, late Phase Two organizations find that they have to infuse increasing amounts of energy into the process to maintain the same results.

THE WALL AND RECYCLING

Businesses who have saturated the market with an existing product have created their own carrying capacity problem just as surely as too many people competing for dwindling resources has. Since everything changes, always, and since everything goes in cycles, it follows that whatever product or service put a Phase One company on the map will eventually become outdated. As a product saturates the market, for example, increasing amounts of energy are needed (in the form of more elaborate or expensive marketing) to find the dwindling supply of consumers who don't know about the product.

Here is another, more compelling example: globally, we are at the wall with the use of fossil fuel. Nature isn't creating any more of it and we are using what is left of it faster than ever. There is more petroleum in the earth's crust for us to tap into, but the cost of extraction, in energy, is getting higher and higher because the "convenient" sources of oil have all been tapped. At some point in the future the cost of extraction of petroleum will exceed the benefits, so we'll invest more of our energy into one of the other technologies already available. Until then, we are simply postponing the inevitable: the need to change the way we think and operate using the earth's available energy resources. And until then, we will continue to heat up the planet, poison ourselves and pay higher and higher prices to do so. Gas is not actually going away, you know, it just changes forms after we burn it.[2]

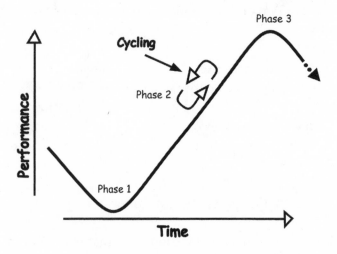

Recycling at The Wall

The difference is that now we are breathing it and suffering the deleterious effects of its unnatural presence in the environment instead of burning it. What will it take to make a change and push through the wall? Unless we face our addiction to oil and embrace a new paradigm about energy (a Phase Three approach) we are likely to learn our lesson through pain, and lots of it.

Unless guided by visionary leaders who not only know how to respond to change, but know how to anticipate it, businesses frequently spend years quite literally up against the wall. Getting over the wall requires change, and change is uncomfortable, scary and sometimes painful. We may exhaust all possibilities before committing to a difficult change in either our personal lives or in the way we manage businesses.

Leaders who are up against the wall and don't know what to do about it have some pretty universal symptoms:

- They are frustrated, baffled and exhausted. "Why isn't this working? It has always worked in the past!" is a frequent sentiment. They are on a witch hunt to find the culprit of the problem—and they find new culprits frequently—but finding them does little to relieve the problem.

- They are defensive. Specifically, they defend the status quo, or they defend why a certain situation is intractable and cannot be changed.

- They report that they are working harder than they have ever worked, with diminishing results.

- They typically have no idea that they are part of the problem.

Sound horrible? It is, but take heart, there is relief in sight: Phase Three. Land called Phase Three the Integrating Phase. In human development terms, we integrate the lessons acquired in our youth with the wisdom that comes from experience. We integrate where we are with what we've learned. Relationships overcome the Wall and enter Phase Three when the people involved reach a new level of acceptance and understanding with each other.

Phase Three is all about change and how to thrive in the face of it. A well known business case that exemplifies Phase Three is the development of the Saturn Corporation. As General Motors cycled back up against the wall in the late 1980's for the millionth time, a splinter cell of engineers, designers, managers, production specialists, etc. set about developing a less expensive vehicle that would compete with Japanese imports in both cost and performance. Building a Saturn meant creating a completely new operating model that was based more on the Toyota production system than on traditional American automobile manufacturing. The project met with huge resistance as it got started, mostly because of fear. By creating Saturn, GM did not do away with the rest of its products under other brands, it just repositioned them. It integrated the values and approaches of the past into the needs of the future.

Phase One companies are about the customer. Phase Two companies are about the product. Phase Three companies are about the process of integrating, combining and rebirthing. Instead of being a linear sequence, the growth curve is a fluid, cyclic process that goes on continually with regard to all human endeavors until the day we die.

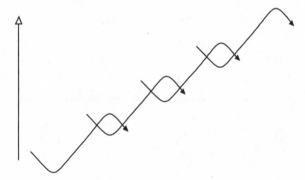

Recycling from Birth to Death, and Then to Birth

Everything that goes around, comes around, and understanding the pattern of change in any organization or organism can help us manage change. In truth, we don't actually "manage" change, we try to anticipate it and prepare for it by exploring likely scenarios for what we will do when it happens. When it shows up, we ride it and wrap ourselves around it. To wrap ourselves around change effectively, we have to understand a bit about complexity.

PART TWO
FAITH AND AGILITY IN ACTION

How do leaders who possess this trait manage to not come unglued when things become overly chaotic, complex or ambiguous? Apparently, there is no one way. Each leader has coping mechanisms and mental models they rely on to make sense out of the world. They have their own way of understanding the change, which allows them to break it into manageable chunks and navigate through the process.

HAVE A LITTLE FAITH (IN CHANGE)

Is Karen Garcia's ability to lead in such a complex system the result of some innate talent, or the result of training, education and practice? How do other enduring leaders who possess this insight develop it? More than most of the other insights of genuine leaders discussed in this book (except Connection), there is little agreement about whether Faith and Agility is "hard-wired" and in-born or if it is acquired through life. Like the serenity prayer says, learning to differentiate between what we have control over and what we do not is critical to our sanity, AND our ability to lead. Of all the insights, developing Faith and Agility tends to be the hardest for leaders who don't already possess it to develop. Part of the reason for the difficulty is tied to how our brains are wired. But there is hope! The more we know about how we are "wired," the better our chances are of changing what we think, feel and how we react.

Research has shown that if you think a given problem will be difficult to solve, you're probably right. If you perceive a situation as too complex to figure out, you're right again. If you think something will be too complex to understand, then it is likely to be true because of your outlook. However, if you believe it is possible to decipher a situation, you can and will. If you believe you can survive and thrive in times of change, you are right.[3]

As entrepreneur, human potential expert and successful businessman Larry Wilson says, "Our brains are perfect, stupid machines. They take in information and respond with whatever is available to draw from. If the only available response our brains have to dealing with a crisis is "Oh shit!" then sure enough, when a crisis occurs, we'll respond with what's available to us." But by rethinking what is, and is not, true to us we can change how we respond."

There is mantra familiar to many of us:

> "If I always do what I've always done, I'll always get what I've always gotten."

Larry takes that mantra and extends it to an interesting and accurate conclusion:

> "...and I'll always do like I've always done if I always think like I've always thought."

Thoughts are things. Thoughts are the stories we tell ourselves to explain the world. When we tell ourselves the story that something is unmanageable, it is. When we relax and embrace the situation, even when we don't understand it, we are far more capable of dealing with it.

THIS IS YOUR BRAIN AND CHANGE...

Scientists are making breakthroughs in understanding the brain almost daily and some of what they are learning will help us understand why we do what we do in the face of change. If we look at the evolution of the brain—and the development of animal life in general—the way our brains developed paralleled the demands placed on them by the circumstances of the environment.[4] Using a "first things, first" approach to development, one of the first and therefore oldest parts of our brains were the structures that controlled autonomic functions like heart rate, temperature regulation, and breathing. These functions just happen without any thought or awareness on our part. A large portion of our brains can stop functioning, yet we can still breathe and circulate blood thanks to these functions. The non-scientific term for this part of the brain is the "brain stem."

From nature's perspective, once the basics have been taken care of and the organism that contains the brain has assured itself of short-term viability, more advanced structures were developed that keep the process fueled and running. These functions take place literally and figuratively a little higher up the tree—in an area of the brain called the cortex and the limbic system. The functions controlled by this area include basic instincts: the automatic reactions of defense, hunger and the need to eat, the primal need to procreate and the instinct of fear. Once this part of the brain developed to nature's satisfaction, even more advanced functions could be developed including structures that allow us to develop rational and emotive thoughts and the ability to apply logic and deduction to our interpretation of the world around us. The neo-cortex, literally the "new brain," was developed.

What does an anatomy lesson on the brain have to do with how leaders lead through change? It means that it takes practice—a lot of it—for some of us to overcome basic primal urges that spring up when change occurs. The further down the tree of our brains we go, the harder it is for us to control our responses to change. The more instinctive or automatic our responses are, the less control and awareness we have of them.

We have an emotional response to change long before it is possible for us to have an intellectual response to it. This is in large part thanks to the limbic system, which controls a lot about how we feel and react to change and complexity. It is called a limbic "system" because it is a system of several separate structures that work together to control and guide behavior.

Scientists say the limbic system does not control our emotions on its own; it works in concert with our higher brains. The limbic system shades all of our emotions. PMS, it is thought, is the result of the limbic system becoming inflamed as hormone levels change in a woman's body. The change shades how someone views the world. For example, the world of business is undergoing radical change in information systems, project management, software upgrades and corporate reorganizations; how people immersed in these changes are coping with them varies from superbly to terribly, depending on the limbic system.

The limbic system is one of the storage areas for emotionally charged memories. Along with the frontal lobes, scientists believe that the limbic system acts as our emotional pain library—the place where we hold on to painful memories so we can avoid those events in the future. Given what we know about the limbic system and its effects on our emotions, it is no wonder why people who have experienced traumatic pain as the result of a change—like watching their home burn down—find changes later in life so upsetting.

Because of its location near our more primitive brains, the limbic system tends to just cruise along with little conscious awareness on the part of the host. For someone who has grown up learning that they are likely to get emotionally hurt when things change, their reaction to sweeping changes at work may make them feel very depressed, anxious or defensive. Because the seat of these emotions is embedded so deeply in the brain, a person experiencing these feelings may not even be aware that they are having an emotional reaction.

The source of our resistance to change may be nature, or it may be nurture. Regardless, being aware of exactly what our reaction is and learning to overcome it is vitally important.

As she grew up, Karen Garcia's limbic system got a good workout and some great programming that made change easier for her later in life. She is from a bilingual, mixed-race family. Her mother was Mexican and her father was Anglo (Karen eventually chose to adopt her mother's surname). The youngest of 8 children, Karen was raised in Dallas, Texas in the 60's and early 70's. When her oldest sister was born, Karen's mother contracted tuberculosis. Her grandmother, who knew little English, raised Karen until the age of five, when her parents took her back to begin grade school.

When Karen entered high school, Dallas had just started busing, and racial tensions among the students and communities in the affected areas grew. For Karen—a bi-racial girl from the poorer side of town—busing was an unpleasant memory. The demands on Karen's ability to adapt to things that were completely out of her control must have been enormous.

When she was 17, Karen opted to graduate early and head out on her own. She ended up in Socorro, New Mexico and got a job fire fighting with the Magdalena Eager Beavers. At the end of the fire season, she wandered through the northwest working odd jobs and saving money. By Karen's own report, she lacked confidence and needed time to find her way into a career. "I traveled all over the northwest working mostly menial jobs. I wasn't really sure what I was good at and less sure about what I wanted to do." Eventually she returned to New Mexico and put herself through school, getting a degree in Wildlife Management from New Mexico State University. After she graduated, Karen took several small jobs before she began her career with the State working in the Environment Department where she eventually rose to the rank of Program Manager of the Compliance section of the Occupational Health and Safety Bureau.

Karen's ability to balance the competing and conflicting interests in a constantly changing political and management environment may have come from being raised in a bilingual, bi-cultural family, or it may come from a developed survival skill that required her to be open to new possibilities when she was roaming and working part-time jobs. Whatever taught her to adapt, she grew quite good at it and her ability to tolerate and embrace change has been a key factor to her success as a leader.

Karen's role today is to help MMD fulfill its mission to:

> *Promote the public trust by ensuring the responsible utilization, conservation, reclamation and safeguarding of land and resources affected by mining.*

If she unabashedly assumed the posture of the environmental watch dog groups, the mining companies would become further entrenched. If she were to take too adversarial a posture with the mining companies, deadlocks would ensue. If she did not hold to the statutes and regulations she is paid to administer and manage, the public would get the short end of the stick. What makes Karen so successful in her role is her ability to see logic in the chaos and to embrace a range of possible solutions to any one scenario.

When the administration of state government in New Mexico changed in 2000, so did the Secretary of the Environment and the Secretary of Energy, Mining and Minerals. Karen's former boss and the Director of MMD, who was responsible for her promotion, was Doug Bland. The year before Doug left, he had to replace the outgoing Mine Regulatory Bureau Chief and he chose Karen for the position. Karen's promotion to Bureau Chief was a controversial move for Doug. She had only been with MMD for three years—a very short tenure for such a senior position—in spite of her having been in a management position with State OSHA. State government, more so than private industry, bases promotions on seniority and tenure, and to go against the prevailing habits of the Division was a risky move politically for Doug. According to Doug, "Karen was at the bottom rung of the MMD hierarchy. When I promoted her I bypassed 2 rungs of the ladder." Doug remembers Karen catching his attention early in her career with MMD. Instead of simply focusing on the tasks she was working on, she would "come to me with questions—complaints really—about why we were dealing with a permitting issue without taking into account a variety of other factors that were linked to the decision." Karen was seeing the complexity of the situation and questioning why the issues were not dealt with more holistically. In Doug's words,

> *Karen saw issues as management problems that needed addressing. The more I worked with her, the more I realized her complaining was really her way of understanding the issues so she could help find solutions to the management problems. She was not getting bogged down in the minutia.*

Doug's comments about what he saw in Karen and why he promoted her are very instructive to leaders who are working on this insight:

> *There were lots of very qualified candidates for this position and the selection was not easy. I was looking for someone with three skills: job knowledge of the [Mining] programs; the ability to work with and develop people in the program; and the ability to deal with all of the issues that would face that particular Bureau Chief. While the Coal [Mine Reclamation] program had around 30 Permits in the works most of the time and the permitting process was a fairly straightforward cookbook type of process, the hard rock [Mining Act Regulatory Program] was still relatively new. The regulations were vague and not as defined in a lot of cases. There were over 100 permits in the works, each one very different from the others.*

Doug continued:

> *I chose Karen for three reasons: First, she had passion for the work. A person in her position can easily be run over by the [mine] operators or just as easily be run over by some of the other departments, internally. To do the job, you have to be passionate about the regulations we enforce and the permits we issue. You have to be passionate about the environment. You have to be an environmentalist who understands that mining has a place in the State and we have to deal with the operators strongly, but realistically. I wanted someone who felt strongly about the environment and the need to regulate the mining industry and someone who I thought could do all that (being a bureau chief) entails.*
>
> *Secondly, Karen has a great work ethic and pride of owner-ship in everything she does. If the job called for her to stay late and pull an all-nighter to complete a report on some permit-ting issue, she did it. If someone needed to go listen to the en-vironmental groups after hours, or travel around the state to hear what people were thinking, she was there.*
>
> *Third, I chose Karen because of how she was with people. She knows how to work with the staff in a way that enhances work-ing at MMD and she knows how to deal with operators and the public. She has the ability to work to people's strengths and focus on their work product. She knows how to be respectful to people who aren't doing so well and help develop them, profes-sionally. I'm a big fan of creating a positive work environment and I thought Karen was the right choice to help do more of that.*

RESISTANCE TO CHANGE

Recent research into what motivates people to change is altering the conven-tional wisdom on the subject. For example, the widely held view that noth-ing prompts change like a crisis turns out to be incorrect. Studies of patients with heart disease suggest that they are reluctant and unwilling to make the necessary changes in lifestyle like quitting smoking or eating fewer fatty foods to prevent further cardiac damage. Up to fifty percent of all cardiac by-pass grafts in patients who have undergone bypass surgery have re-clogged arteries within a few years. Angioplasties reclog within a few months. The patients win a new lease on life, yet over fifty percent of them don't change the lifestyles that created the cardiac disease in the first place.[5] It would seem logical that such a crisis as impending heart failure would create a high level of motivation for changing, but in fact, it does not.

Large businesses can hit and stay at "the wall" a lot longer than a cardiac patient. Endlessly recycling the same ineffective approaches that don't work is sometimes hard to see because it happens over the course of years or even decades. A now famous rescue from the brink of disaster and bankruptcy illustrates this point. In 1979-80 General Motors Chairman Lee Iacocca—with the support of the Union of Automobile Workers (UAW)—got the United States government to bail out General Motors. By offering $1.5 billion in loan guarantees and ultimately eliminating 50,000 blue collar jobs, the government was able to keep GM in business through the Arab oil embargo, lagging automobile sales, and the worst recession in decades. GM was the weakest of Detroit's big three auto manufacturers, losing between $6 and $8 million a day at the zenith of its problems. In a magnificent display of charisma and bravado, Chairman Iacocca starred in no less than 61 television commercials designed to increase sales and improve public perception. Iacocca's efforts notwithstanding, it was the single largest corporate bail out of all time. Now, a quarter century later, GM has completed the cycle and is once again in trouble. The company has asked former Chairman Iacocca to once again be its spokesman as the company scrambles to seek relief from many of the same ills that plagued it in 1980. New day, same problem. Crisis does not inspire change at the corporate organizational level either—at least not without a change in mindset.

VIRGINIA SATIR AND THE CHANGE PROCESS MODEL

From a human performance standpoint, "change management" has several distinct phases. An easy way to understand the emotional process of change comes from the great work done by Virginia Satir and her research into death and dying. Satir's theories and viewpoints have been widely embraced by the change management community. Her work centered on an astute observation that human reactions to change are similar to our reactions to death.

While most change does not represent death, we have an emotional reaction to it as if we were resisting or fighting the possibility of death.

Satir's premise was this: change is not an event, it is a process. As with any process, one has to go through it in order to integrate it instead of being constantly affected by it. But going through change—instead of running around it—is painful. There is hope, however. If we go through change instead of resisting it, we learn how to respond better when the next change occurs. Like George Land and his growth curve, Satir used a curve to describe her view of the change process as well, although her curve looks different than Land's.

Her model is illustrated with only the two axes labeled. See if you can figure out what she had to say about change before reading on.

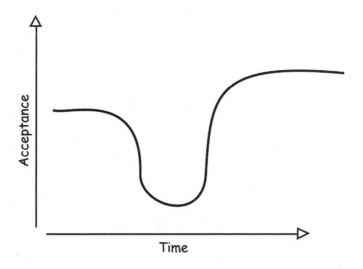

Virginia Satir's Loss/Response Curve

Notice that the two axes in this model are time and acceptance—implying there is a connection between the time when a change occurs and our ability to accept it. Notice also that the end-phase of this curve suggested that our level of acceptance actually increases once we go through a change.

Before any change occurs, we are in the status quo (the far left of the diagram). Then suddenly a new element is introduced into the system. At first we deny that anything has changed. Then we resist the change as we come out of denial, and our level of acceptance goes down dramatically. We hit rock bottom about the time chaos takes over. By "chaos" I mean a period when what has worked before now doesn't, and when what used to be true no longer is true. Chaos is the time when what was predictable no longer works. As we grapple with the confusion, a new pattern of survival starts to emerge. A "Transforming Idea," as Satir called it, takes shape. Over time, that transforming idea morphs into a new way of understanding the world. Eventually, our level of acceptance starts to increase. We have embraced a new reality—the far right of the diagram. Notice how the right side of the diagram is higher than the left?

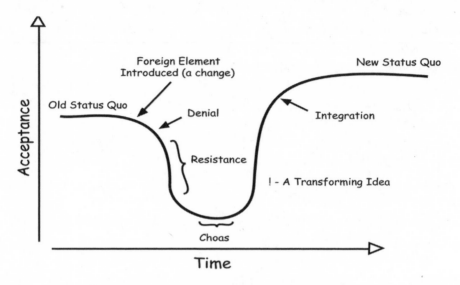

Stages of Loss and Acceptance

That's because Satir's model is based on the belief that, if we go through the process, we emerge smarter, prepared, experienced and more able to cope with the next change.

Satir's model is an optimal picture of how people adapt to change. Unfortunately, all too often we see people and groups get stuck in the denial and resistance phase of this model far too long—sometimes indefinitely.

It is likely that the problems GM has and is facing are endemic of the entire automotive industry. With hundreds of thousands of workers expecting to retire on pension plans and in the face of escalating costs of car components and labor, the industry has been resisting change long enough. To be fair, the "change" they are resisting is enormous: scrapping the production and business models of the past 100 years while embracing a new, leaner, more competitive job market where efficiencies can be gained by shipping key processes off shore for one tenth the wage and reducing what they offer in terms of retirement and pension.

Regardless of whether the loss is on an organizational or personal level, Satir's message is clear: go through change, not around it. You are likely to feel some pain either way, but avoiding it just prolongs it. Or, as Winston Churchill put it:

If you're going through hell, keep going...

CONTROL: PARADOX AND ILLUSION

Of all the demands of leadership, none is more convoluted, complex and cunning than learning how to—and when to—exert influence on an organization, person or system. It's a conundrum; too much control and team members give up all of their authority out of frustration or quietly check their brains at the door when they come to work. On the other hand, if leaders aren't involved enough, employees feel like they are swinging in the breeze with no support, no help and no mentoring. If it is true that we learn most of what we know through experience, than how can a leader allow their employees enough leeway to have valuable learning experiences without negatively affecting the organization's results?

The answer is, it depends. What applies to one person in one situation does not apply to the same person in a different situation. How Karen Garcia navigates through complex regulatory decisions with her staff depends on a long list of variables. Leaders who learn to successfully navigate these types of issues learn one universal lesson over and over again: none of us actually controls anything other than ourselves. The best we can hope for is to influence others.

Control is a dangerous intoxicant for leaders. New managers who are eager to prove themselves may "take the bull by the horns" on their early projects and oversee every detail of how work is performed. Eventually, their success gets noticed and they get promoted. As their careers progress, they are expected to handle an ever increasing workload, more and more projects. But as we saw in George Land's growth curve, their ability to handle the workload in the same way that worked for them in the beginning eventually meets diminishing returns. Without employees who know how to think and act absent of constant guidance, most managers eventually fail. Many senior leaders survive for years—even decades—working as micromanagers.

But as we've seen, change is inevitable and what used to work is bound to eventually wear out.

Leaders who don't tame the beast of control—meaning get a handle on their own egos and insecurities—inevitably fall from grace. In their wake they leave a trail of frustrated people, or dependent employees incapable of cogent independent thought, or a string of broken promises and unfulfilled potential.

What do we really have control over? Our kids? Nope. Our spouses? Most definitely not. Employees? Sorry. Each of us has control—and I use that term very loosely—over ourselves, period. Being able to control anything else is an illusion. We mistakenly insert the word control for what we can really and frequently do, which is influence. Can you influence the decisions and actions of your kids? You bet. Can you influence how your spouse behaves towards you? Absolutely! You have control over the only thing you need to have control of to be successful: you.

Our need to control typically comes from one of two places: confidence or fear. Confidence and fear both arise from our perception of ourselves and our assessment of specific situations. When we are confronted with a task that is familiar or easy to solve, we are confident. The problem is that confident leaders frequently fool themselves into thinking that those around them will learn by watching. We learn most effectively from doing, not watching, so the strategy rarely works. If a task is perceived as risky or dangerous, we can become controlling because we don't want to fail, but once again, control hinders learning.

Whether through confidence or fear, our attempts to control almost always have the same end result: a lack of learning and experience for those that need it. Worse, if we start to think that we are successful "controlling" a situation, this success has the effect of falsely inflating our confidence, which in turn leads us to believe that we can have more influence on others than we actually have.

Letting go of the illusion of control is part of what having faith involves: a realistic view of what we have control over and a faith that all we need to have control over to be successful is ourselves.

COMPLEXITY

> *"Abandon the urge to simplify everything, to look for formulas*
> *and easy answers, and to begin to think multidimensionally, to*

glory in the mystery and paradoxes of life, not to be dismayed
by the multitude of causes and consequences that are inherent
in each experience to appreciate the fact that life is complex."
– M. Scott Peck[6]

Understanding complexity requires a "both/and" mindset. What we see and study can sometimes be reduced to the simplest principles. There is wisdom to this approach, particularly when trying to understand the complex questions that confront each of us as we try to make sense of the choices that face us in life. "Complexity" on the other hand exists in everything, and learning to embrace it is just as important as trying to simplify it. The question is not, "Is this a complex situation that can be simplified?" but "What can be learned from this situation's complexity and from its simplicity?"

"Complexity" is not the same as "Complicated." A complicated task can be simplified to actions, calculations or reasoning, which usually decreases the difficulty of completing the task. Solving complicated problems is best accomplished by those who have prior experience sorting out similar complicated tasks. Every day examples of complicated tasks include building a skyscraper, sending a rocket into space or taking a team to the summit of, say, Mt. Everest. Each of these tasks can be broken down into steps or discrete tasks. Complexity, on the other hand, cannot be reduced, decreased or simplified as a result of working on it. Examples of complex tasks include child rearing, reforming healthcare and coaching.

Building the Taj Mahal, located in Agra, India, qualifies as a complicated, but not complex, task. Made entirely of white marble, this structure is considered one of the eight wonders of the world, a building of unparalleled symmetry and economy. The Taj was completed after 22 years of construction in 1648 and was designed by an architect named Ustad 'Isa—a well known and revered architect of the time. Historians believe that Master 'Isa was the lead architect on the project with a team of designers from Persia, the Ottoman Empire and Italy. Even though new, intricate design details were integrated into the design of the building, the designers were able to draw upon their previous experience and their considerable expertise to solve the technical and structural issues associated with building the structure. They knew and followed a prescribed process for constructing the edifice similar to the processes they had used on countless other projects.

Now that we have become expert at it, sending a rocket into space is complicated, but not complex. It requires completing a number of complicated and intricate calculations, acquiring and assembling the necessary materials, and launching it in a prescribed manner. However, the procedures for performing these tasks are based on making a series of determinations that are known, established and can be laid out in a linear sequence.

Raising children qualifies as a complex task. Try as we might, each child requires special attention in unpredictable ways and at unpredictable times. How our children turn out is equally mysterious, involving chance and countless variables that can't be predicted such as genetics, the personality features of the child, nutrition, the external environment, and so on. Similarly, the solution to healthcare reform requires more than an advanced knowledge of economics, politics, business, medicine, or sociology. The interlocking issues of economics, legislation and governance, regulation, culture, education and insurance make the issue complex and complicated.

Complex tasks defy simplification; they remain complex no matter how we look at them and no matter how much we try to simplify them. When confronted with complexity, those of us who like to think we have more control than we actually do will find ourselves frustrated, because a truly complex situation is beyond ours, or anyone else's ability to control. Since it can't be reduced to a simple formula, complexity is best addressed through an incremental approach founded on the knowledge that complexity can't be reduced, but it can be overcome. Think back to the discussion about George Land's growth curve in the previous part for a moment. Nothing generates recycling at the WALL like trying to use complicated problem solving to address a complex issue. When companies (or governments) try to use simplified thinking to deal with complexity, they recycle endlessly or until the customers defect, employees leave, the money runs out or the system breaks down.

Using the definitions and language established earlier in this book, solving complicated problems is a skill. Solving complex problems is part of the insight of *Faith and Agility.*

Dr. Elliott Jaques and his colleagues devised a model for organizational development that describes the connection between complexity and leadership called The Requisite Organization.[7] Jaques believed that successful, healthy organizations worked constantly to balance 4 main factors that drive and guide Requisite organizations:

- Processes that reinforce accountability throughout the organization, regardless of position;

- Jobs, defined by their level of complexity and the time horizons people have to think in terms of in order to be successful;

- MAH's or Management Accountability Hierarchies – the structures and systems in organizations that define accountability and who is responsible for what;

- The capacity and capability of the organization's people relative to the work they perform.

When the system is well ordered and people are assigned to tasks that roughly parallel their ability to handle and manage the various levels of complexity, Jaques suggests, people perform at or near their peak performance level and the organization prospers. Jaques divides the ability to think and manage complexity into six "strata" based on how complicated the task is to complete and the time frame required to complete it:

Stratum I – People whose job it is to follow a predetermined path to a goal. These are employees who understand procedures and know how to follow them. Stratum I employees revert to known dogma or procedure when a situation becomes ambiguous; and they generally manage tasks in time frames ranging from hours to days.

Stratum II – People who detect patterns and anticipate problems through the ongoing accumulation of data and information. When a Stratum II employee sees a problem that requires decision making, they reference other decisions that have been made under similar situations to make the current decision. Stratum II employees tend to manage tasks and think in terms of weeks or months.

Stratum III – These are employees who manage projects following a pre–established process, without a lot of detail. Jaques and his colleagues call these projects "serial projects"; the steps to take are unclear but the project's tasks can be defined and executed in a serial, or linear progression. Stratum III employees tend to be comfortable thinking in terms of months and years.

Stratum IV – Employees who can oversee and manage multiple, complex projects simultaneously are Stratum IV leaders. These employees tend to view their tasks as multi-year processes.

Stratum V – Instead of working in a sequential, procedural or prescribed way, Stratum V employees view things systemically and abstractly. They can visualize an entire business process and may work more on clusters of tasks simultaneously without consciously knowing the interrelatedness of the subject. Stratum V employees see their tasks from the perspective of eras or decades.

Stratum VI – The employees focus their energies on the linkages between a number of inputs including business processes, the environment, the culture and capability of the overall company. Stratum VI thinkers look at things from a truly long–term perspective—measuring time and task completion in multiple decades.

By Dr. Jaques definition, Karen Garcia is required to operate and lead somewhere between Stratum IV and Stratum V. She has to manage multiple projects without a lot of detailed information (unless she and her employees determine how to create information through research and study) and she has to be able to grasp and visualize completion of projects over the time spans of many years. For an organization to be successful, it is important to match the right people to the right jobs. This assures that they are in jobs in which their ability to manage complexity is commensurate to the tasks they need to perform.

PART THREE
THE PRACTICE

"God grant me the serenity
to accept the things I cannot change;
the courage to change the things I can;
and the wisdom to know the difference"

FOR ASPIRING LEADERS

Keep the Faith – Things Will Change

One of the most fascinating elements of change is that it is rarely expected before it happens, but once it does, looking at what has changed makes almost total sense. Change is frequently precipitated by a series of small, subtle and apparently unrelated events that collectively influence something enough to generate a change. To illustrate this point, let's take a personal approach. Think back to what you were doing for a living and in life five years ago. What were you doing for work? What did you do with your free time? How were your relationships? With whom did you have relationships? Did you have friends that you thought you'd have forever? What were your goals then? Where were you headed? Five years ago, where did you think you would be five years hence?

If you are like most of us, you will notice that you are not at all where you thought you'd be. Your interests have changed. Your career may have taken an unexpected left or right turn in a new direction that was completely unexpected. Your friendships and relationships have taken equally unexpected turns; some of them have deepened in surprising ways over the past five years while others have faded some with time. Things have probably not turned out as you would have predicted, but barring a major life catastrophe, an unbelievable run of back luck or sudden death, most of what has happened to you probably makes sense when viewed in retrospect. And what has precipitated the change was more than likely a series of small events that all led up to the moment when change occurred. In some rare cases, things may not have changed at all for you—or if they have, you don't notice them. Each of us goes through periods of relative calm and stasis. If you're in between transitions, enjoy the calm and rest up, for that time will pass, too.

What to Do:

Don't get hung up on picking a direction and pushing for change to happen in a specific way. There are two reasons for this advice: First, you are but a small piece of the large cosmic pie that is changing and therefore you have only a small effect—and only the smallest piece of control—over the changes that are occurring. Secondly, if you are an aspiring leader who has moderate influence in your organization, your role is usually to react to changes and produce consistent results, whatever the change is, rather than direct the changes. If being noticed is important to you, don't push it, just adapt to the changes productively and quickly.

To Truly Add Value, Take Alvin Toffler's Advice

Take charge of your own learning. Amidst change, the leaders who know how to independently acquire the skills to be more valuable to their business are the ones who get noticed. Don't wait for a mentor, find one and recruit them to help you. Don't wait to be asked to go to a training that you need to become better at your evolving job, ask to be sent. And if you meet resistance, consider sending yourself.

Choose well. Be judicious and cautious with how you allocate your time, particularly in times of change. Prioritize activities that support and facilitate the business. Choose carefully when to apply your full attention to a task and when to simply complete it to a satisfactory standard. Your ability to manage your time, identify key priorities and apply differing levels of attention to different projects will be noticed.

Don't sacrifice relationships for tasks. Leaders lead people, not things. Preserve relationships with everyone in your sphere. You have to be able to work effectively with even the most difficult people. Never dismiss someone out of hand as unimportant.

Notice Your Own Resistance to Change

There is a misperception that those who resist change are obstructing it. Not always. Resistance is a normal reaction to change and we all have it to varying degrees depending on our position or proximity in relation to that change. Think of Satir's Loss/Response curve: Before we can embrace a new possibility, we have to resist it, then grieve it before we can begin to accept it.

What to Do:

Don't bypass your feelings and emotions about change, work through them. How does one work through them? Use trusted colleagues as sounding boards and coaches to express your feelings, concerns and fears about the changes you are witnessing. As you work through your personal feelings, notice how some of your concerns stem from emotionally based fears. Challenge yourself to see those emotionally based fears for what they frequently are: little dramas we make up as rationalizations for why things should not change. Try and influence the direction of change instead of stopping it.

Be Optimistic

Harvard Business School change expert John Kotter is one of the foremost thinkers and researchers about the human dynamic in changing organizations. Professor Kotter says, and I agree, that change is less about creating a good strategy or effective systems and culture in an organization than it is about the organization's resilience going through change. Kotter says the most critical issue in times of upheaval is the response and behaviors of the people in the midst of the upheaval. If they are pessimistic or preoccupied with fighting the change, the process is likely to be more drawn out and much more painful. If on the other hand, they think and behave optimistically, everything works out better. A simple but critical behavior everyone can exhibit in times of upheaval is to focus on the moment at hand.

What to Do:

Deal with what is real and what is tangible, not with what is a product of your imagination or what may happen the day after tomorrow. By living and working to make the best of what IS, you exert perhaps the best and certainly the most supportive behavior needed in times of change.

Studies have supported Kotter's assertion that people who view events occurring around them optimistically are more likely to see what is happening objectively and are more able to adjust to changes. I am not suggesting you play Pollyanna or pretend that nothing is happening. You have to go through the process of accepting change, and that may be painful. Once you are able to do so, plot a path through whatever is happening and develop possible scenarios that lead to a positive outcome. Find the silver lining and work towards it.

Resist When Resistance is Called For

Just because Karen responds well to all sorts of changes does not mean that she agrees with all of them. She doesn't. Karen frequently finds herself in the role of having to implement changes she is not in favor of as a result of actions taken by the governor, the secretary of the environment, or the legislature. "When I disagree with something that is happening, I say so, but some of the difficult decisions we need to make (as a state) take time to come to, and sometimes we have to wait."

When Karen disagrees, she fights when fighting is called for. She states her opinion for the record when fighting will be more destructive than productive. She lobbies for support for alternatives when she thinks doing so will produce a better result. But at the end of the day, Karen makes change work—even if she is not in favor of its direction.

What to Do:

Not all change is necessary, good, or productive. If you resist or state your disagreement, make sure you do so in a responsible fashion that shows you are making the best interest of the business your priority. The delivery of your ideas is up to you; the reception of your ideas is up to whomever you are talking to. If you decide to push against the change, separate your opinion about the situation and how well received your ideas are from your ego. Understand that, provided you state your opinions responsibly and professionally, how they are received is not about you. By far, the highest percentage of "victims" in a change process in an organization are those who personalize it. What is happening to the organization may or may not affect you, but it is unlikely the change is ABOUT you.

A Change Resistance Checklist:

• Survey the situation. Do you have the necessary resolve to push against the change? Does your opinion truly count enough to make a difference? Is your perspective on the situation going to be seen as credible and useful or misinformed and a waste of energy? By pushing against the change, are you more likely to hurt yourself or improve the situation?

• Survey yourself. Are you merely upset about the effects the change will have on you, personally? If your concerns are for the organization, but the change will be inconvenient for you, are you ready and equipped to explain that your resistance is in the best interest of the organization and is not just self–serving? Is it possible your opinion matters more than you are willing to admit? Don't rationalize or make excuses for not speaking up. If your opinion needs to be heard, say it!

• State your ideas and perspectives clearly. Provide good backup information to support your ideas. Do your best to make sure what you are saying has been heard, then let it go. If you can't let it go and you vehemently disagree with what is happening, decide what you feel you must do in your own best interest. It is usually better to leave than it is to stay and be angry. The biggest mistake of people who choose to resist change is to assume that change in organizations is a democratic process. Usually it isn't. Senior managers will typically discuss potentially disruptive changes and study them from every conceivable angle before announcing them publicly. Once this has occurred, their hope is that the employees will understand and support what is happening. In rare instances, middle managers or less senior employees will be asked for their opinion and input.

Know the Difference Between Complex & Complicated, and Act Accordingly

How leaders address complex versus complicated tasks varies significantly. Leaders at the most senior levels in organizations are more frequently the ones who diagnose the nature of an opportunity or problem and then determine who should address it, and how. Asking one's self, "Is this a complex problem or a complicated one?" can help determine how to approach it. On the other hand, misdiagnosing an issue can have a detrimental effect on its ultimate solution.

A promising example of an effective solution to a complex problem can be found in the over 95 health care facilities across the country that are adopting the Planetree System as a means of patient care. Planetree is an internationally recognized system that is proving to be an effective solution to both healing and healthcare management. Planetree has taken the notion of health care and turned it on its ear. By embracing a truly holistic approach to patient care, facilities using the Planetree approach are posting significantly better results financially, medically and preventively than similar facilities using the traditional approach to health care. Foremost among the improvements noted for facilities using the Planetree system is the effect of a "healing environment" on surgical recovery patients and for the issue of pain management in post–operative patients. Roger S. Ulrich, Ph.D. is the director of the Center for Health Systems and Design at Texas A&M University. According to Dr. Ulrich, "Studies have shown that stress suppresses immune function and often is expressed in upper respiratory infections," Ulrich says. "It stands to reason that patients undergoing surgery have high stress levels that can affect the immune system, impact wound recovery and possibly determine the probability of infection. Patients who are exposed to stress–reducing interventions in a healing environment show reductions in anxiety and increases in immunity that can be measured. The medical community is more accepting of the fact that having a patient look at a white ceiling and having nothing better to do than counting the tiles is not a good thing."[8] In a study comparing 12 Planetree affiliates 12 months prior to and 12 to 24 months following implementation of the Planetree model of care, significant average increases in overall patient satisfaction were found as well as a willingness to recommend the healthcare facility to family and friends, and a likelihood of returning to the facility. It also appears that the Planetree model may also be responsible for fewer medical errors and lower infection rates. The elements of the Planetree system:

- Human Interaction: Planetree is about people caring for people
- Empowering Patients through Information and Education
- Architectural Design Conducive to Health and Healing
- The Importance of the Nutritional and Nurturing Aspects of Food
- Spirituality: The Importance of Inner Resources
- The Importance of the Human Touch
- Healing Arts: Nutrition for the Soul
- Complementary Therapies: Expanding Patient Choices
- Healthy Communities: Expanding the Boundaries of Health Care
- The Importance of Family, Friends and Social Support

Instead of viewing healing as an issue of science, the Planetree model begins by assuming that healing is an issue that is far more complex. Instead of reducing the complexity, Planetree acknowledges it by including many of the pieces that affect healthcare in the system.

What to Do:

If it is a complicated problem, unpack it by pulling out all the pieces of the problem. Then work to simplify them. Try and find the source of the problem and see if you can start unpacking it there. If it is a complex problem, chunk it down, that is, separate the tangled issues of the problem as much as possible and go to work solving discrete components. Deciding what kind of problem you are dealing with will save you immeasurable time and energy. If it is complicated, reduce it to its parts. If it is complex, determine the inter-relationships of the parts and your desired outcome and proceed on a basis that gives you as much of what you want as possible. If you want to know what hitting the wall feels like personally, try applying complicated problem solving methods (reducible to simpler or more defined chunks) to a complex problem (not reducible, multi–faceted, chaotic). Save yourself some heart-ache; before diving in to a problem, do your best to figure out what kind of problem you're dealing with. Complex problems require untraditional solutions and input from many different people with different perspectives. Our own preconceived notions about what works and what does not work when solving complex issues are an impediment to working through complexity.

FOR SENIOR LEADERS AND COACHES

Where is your organization on the Growth Curve? Take another look at the growth curve explanation. Where is your business? Given where it is, what are your plans to push through to another level and what precautionary measures can you take to make sure your transition from Phase Two to Phase Three (through the wall) is a smooth one? If you are comfortably ensconced in Phase Two, what can you do to maintain the status quo? If you are entering Phase Three, realize that what people most need is a positive vision of the future. You may need to describe it for them, over and over again.

What to Do:

Have these discussions with your trusted advisors and your management team. Debate where you are and the best way through it. Don't worry about who is right or wrong; encourage thinking and creativity. Once you decide on a strategy, engage them in helping you achieve the plan.

Not All Change is Better In Small Doses

In an effort to mitigate the effects of change, founding senior leaders often attempt to soften the blow of change by doing it very slowly over an extended period of time. Sometimes, however, it is better to completely change the situation quickly. Responding to change is an emotional process that requires a shift in behavior, and there is research showing that sometimes it is more effective to ask people to make major shifts instead of changes in small doses. Dr. Dean Ornish, a professor of medicine at the University of California at San Francisco and founder of the Preventive Medicine Research Institute in Sausalito, California noticed that the effects of incremental changes in diet on patients were less effective than radical changes. In the incremental change scenario, patients felt deprived of their favorite foods, but they did not get positive reinforcement quickly enough in the form of weight loss, since the changes they made were only incremental and weight loss occurs more slowly. Radical diets requiring complete shifts in behavior and habit produce better results in diets, because patients feel less deprived and they can quickly see tangible results.

What to Do:

Rapid organizational change instead of incremental change can be very effective if leaders have in place the following structures and support mechanisms before proceeding:

- An aligned, articulate and committed leadership team who supports the change effort and can help employees move quickly through the loss response curve;

- A process for either keeping clients, customers and even suppliers informed of the rapid change initiative or a process for insulating them from all of the changes so they don't become unduly concerned;

- A clearly defined explanation that can be posted, discussed, blogged and otherwise disseminated through the organization about why a rapid change approach was used instead of an incremental one;

- A plan to move, remove or re–assign key players who will be unable to adapt or align themselves with the change effort quickly enough;

- Clearly defined metrics and measures to show whether or not the plan is working and how it needs to be modified
over time.

FOR BOTH ASPIRING LEADERS AND MENTORS

Choose Your Pain.

When confronted with a wall, here is what to do: CHOOSE YOUR PAIN. Staying stuck is going to be painful. So will be trying something new—particularly if it fails. Either scenario has its own brand of pain. What are you willing to risk to get what you want? Choose. Don't tell yourself you don't have choices, you do. The most tragic of all circumstances is when a person or organization is at the wall and, instead of confronting the issue, they recycle countless times trying different variations on the same theme to surmount the wall.

Know Your Own Control Triggers

The question is not IF you can act controlling, but whether your need to control interferes with your people's ability to produce results. There is no need to be apologetic or remorseful for being controlling. At some point in the life cycle of your organization, it is entirely possible that your ability to control a situation was critical to the organization's well being. If you are working on a project or managing a company by organizing and prioritizing all of the details, restricting communication so that it flows through you, or making most of the decisions, know that doing so comes at a cost in exchange for the control you gain. While exerting control can be critical when getting your organization through tough times, continuing to manage the organization from a control position is very difficult to sustain. Worse, it creates dependency on whoever is in control. I have worked with six companies who were making the transition from being run by a founding senior leader to being run by a senior management team. In each case, the most difficult element of the transition was the senior team's ability to truly think and act independently without the input or leadership of the founding senior leader. In fact, organizations where the senior team is so habituated to following directions from the founding senior leader often require a new senior team since the old one just can't make the transition to thinking and acting independently.

Control is a trade–off. The more you have, the less the people around you learn about how to make decisions or execute plans. The less you have, the more those around you will learn from experience. The more you have, the better you will feel about mistakes when they occur because the mistakes will be yours. The less you have, the worse you will feel about mistakes since you have no ownership in them.

What to Do:

Be aware of when you are fooling yourself about your need for control. If you want to create a senior team that can function without your constant leadership be aware of the following pitfalls:

- Saying, "I trust your decision, just run it by me before you make it." What you are really saying is that you don't trust whoever is making that decision. Incidentally, there is nothing wrong with NOT trusting someone else's ability to make the kind of decision you think is important, but don't fake it.

- Waiting until after a decision is made (by the senior team) to state your opinion, particularly when you disagree with the decision. If you want to let the team make the decision on their own, then let them do it and learn from it without additional "I told you so" input. "I told you so" feedback doesn't help anyone except perhaps to give you some odd sense of satisfaction. If you disagree with a prospective decision that may be made by the senior team, say so or don't, but support the team's process in the end and be there to help them clean up the mess, if one is created.

Instead, follow these two guidelines:

- Pick your role and stick to it. Leaders who want their senior teams to grow and become more capable have a hard time picking how they want to participate and sticking to it.

If you want to approve/disapprove any decision made, but you don't want to have to be the one to think through the choice of decisions, then do that. If you want to do nothing other that to watch how the senior team does managing the company without you for 6 months, then do that (I don't recommend this approach, incidentally). If you want your opinion to be of equal weight to the rest of the team, then do that. Whatever your role will be, pick one and do your best to stick to it.

•   Make sure people know what they have control over and what they don't. Don't think giving someone a false sense of authority as a means of bolstering their self confidence is helpful—it is not.

Manage Creative Tension – Don't Eliminate It

In the creative communities of the performing arts, design, advertising, and architecture, the phrase "creative tension" is frequently used to describe an important ingredient critical to innovation and design genius. Creative tension exists whenever people with passionate views on a particular project or problem disagree about how to address the issue. If everyone is firmly entrenched in an ego–based need to be "right" or prove their point to the exclusion of listening to the perspectives of others, there is just tension. Creative tension exists when there is a shared belief that everyone's perspective is of value, even if they disagree.

In times of change, creative tension can be a key driver for organizational transformation. By articulating their vision, each person involved in the process gains new insights into the possibilities, if not the solutions. By listening to the visions of others, new insights are gained (which also enhances relationships of the people in the group). Creative tension most commonly exists between those who seek to maintain the status quo (what helped the organization achieve success) and those that have a new view of the future. One of the problems of managing creative tension during leadership transitions is that the founders have hard data to support their defense of the status quo while the aspiring leaders only have an educated guess about what might work in the future. Interestingly, most founders started their companies with no more than an educated guess.

Organizations without any creative tension eventually experience declining results. Without an internal mechanism to challenge the commonly held beliefs, organizations frequently stagnate. I call this "drinking too much of their own Koolaid" because these organizations eventually take on a cult–like feel that is the result of everyone sharing a common, often outdated, paradigm about the work they do and the solutions they offer customers. These types of organizational cultures become intolerant and even indignant when anyone challenges the status quo.

Well managed creative tension means that the interests and ideas of both groups are blended in many of the organization's strategic decisions. What worked and what might work meet at a crossroads where success is more possible and innovation almost guaranteed.

Managing the tension between these two types of people is not only healthy—it is essential. The objective in managing creative tension in organizations is NOT to eliminate it. Imagine a one–party system of governance. We grow from the debate of multi–party systems. Without creative tension in our system of governance, we would be an empire or worse, a dictatorship. Likewise, the aim of constructive tension between Founding Senior Leaders and Aspiring Leaders is to grow and learn in a way that benefits the entire enterprise. Such tension is critical to the success of any business.

FAITH AND AGILITY

Add Value...

- Embrace changes as they occur when you can.
- Resist changes when every logical, non-emotional fiber in your being says the change is not in the best interest of accomplishing an end result.
- Learn as much as you can about alternative problem solving techniques, especially for dealing with complexity and chaos.

Inspire Others...

- Be the calming, optimistic influence that helps smooth the way through change and complexity. Use your Connection skills to help those who are fighting change learn to relax into it.
- Assume it's never too late to change. As Ghandi said:"Be the Change" —it begins with you.

Change the World...

- Look at the BIG PICTURE and have a plan. Think, plan and act with the end in mind instead of what may or may not happen tomorrow.
- Successful leaders plan six, twelve or even twenty-four months in advance.
- Notice patterns and trends, work to anticipate change. Lead change instead of following it.

SECTION THREE
COURAGE THROUGH SERVICE

This Section In Brief:

Vision is certainly a desirable thing for a leader to have. But Courage Through Service is the insight that turns that vision into reality. When leaders have vision, they must also have an innate belief in their ability to attack a problem and make it better. That innate belief is confidence. When an enduring leader has confidence and a desire to make a difference in whatever way he can, magic happens.

Confidence without direction is hubris. The desire to make a difference without confidence is just a fantasy. Together, they inspire. Nothing motivates employees like working for or with a leader who is inspired to make a difference. The sheer force of their conviction and will enrolls and attracts those around them. Nothing builds confidence like trying something difficult or risky and succeeding at it. The better we become at trying difficult things, the more capable we feel and the more willing we are to try something challenging again. Research shows that confidence can be developed. One of the best ways to develop it is through a mindset of service to others.

Leaders who possess this insight have learned to temper their desire to make a difference with an understanding that things happen when opportunity and timing converge. Until timing and opportunity do converge, they provoke opportunity by doing things that serve others. For more information on how to develop a practice that builds confidence in one's ability to make a difference, turn to page 126.

PART ONE
TO SERVE, TO STRIVE
AND NOT TO YIELD

The uninterrupted supply of machinery, weapons, food and supplies from North America to England was critical to holding the German juggernaut at bay during World War II. The task of delivery fell on the merchant marines and private shipping lines of the U.S., England, and Scotland. Germany understood how important this supply line was, which is why U-Boat captains trained their sights and torpedoes at supply ships making the crossing from the States to the United Kingdom more than they did on war ships. The toll the U-Boat captains extracted was enormous in both supplies and loss of life. The loss of life was what most concerned Lawrence Holt. Holt was the owner of the Blue Funnel Shipping Line, a fleet of freighters that he had made available, along with the crews to run them, to the British government to keep supplies moving. Ships could be replaced, but lives could not.

When Holt surveyed the problem—loss of life of his ship's crews—he discovered a disturbing trend: the old salts were surviving at a much higher rate than young crew members. Holt called a meeting of the more experienced and more senior members of his crews to ascertain what was happening to the younger crew members when their ships were sunk. The discussion revealed several patterns:

- The older sailors knew their limits and knew how to pace themselves when stranded in life rafts or in the water for extended periods of time.

- The older seamen were familiar with the discomforts of being at sea while the younger men were not. Being stranded at sea seemed overwhelming to the young men—not because the rigors of being stranded were so difficult—but because being stranded was a completely unfamiliar and uncomfortable experience to them.

- The younger men were overcome with a sense of dread and fear when their ships were sunk. The old salts knew if they just used common sense and patience, they would be rescued.

And finally,

- The younger seamen were more likely to lose hope when they were stranded at sea. When they lost hope, they lost their lives.

To prepare his seamen for the dangers of their work, Holt hired an educator who had developed a reputation for his ability to bolster confidence in youth using a combination of physical and intellectual challenges and teamwork. Each seaman was expected to go through a short survival and confidence course prior to going into service. The results were dramatic and immediate. Loss of life of stranded crews went down dramatically, especially among the younger seamen.

After the war, Holt hired the educator who had unusual theories about developing character in youth to develop a 28- day course for all of his new, incoming employees as part of the Blue Funnel Line's seamanship school in North Wales. He named the course "Outward Bound," and an educational movement was born.

The educator Holt had hired was an expatriated German Jew named Kurt Hahn. The son of a well-to-do German industrialist, Hahn was arrested for criticizing the Nazis in 1933 after witnessing a brutal civilian beating by German soldiers. He was released on the condition that he would leave Germany, which he did. These events, in particular the gang mentality of the Nazis, had a profound effect on him, so much so that he patterned part of his educational philosophy on the belief that people need the courage and wherewithal to think and act for themselves, especially in times of adversity.

On the urging of friends and admirers, Hahn eventually founded his own school in an abandoned castle in Scotland, which he called Gordonstoun School. Hahn saw education as a lot more than the pursuit of academic knowledge. Post World War II Europe was suffering from a loss of self-esteem as much as from the physical losses levied by the War.

Based on what he was seeing, Hahn identified what he referred to as "The Six Declines" of Modern Youth:

- Decline of Fitness due to modern methods of locomotion

- Decline of Initiative and Enterprise due to the widespread disease of 'spectatoritis'

- Decline of Memory and Imagination due to the confused restlessness of modern life

- Decline of Skill and Care due to a weakening of craftsmanship

- Decline of Self-discipline due to the ever-present availability of stimulants and tranquilizers

- Decline of Compassion due to the unseemly haste with which modern life is conducted or as William Temple called it "spiritual death"

To counter these declines, Hahn developed what he called the "Four Antidotes":

- Fitness Training (e.g., to compete with one's self in physical fitness; in so doing, train the discipline and determination of the mind through the body)

- Expeditions (e.g., via sea or land, to engage in long, challenging endurance tasks) to catalyze teams and teach the importance of human relationships

- Projects (e.g., involving crafts and manual skills) that brought the team together and gave them something to strive for

- Rescue Service (e.g., Surf Lifesaving, Firefighting, First Aid, etc.)

The school became a capable and effective rescue service for ships at sea. To prepare crews of students for the rescue service element, specifically for boarding a vessel or evacuating it, on-land obstacle courses were constructed for the students to practice climbing cargo nets or doing zip-line rescue transfers. These initial on-land courses became increasingly popular as physical conditioning and teambuilding exercises that had the added benefit of building a student's confidence. Modern-day versions of these courses are the thousands of challenge courses—or ropes courses—in use today around the world. Challenge courses are used in every conceivable educational context today from corporate teambuilding programs to team problem solving courses on the T.V. show "Survivor."

Hahn's wisdom about the needs of youth and his educational philosophy addressed the whole student—not just the academic one. As he said, "there is more in us than we know. If we can be made to see it, perhaps, for the rest of our lives, we will be unwilling to settle for less."

When the Kennedy administration started the Peace Corps in the early 1960's, it was decided that each Peace Corps volunteer should undergo an orientation training program that would build up the confidence and self-reliance of volunteers before sending them off on assignment. They turned to a student and adherent of Hahn's philosophy to develop their training program. At about the same time, a handful of American educators and philanthropists brought back Hahn's philosophy to schools and inner city youth, also calling the cutting edge programs they created Outward Bound. Today, Outward Bound is an international education and character development movement with schools, pilot programs and partnerships all over the world. Outward Bound's results have been remarkable. Never before had an educational movement used the wilderness to such great effect in the development of character and skill of young people. Outward Bound graduates include at-risk and adjudicated youth, business leaders, the 1998 U.S. Olympic Volleyball Team, survivors of cancer, schools committed to systemic reform, college students in transition, and "regular" students and professionals interested in testing and developing their mettle through the out of doors. It's motto: "To Serve, To Strive and Not to Yield."

Lawrence Holt discovered an essential truth of human behavior: confidence matters. A lot. It affects our behavior so much that it can mean the difference between life and death. It can also mean the difference between being a successful leader and one who fails through lack of direction, lack of resolve or lack of inspiration. When everything falls apart, confidence coupled with a desire to make a difference can carry the day.

Jon Mark Howard learned about Outward Bound from a favorite high school teacher who had gone to the mountains of North Carolina to take a pilot Outward Bound educators course. The teacher came back to school energized by what he had learned. At that time, the North Carolina Outward Bound School ("NCOBS" to Outward Bounders) was one of a confederation of six Outward Bound schools scattered across the country running everything from classic 21-day multi-element wilderness trips to special contract courses for schools and special populations. NCOBS was known for taking students on rigorous "shakedown" hikes that involved hiking and navigating off-trail through the steep gorges and mountains of western North Carolina. These "bush-pushes" were usually done as part of the Main phase of an Outward Bound course, which was preceded by the Training phase. During Training, novice students were exposed to the fundamentals of backpacking, expeditioning and wilderness navigation. Training was frequently culminated by a day on the base camp's ropes challenge course where students got to practice self-protection and self-rescue while going through a series of events 20, 30 and 40 feet off the ground. Following Training, students went on their Main expedition where they were expected to take on more of the management and decision-making of the course. In addition to lengthy, all night bush pushes—frequently performed on hands and knees to get through the thickets of rhododendron—the Main phase of the course was also where students learned more advanced skills like CPR, First Aid and rock climbing. During the Final phase of their course, students were expected to work together to plan, navigate and safely run a brief expedition without the assistance or sometimes even the presence of their instructors.

Whether the course was run from Pulling Boats (modified whaling vessels powered by sail and oars) in the island archipelago off the coast of Maine or in the high mountains of Colorado, Outward Bound's curriculum always included Training, Main and Final phases.

Based on the same fundamentals of Hahn's thinking, Jon's teacher started running courses that combined learning of wilderness skills with teamwork and the immediate application of those skills on weekend wilderness expeditions. Just like a real Outward Bound course, as the student's skills increased, they were expected to assume increasing levels of responsibility for their own safety and learning. In the end, the feeling of confidence in themselves and their ability to confront and overcome adversity was magical. All of this happened in the greatest classroom on the planet—the outdoors.

Jon was hooked. He had always loved being outdoors, he loved the lessons he was learning and he loved how he and his peers learned to work together to overcome the obstacles and challenges that presented themselves on the trips. In the summer after he graduated high school and before going to college, Jon attended a full-blown Outward Bound course. Thus began a lifelong connection with Outward Bound that would see him rise from a fledgling assistant instructor to the President of Outward Bound Discovery—a series of programs and schools that work with at-risk and adjudicated youth across the U.S.

Since his transformative experiences on the course, Jon Howard's life has been devoted to what Outward Bounder's call "The Four Pillars": Service to Others, Self-Reliance, Confidence and Craftsmanship. He is a master expeditioner and marathon canoe paddler. While he is most at home in the swamps and rivers of his native Florida, Jon has gone on expeditions across North America equipped with little more than the confidence he has gained from being a part of Outward Bound and a deep seated trust in his own abilities and the abilities of his expedition mates.

Jon's confidence and will to make a difference in the world have made a lasting and indelible impact on Outward Bound. This quiet, unassuming man has touched the lives of hundreds of staff and literally thousands of kids, all through his confident leadership and his deep desire to make a difference. Outward Bound programs in Florida are accredited by the Department of Education in the State of Florida, thanks to Jon's leadership and vision. He created a prevention program for at-risk youth—FINS (Families in Need of Service)—that became a national template for combining Outward Bound principles with crime prevention. As Discovery's president, Jon has had to

The Old Outward Bound Logo, Used Around the World...

lead his programs and the school through one of—if not the—most trying era in the history of Outward Bound as it tries to redefine itself.

Yet, no one who meets Jon for the first time would ever guess he is one of Outward Bound's most tenured employees or that he holds one of the highest positions in one of the most esteemed educational institutions in the country. He exerts his influence and leadership in a humble, soft spoken way. He leads his staff in the same way a master Outward Bound instructor leads a crew on a typical Outward Bound expedition: showing them skills and intervening when the need arises, preferring to remain in the background whenever possible. As an elementary school teacher, an Outward Bound Instructor and a director of programs at both Outward Bound and the American Youth Foundation, Jon's entire life has been one of service to others. Jon's confidence coupled with his willingness to make a difference in his organization and in the lives of others makes him a classic example of an enduring leader and the embodiment of this trait, the Confidence to Make a Difference.

THE POWERFUL COMBINATION OF "CONFIDENCE" AND "MAKING A DIFFERENCE"

When I was researching the insights of enduring leaders, this one was the hardest to define and name. Very few of the competencies I surveyed men-

tioned "confidence" as a key competence and no one listed "making a difference" as a competency. Numerous organizations listed vision, and the ability
to visualize the future. Almost all organizations referred to the importance
of having leaders who inspire or motivate, but these attributes cross over all
of the competencies of enduring leaders, and are discussed throughout this
book. Many of the leadership competencies I surveyed used terms such as
"forward looking," "determined," "courageous" and "ambitious." Over half of
the organizations in my study listed "inspires high performance" as a leadership competency. Others listed "motivates and generates exceptional performance in employees." Is each one of these adjectives a competency? Maybe,
but what drives each of them is something deeper. What makes someone
courageous, ambitious or inspiring? What do leaders who possess these
things actually do? I think they approach work and the world from a mindset that is based at least to a degree in confidence in themselves.

In all of the leadership competencies I studied, not one directly referred
to "makes a difference" as an important attribute, skill or trait of leaders.
Instead, they used words and phrases such as "vision" or "forward looking"
or "sets high expectations" or "has a clear plan for the future." If someone
asked you, "How should we teach people to have a clear plan for the future?"
or show them how to be "forward looking". How would you do it? My bet
is you would find more fundamental behaviors for the person to work on
as a means to become better at visualizing and creating plans for the future.
You would do what learning experts describe as "chunking down," breaking
down the concept of "vision" into elemental building blocks of what having
vision really entails. Underneath the skills of "setting high expectations" and
"having a clear plan for the future" lie the pair of traits we are going to discuss in this chapter: Having the desire to make a difference combined with
the confidence to do so.

So what about the need for leaders to be "inspiring" or "motivating"?
Doesn't charisma count? There is no doubt that working for a dynamic, in-
spirational leader is fun and exhilarating, but does a leader have to be those
things in order to be effective? My interpretation of the data on leadership is
that there are a variety of skills that leaders who motivate must have such as a
relatively high degree of honesty and general job competence, but what truly
motivates people falls into two of the five insights of enduring leaders—having the confidence to try and make a difference and having the emotional
intelligence to make connections with people. Each leader creates inspira-

tion and motivation in their own way, using their own unique blend of innate traits and acquired skills to bring out the best in people. However, any combination of skills is more likely to be motivational when in the hands of a leader who has confidence.

Confidence alone is a great attribute, as we can all testify when we feel it. There is nothing more exhilarating than approaching a difficult task with the adamant belief that we will be successful, whatever challenges or pitfalls await us. But confidence alone is not an insight of an enduring leader. Confidence without a vehicle for accomplishment is like putting a high performance racing engine on a go-cart. The engine will make the cart go faster, but the engine will never reach its full potential because it's not attached to the right vehicle. That vehicle or focal point for direction in leaders is the willingness to make a difference.

Confidence is the trait that allows enduring leaders to get up each morning and attempt to do something important. This happens when they are doing something that they believe will make a difference. Having a vision is an important skill for some leaders, but a vision without the confidence to attempt to achieve that vision is just fantasy. Confidence, coupled with a desire to make a difference, is the energy that drives leaders to attempt to achieve a goal.

CONNECTED COMPETENCIES

The competencies frequently connected with the Confidence to Make a Difference include:

- Visualizes Success
- Creates and works towards a positive future
- Provides a clear vision for others
- Understands current capabilities versus future needs
- Prioritizes accordingly
- Has vision
- Plans for the future
- Inspires and motivates others
- Appropriately challenges others

The traits of Passion and Timing and Self-Awareness and Personal Mastery may also generate motivation and inspiration in others, but the Confidence to Make a Difference is at the core of the competencies listed above. Employees are inspired by hard working leaders, but unless those leaders have a vision for how to make a difference in some way, hard work may look like blind compulsion. And while people in general are more likely to work well for a leader who can connect with them personally (the ability to do this lies in one's Self-Awareness and Personal Mastery), again, unless there is an important mission or task to accomplish, they are likely to be less inspired or motivated. Vision, as I have already mentioned, is a distinct and important competency for leaders and can be considered synonymous with the notion of making a difference. Anyone can dream up a vision, but confidence is what turns a vision into a reality.

The shoulder trait between Courage Through Service and Connection is Vision. Developing a vision requires having the confidence to see a hopeful and possible future combined with the ability to articulate that vision to those around you. Exercises to help develop Vision can be found in The Practice of this section and in the section on Connection.

PART TWO
COURAGE THROUGH
SERVICE IN ACTION

The most dramatic modern day example about the importance of confident leadership happened in the events immediately after terrorist attacks on the World Trade Center on September 11, 2001. The mayoral primaries for the city of New York were also on this day—the beginning of the end of Rudolph Guiliani's tenure as the city's mayor. But on that day, the world changed and Guiliani's hardest 80 days in office began. By most accounts, Guiliani had been a great mayor for the city, reducing the welfare rolls, increasing property values and improving communities throughout the city. The public perception of his personal life and character was less positive. His character had been called into question on a variety of issues—from how he managed marital problems and personal relationships to public temper tantrums directed at subordinates when things were not to his liking. Whatever the public's criticism of Guiliani before September 11th was, it disappeared as he confidently and masterfully handled one of the darkest hours in American history.

For most of the day on September 11th, President Bush was being whisked around the country on Air Force One and was out of reach of network television. In his stead, Guiliani became the face and voice of leadership for the U.S. Guiliani's confidence carried the day. "Tomorrow New York is going to be here," he said. "And we're going to rebuild, and we're going to be stronger than we were before.... I want the people of New York to be an example to the rest of the country, and the rest of the world, that terrorism can't stop us."

He gave Americans hope that somehow we would not only survive the attacks, but come back stronger and better for it. But Guiliani's confidence wasn't all that he showed us. He set up a command post as close to ground zero as was possible, and he dove into the details of the recovery and rescue of the victims of the attack, managing logistics and helping to coordinate the various recovery efforts being made by the hundreds of civil, local, state and federal agencies and organizations. When he spoke on television—frequently covered in the dust from the aftermath of the attacks—he addressed the facts as he knew them clearly and compassionately. He also served as a model for a nation of people who were not sure what to feel or how to express it. In the numerous press conferences and special announcements immediately after the attacks, Guiliani was neither stoic nor overwrought with emotion. He was himself. When specific announcements about those presumed dead or missing were shared, his voice quivered, full of the emotion that reflected the magnitude of what had happened. He prepared us for the inevitable and helped us grieve, conveying the horror of the event genuinely. "The number of casualties will be more than any of us can bear," he said. He offered and received lots of hugs, on and off camera, visibly demonstrating the emotional impact of the events on him, while still leading and guiding us. Through it all, he reminded us that we would recover. When asked how much of his presence and confidence was a bluff, Guiliani responded, "Look, in a crisis you have to be optimistic. When I said the spirit of the city would be stronger, I didn't know that. I just hoped it. There are parts of you that say, 'Maybe we're not going to get through this.' You don't listen to them."[1]

Mayor Guiliani's confident presence, humility and self-assuredness helped quell panic and began to restore hope. His belief in the resilience of the human spirit in the face of overwhelming tragedy helped many Americans find hope and light in the darkness of September 11th. Though his behavior and actions on 9/11 were remarkable, that same ability to confidently try to make a difference exists in hundreds of thousands of leaders throughout the country. They work as CEO's and sous chefs, policemen and project team leaders, civic leaders and kindergarten teachers. Mayor Guiliani's message served as a call to action for all of us to get up, dust ourselves off, and start picking up the pieces, which is exactly what we did.

CONFIDENCE

Confidence is a belief that shows up in behavior. It is this belief that keeps enduring leaders going when they hit setbacks and resistance. Leaders who have the confidence to make a difference are willing to take a stand for what they believe in, even when those around don't believe in the possibility of success.

Confidence—coupled with a desire to make a difference—outweigh education or prior experience as a means to achieve results. Many of the most successful businesses, enterprises and social movements in the world were founded and run by people whose only qualification was their confidence and vision. Expertise and knowledge help make a leader, but without the confidence to put those attributes to work, we're still driving a go cart with a high performance engine.

In 2001, Outward Bound Discovery faced the closure of most of its state-funded programs due to a $900 million budget shortfall in the State of Florida's annual budget. At the time, Jon Howard was serving as the acting Director of Programs for Outward Bound Discovery while his boss Mike Muley was undergoing treatment for cancer. The state threatened to do away with all "low risk" youth programs—Outward Bound had 4 such programs at the time totaling well over $4 million of the school's $7 million dollar revenue. Saving the programs involved contacting key legislators and senior members of the State of Florida's executive branch. Making these contacts and influencing the outcome required the skills of an experienced lobbyist like Mike. Jon and Mike had developed a complementary working relationship over the years; Jon handled all programmatic and operational issues of Florida programs while Mike handled lobbying, liaisons with the state and managing relationships with the power brokers who controlled Outward Bound's purse strings. During the 2001 crisis, Jon had to jump into a new role with absolute confidence and no experience. Jon's natural humility—not to mention his high value on personal integrity—kept him from trying to "fake it to make it." Instead, he approached the situation like this: "I just figured it was another Outward Bound Course and I had graduated from Main to Final. It was time to get out in the deep end and see if I could swim." As anyone who knows him will testify, one of the most remarkable characteristics of Jon is his unabashed willingness to tell the truth about his own abilities. When he was unsure of what had happened in previous conversations or negotiations between Mike and the State, he said so. When he was unsure about which direction to take, he called board members and colleagues who had similar but unrelated experience and listened to their council. Jon and Mike had 60 days to work through the issues and secure Outward Bound's funding, and they did it.

In his own words Jon explains:

> *I remember thinking 'Oh my gosh, what am I going to do?' on the one hand and telling myself that there was no way the whole thing (Outward Bound) was going to go down during this time period. I didn't want to let Mike down. I also knew the magnitude of the responsibility to each of the programs. It was important to provide stability to the bases and all the staff who were being told they wouldn't have a job. I knew I didn't know what needed doing in some cases, but I also realized that ultimately, I knew what we were trying to do for kids in Florida and I believed in what we did. I had a lot of confidence that I could explain to anyone why we were important to kids in the State, and that kept me from ever feeling intimidated. I was confident enough with what I did know to tell people what I didn't know and I think that helped.*

It is not uncommon for people to pick careers that allow them to pursue those things they are most interested in learning and Jon Howard is no exception. His leadership of Outward Bound Discovery has been a powerful element in developing his own confidence. As he said,

> *One of the biggest students of Outward Bound has been me. I have always felt like I could figure things out and find my way through, but I never took doing so for granted. I think people mistake my saying "I don't know how to do that" for a lack of confidence. I think my confidence allows me to state what I don't know how to do or admit to what I am not good at. For me, one of the first steps towards learning to do something is to acknowledge that I don't know how to do it. I guess people aren't used to someone having confidence who is always admitting*

to what they can't do. I think my confidence comes from really understanding what I am not good at; not by ignoring it or pretending it doesn't exist. Being realistic about my skills makes it a lot easier to figure things out. I'm O.K. acknowledging what I don't know, but I'm also confident that I have the skills I need to solve big problems. Between the two, I know I have what it takes to be successful.

Like Mayor Guiliani, Jon finds a confident, centered place to lead from in times of crisis not because he pretends there is no crisis, but because he is willing to work through the crisis. The net effect of this style of leadership is enormous credibility for having the willingness to admit there is a problem and the confidence that it can be overcome.

CONFIDENCE, ARROGANCE OR HUBRIS?

In his book, *Jack, Straight from the Gut* celebrated leader and business man Jack Welch says, "There's only a razor's edge between self- confidence and hubris." Confidence is not the same as arrogance or hubris, but these attributes may look the same at first glance. Hubris is arrogance and unfounded or overstated pride. Confidence, true confidence, is self-assuredness tempered with humility. Why? A confident leader can accept the possibility that failure could be a potential outcome of their efforts, but the prospect of failure doesn't keep them from striving to achieve. A confident leader who does not see the potential for failure in difficult pursuits is dangerous, because they are blind to the hazards they may face along the way. If they can't see the risks, they are less likely to develop a plan to overcome them. Mayor Guiliani's comments, in whole, revealed his confidence. President Bush's comments, as you'll see below, were just hubris.

Guiliani spoke of recovery and rebuilding, giving everyone listening a verb—"rebuild"—that made sense. Bush's first directive to the Joint Chiefs when they met after the attacks was "I wanna kick some ass!" On television, he talked about killing those responsible, stating, "I want justice. And there's an old poster out West, I recall, that says, 'Wanted: Dead or Alive.' " Were we supposed to round up a posse and go look for someone to kill? Confidence without a mission is just hot air. The desire to make a difference without the confidence to do so is just day dreaming. But when a leader has both of these attributes, they can change the world, or at least their part of it.

Arrogance and hubris may look like confidence and in fact may come from a sense of pride, but true confidence comes from a more balanced world view that reminds us not to take ourselves too seriously. Confidence is a belief in ourselves as a result of what we have learned. Arrogance is an ego-based need to demonstrate to others that we are exempt from the same standards as those around us. People who are feeling arrogant don't think that the rules apply to them in the same way that they apply to others. Hubris and arrogance are high-handed human failings.

Politicians are by no means the only practitioners of hubris. When professional athletes use steroids to enhance performance, regardless of the fundamental flaws and legality of so doing, they are performing an act of hubris. Business leaders who have generated consistent wealth and value for shareholders and stockholders can go from being confident to arrogant in no time if they allow their own success to go to their heads. Anyone who becomes disconnected from the real world is more likely to develop hubris. This might explain why so many public figures seem to be parodies of themselves. Managers who manage from behind their desks, or entrepreneurs who have allowed their business success to go to their heads are both candidates for hubris. When we are exposed to hubris, we notice it even if we don't have a word for it. The word we most frequently attach to it is *bullshit* and after a while, listening to bullshit becomes exceedingly boring. Confidence draws people in; hubris eventually sends them running.

Newly developed confidence can become hubris or arrogance—particularly if egos or hurt feelings are involved. In the mid 1990's, I helped to develop a group of newly promoted executives into a high- performing team. The group was comprised of senior officers and executives for a very large professional services firm. Most of them were under 40, all but one team member was male, and most of them were new to their positions. They had been part of a remarkable and rapid turnaround in profits, culture, employee retention and customer satisfaction, which is why they had been promoted to officers and senior executives in the company. In the early stages of the turnaround, virtually every team member had been the subject of unpleasant confrontations, dismissals or character attacks from employees who were affected by changes in the company, disagreed with the changes that were occurring or were resistant to the point of becoming combative about where this team was taking the company. These confrontations and attacks

ranged from inappropriate personal attacks in meetings to lengthy anony-
mous diatribes referring to specific team member's personal lives, family
members and even speculation about their sexual preferences.

Although such attacks come with the territory in the course of a major
change initiative, they are never fun, easy or painless. In this case, the attacks frequently made a big impact on team members. Some members had
to work very hard not to succumb to the criticism and start doubting themselves. During the messiest and most stressful part of the turnaround, our
meetings would dissolve from plotting strategy and reporting on progress
to very emotional and honest conversations about the effect various attacks
had on members of the team.

Like a good Outward Bound Course, the adversity of the experience built
the team's skill level in managing and leading change, which in turn built
their confidence. Under their leadership, the turnaround made steady progress over the next several months, but so did their hubris. As their confidence increased, they became increasingly impatient with the staff who had
aided them in the transformation. They started to behave like a clique, excluding key staff in decisions that only a few months ago they would have
been involved in.

In retrospect, I think what happened was this: the executive team compensated for the painful treatment they had received during the turnaround by
becoming angry and passively aggressive.

During the height of their hubris, they decided to acquire a competitor,
orchestrating the purchase within the period of a few months. The pace of
the acquisition and their over-inflated confidence in their management and
leadership skills led to incomplete pre-acquisition due diligence. The owners of the acquired business needed reassurance and coaching in how to
integrate it into the new, larger corporate model. Instead they got arrogant,
insensitive treatment. The treatment ruined any value that could have come
out of the acquisition and the entire business unraveled over the course of
several years. By the time they knew they were in trouble, they had already
damaged many of the relationships they desperately needed beyond repair.

Nothing fails like success. And the agent to this failure is hubris run
amuck.

REWIRING CONFIDENCE

Where does confidence come from? We aren't born with it, although some of us are probably predisposed to have more of it than others as a result of how we were raised. The kinds of life experiences we have had certainly play a part in how much confidence we have and what exactly we have confidence in. Whether through experience, how we were raised, or how we are wired, confidence begins with a desire to learn or do something. Then, our confidence grows with lots and lots of practice.

Confidence begins with that instinct and primal urge we commonly refer to as will. As an instinct, will is what motivates us to try something we have not tried before. Without will, the human species might not exist. When we lose the will to live, we die. When we lose the will to try, we quit. Understanding how will plays out in real life is subtle because our will is linked to our intentions, and we frequently develop our intentions in a completely unconscious way. Do human babies learn to walk because they have a will to walk? Do they develop an intention to walk? Yes. They become inquisitive about the world and they desire to see more of it. Amazingly, none of this process is conscious. It just happens.

Will is often associated with "free will," but in fact the two are entirely different things. All animals have will, in their case often called instinct. Only humans develop "free will," as we shall see, and free will is not necessarily as liberating as its reputation.

The first three years of life for babies is a feast of unfettered and instinctual learning. Infants are continuous learning machines with no filters, buffers or barriers between what is happening around them and what they learn. As they continue to grow, a new awareness starts to develop and the party is over. Scientists call this new awareness "cognition" which is defined as the awareness of thinking. As we become increasingly cognizant of our environment and ourselves, we start to make choices about what we learn and how we interpret experience. We go from just learning to being aware of our learning, to making decisions about what the information we are learning means, to choosing whether or not we want to learn something in the first place. We build filters and buffers that temper, focus and occasionally inhibit our learning. In the context of confidence, our cognizant minds are at once our worst enemies and our best friends as they help us—and force us—to make choices about what we learn. "Will," pure and simple, has been replaced with "free will", which isn't really free at all.[2] At the beginning of this section the story of seamen on the Blue Funnel Line described a problem of confidence that led to younger, less experienced seamen giving up in what they perceived as a hopeless situation, being stranded at sea. Some of them lost the will to fight to survive. Yet, as this example proved, having the right mindset to survive being stranded at sea was the single most important survival tool to have.

How we interpret a situation is critical to how we respond to it, and our interpretations of events in our lives is one of the major contributors to how much confidence we have. Each of us has a different window on the world—or a different view of the world. That world view is the result of all of the previous experiences we have had—from what we have learned to how we were raised. From what we feel to how we think. We assign different interpretations to the same events, so our opinions about a common experience can vary substantially. If our window on the world is that being stranded in a life raft in the North Sea is a fatal event, then we are less likely to survive it than if our window on the world tells us that surviving a U-Boat attack and ship sinking is entirely possible.

Transforming negative interpretations—changing our windows on the world—is at the heart of what Outward Bound and Kurt Hahn were teaching. By placing people in stressful situations and unfamiliar environments and helping them develop the skills and tools to cope with adversity, Outward Bound participants learn to generalize what they learn on an Outward Bound course to how they live their lives. When our outlook is more positive, we move through the world with more confidence. When we believe we can be successful, we are more likely to become so.

Changing the way we think, particularly about ourselves, is no easy task. But it's possible. Ask any Marine who has just finished basic training. Ask any football player who has made the cut after pre-season training. Ask any mountaineer who has survived a night above 18,000 feet without a sleeping bag or a tent. Ask a single mother. Ask a cancer survivor. Their experiences may or may not have been positive, but they all have an increased awareness of their own strength, determination and fortitude to overcome adversity. Confidence is a matter of practice, particularly for those who don't feel like they have much of it.

Before we can develop more confidence, we have to have the will to try.

And each time we muster the will to try, we learn how we can make a difference which of course builds more confidence.

Our minds and our thoughts, conscious and unconscious, play an immense role in how we develop the insights of enduring leaders. Understanding them—or at least how to re-wire them—is critical to the practice of enduring leadership.

DROWN PROOFING

Will is what motivates us to try, and as we try, we develop the willingness to try more difficult and complex activities. When we confront a difficult challenge, we weigh the options for if and how to address it based on a number of factors including:

- Our previous experiences, both positive and negative, in addressing challenges like it.

- What we know about our chances of success based on our experience or the experience of others who have faced a similar challenge.

- The perceived risks and rewards of addressing that challenge.

- The energetic, physical and emotional stress we are likely to incur as a result of addressing it.

- If the potential pay-offs are high enough, we go for it. If we fail, we either choose to try again or we give up.

Frequently, the risks we most need to take are the ones we are most unwilling to take. Psychologists who work with patients who have chronic anxiety or an unfounded fear or phobia of something help them overcome it using what they call "successive approximations." In mathematics—the field from which the term originated—successive approximation is a method of determining the value of an unknown quantity by repeatedly comparing it to known quantities. In the practice of psychology, successive approximation therapy is based on the idea that by exposing patients to incremental doses of whatever causes their anxiety, they begin to develop the confidence in themselves to overcome whatever they were afraid of. In other words, practice makes perfect. If a patient has a paralyzing fear of being in open spaces, the therapy might involve placing them first in a small room with no windows and a number of familiar objects that remind them of what is safe—like a favorite chair. Next, the patient is placed in a larger room—perhaps with windows looking out on the outside world, again with their favorite chair. After becoming comfortable with this new environment, the chair is removed so the patient has to learn to find safety and security in some new object. With each successive experience, the therapist helps the patient learn to find comfort in each environment and remind them that the world will not end and they will not be lost if they don't have their favorite chair or if they can see the outside world. The therapist desensitizes the patient to each new environment, much like an Outward Bound student who has never spent the night in the woods learns to become increasingly comfortable with their new environment through practice and continued exposure.

In the real world, we expand our comfort zones in much the same way. We learn to ski on an easy ski slope before challenging ourselves with a steeper intermediate slope. We manage a smaller project before trying to manage a larger one. With each successive experience we become more confident. Instead of having a therapist, we rely on the feedback and viewpoints of those around us to tell us when we are making progress, if we are not aware of the progress we are making on our own or if we are being realistic about the progress we are in fact making.

An interesting adaptation of Kurt Hahn's educational philosophy was the teaching of drown proofing as part of a Peace Corps volunteer's final exam. Freddie LaNue was the former swimming coach for Georgia Tech and the inventor of drown proofing training. Confident to the point of being overwhelming, Freddie—who referred to himself as "the rambling wreck from Georgia Tech"—taught the course with great flourish and drama. True to the Outward Bound philosophy, the purpose of drown proofing was somewhat utilitarian, but it fit with the notion of building the volunteer's confidence in themselves in trying circumstances. The concept of drown proofing was simple: learn to breathe and stay alive in the water indefinitely without expending any more energy than absolutely necessary. For those who were comfortable in the water, drown proofing was merely an exercise, but for anyone who was not totally comfortable in water, drown proofing was like a final expedition. After learning a variety of drown-proofing skills that were in themselves successive approximations, the final test of the course involved Freddie tying the legs and arms of each volunteer together, then pushing them in the pool so they could demonstrate the skill for up to 10 minutes. Whether Freddie LaNue or Kurt Hahn knew it, they were teaching students by de-sensitizing them to the panic that comes when someone thinks they are going to drown. They were using successive approximations before the term was invented.

If building confidence is this simple—practicing progressively more difficult tasks until we master them—then why do so many of us struggle with self-doubt and insecurity? Of all of our windows on the world, our views of ourselves, our self-perception, is the most difficult window to look through and see a clear image. It is much easier to see and even measure the growth of others than it is to do the same with ourselves. We are left to try and decipher what our own progress is based on what we see and what the feedback from the outside world—our friends, colleagues, supervisors and coaches—tells us.

Confidence, like competence, is a matter of genetics and upbringing. Not all of us are capable of being astrophysicists, but confidence can help us achieve more than we might otherwise achieve if we did not have it. Sometimes, we overshoot in our self-assessment of our skills due to overconfidence. If you have ever stood at the top of a ski run that you just knew was beyond your ability, you know the feeling. Likewise, if you have ever been in a job that you were under qualified for and there was not adequate time to learn the job, you'll recognize the feeling. Just as debilitating—but likely a less dangerous approach—is when we undershoot in our self-assessment of our skills due to lack of confidence. But as the saying has it, nothing ventured, nothing gained. We have to be willing to try if we want to grow, and if our lack of confidence keeps us from even trying, we limit our growth and our learning.

MAKING A DIFFERENCE

It's convenient that making a difference both requires confidence and builds more confidence. One great way to begin building confidence is to try and make a difference in the world by improving someone's life or by making your community better. But making a difference has a broader definition than you might think. It likely already applies to you and your company.

Examples of ordinary companies doing extraordinary things—and motivating their employees in the process—abound. Southwest Airlines provides affordable travel and predictable service to customers. Medtronic is a global leader of medical technology, and they are also a global alleviator of pain and suffering while improving the lifestyles of their employees. Red Hat is the leading designer of Linux products. They also support independent software designers who are part of the open source community and promote the sharing of technology.

These companies and hundreds like them don't define their success simply by ROI or quarterly earnings; they believe they exist to serve a higher purpose. By telling the story of how they make a difference, they provide their employees with critical strategic information about how the business runs and what its priorities are. In turn, having this information allows the employees to make intelligent, independent decisions about how to serve the company and the customer. By making intelligent independent decisions, their confidence goes up, and so do the company's results.

FATE AND FAITH – CREATING CONVERGENCE

The ability to make a difference also requires a degree of serendipity, or "convergence." When the right combination of opportunities, events and occurrences come together, making a difference becomes a lot more possible. Therefore, one element of making change is the trait of timing (refer to Section Five if you're interested in more on developing good timing).

What if Kurt Hahn—the founder of Outward Bound mentioned at the beginning of this section—tried to found an educational movement today based on the "Six Declines" and the "Four Antidotes" to the decline of modern youth? These declines, again, are:

- Decline of Fitness due to modern methods of locomotion (moving about)

- Decline of Initiative and Enterprise due to the wide spread disease of spectatoritis

- Decline of Memory and Imagination due to the confused restlessness of modern life

- Decline of Skill and Care due to the weakened tradition of craftsmanship

- Decline of Self-discipline due to the ever-present availability of stimulants and tranquilizers

- Decline of Compassion due to the unseemly haste with which modern life is conducted or as William Temple called it "spiritual death"

Hahn's "Four Antidotes," again are:

- Fitness Training (e.g., to compete with one's self in physical fitness; in so doing, train the discipline and determination of the mind through the body)

- Expeditions (e.g., via sea or land, to engage in long, challenging endurance tasks) to catalyze teams and teach the importance of human relationships

- Projects (e.g., involving crafts and manual skills) that brought the team together and gave them something to strive for

- Rescue Service (e.g., surf lifesaving, fire-fighting, first Aid, etc.)

Would these same words be used today to refer to the needs of youth in the United States or any developed country? Probably. But would the same approach work? Probably not. The interest in Hahn's educational philosophies and approaches came at a time of intense examination of nationalism, the responsible application of technology and the sunrise of the cold war. In Post-War England, Hahn's focus on the character and confidence of young people also resonated with a country that had lost so many young men. Hahn's work—while noteworthy and as fitting today as ever—occurred at an ideal time. The collision of circumstances to create an optimal moment for something to happen is what physicists and cultural scientists both refer to as a "convergence." The conditions and circumstances of one event—the creation of Outward Bound—converged harmoniously with Europe's post-World War II reconstruction. Each of the two events brought additional attention and momentum to the other.

Making a difference does not require convergence, but it helps. There is no simple formula for when or if a leader's desire to make a difference is going to converge with a greater need inside a social network. Frequently, the events that converge come from totally unrelated events. When a critical need in a social network is dramatically filled, there are usually several enduring leaders fueling it. A youngster named Bill Gates set up shop in Albuquerque, New Mexico to perfect an operating system he thought would revolutionize computing 20 years before the advent of the internet, but when his work converged with the needs of the social network, Boom! Rudy Guiliani had been an effective leader in New York City for many years before the events of 9/11, and he most assuredly wishes those events had not occurred, but when the attacks happened, there was a convergence of his presence and the need for leadership in the moment.

Enduring leaders don't wander about looking for a need somewhere in a social network so they can go figure out how to make a difference. Instead, they attach themselves to an idea, cause, vision or ideal and they pursue it with passion. If the idea is premature to the need, they move on until the time is right to come back and further develop the idea. Leaders who have confidence may not be able to create the right conditions for a convergence that allows them to make a difference, but they can certainly stir things up. Stirring things up takes a lot of confidence, as we shall see.

Enduring leaders may "make a difference" through what they do, but they are just as likely to make a difference by what they don't do. In either case, enduring leaders who practice this insight don't have every move of their careers or lives worked out before they try something. What they *do* have worked out is that they want to make a difference—and that desire helps to guide them.

In the mid-1990's Jon Howard felt he had reached a plateau in terms of his career at Outward Bound. While he held out some hope of being named as the successor to his boss, Mike Muley, Jon was equally interested in his own learning and growth, and it appeared he had learned most of what he could at Outward Bound in the Associate Director position. After over 20 years of working for Outward Bound—practically his entire adult life—Jon left Outward Bound for a lateral, if not slightly lower position as one of the program directors for the American Youth Foundation and to pursue a masters in educational leadership. It was a painful decision for Jon, but, he says,

> *I knew Mike was going to retire in his position, and I understood why—he was brilliant at his job. It looked like he was going to recover fully from the cancer, or so I thought, so I didn't feel like I was leaving the school, or Mike, in the lurch. I was worried about stagnation professionally. If I wanted to continue to grow, I had to leave even though I wasn't sure it was a good move at the time.*

Jon's departure from what were at the time named "Florida Outreach Programs" shocked everyone. He was practically an institution within the organization and his departure stirred things up. Jon's intent was to further his own professional growth—not create havoc at Outward Bound, but his timing and the timing of the school's careful re-examination of itself converged. The confederation of Outward Bound schools scattered across the country had been struggling for several years with increased competition for funds and students. Imitation is a form of flattery. A number of character and confidence development programs for various populations and niches had sprung up all over the world since Outward Bound's inception, which eroded its market share. A number of former Outward Bounders had left the schools over the years to found or go to work for various adventure learning and travel companies. These companies were also competing for Outward Bound's core clientele. Independent of Jon's decision, Outward Bound's trustees began to look at how to reconfigure the schools to keep overhead down and quality up.

Within three months of Jon's departure, Mike Muley died of cancer. To replace Mike, the school undertook a protracted search process and Jon was one of several finalists. Within months of him assuming the reigns as the director of Florida Programs, Outward Bound started a multi-year process culminating in 2005 where all but one Outward Bound school and two Urban Centers in the U.S decided to merge and reorganize around populations and niches instead of geographies. Jon moved from being a Director to a President as a result of the reorganization.

> *I guess I needed to leave in order to come back."* Jon said. *"I don't think that I would have been hired as Director had I remained. I think my departure helped everyone see just how serious I was about my career and interest in growing professionally. I had it all charted out, I was going to work for AYF and then go back to grad school, get my masters, and then teach. It's interesting how it all turned out.*

Jon didn't have his career plotted out, but he did know he wanted to make a difference and he had the confidence to believe he could do that anywhere—even some place where he was a newly hired manager instead of a school president.

Making a difference happens when confidence converges with conviction, when vision merges with passion, and when a belief in one's self allows them to put themselves in the middle of what matters. There are those who believe that what we accomplish is due to faith, or fate, or luck, or hard work, or the mysterious spin of the universal roulette wheel, or all of the above. What is unassailably true is that making a difference begins with a desire to do so. Confidence is a belief.

Believe....

PART THREE
THE PRACTICE

FOR ASPIRING LEADERS

Accumulate Experiences

As basic as it sounds, the best way to build confidence and learn to make a difference is to get up each morning, put your socks on and practice living a full and helpful life. The theory of successive approximations says that if we are repeatedly exposed to the same stressful event, we will develop coping mechanisms to handle that event with less and less stress.

What to Do:

To build confidence, we have to fill our lives with experiences. And if we want to make a difference, not just any old experience will do. We have to fill our lives with meaningful experiences.

If you need a more specific guideline, use Kurt Hahn's Four Antidotes. They are more relevant today than ever:

• Compete with yourself—not the world. If you measure yourself against someone else, you may be able to set a high standard, but it's the wrong standard. We all have people we look up to or try to emulate, but when we compete with people who have a skill we want to develop, competing with them makes it difficult to be coached by them. Practice those things that are important to you and mark your own progress against yourself. Hahn's first "antidote" was originally based on self-competition in physical conditioning, but his point was to develop discipline through rigorous attempts to improve oneself against previous best efforts. Through this self-competition, his student's confidence in themselves went up. By competing with ourselves, we are competing against the most difficult adversary we have. One note: Competing with yourself has one major drawback. It is hard to accurately assess your own progress. For this, I rely on the feedback and observations of a few trusted advisors who know me and can tell me when and if I am making as much progress as I think I am. The reason assessing our own progress is so difficult is, I think, because when we do battle against ourselves we may expend a tremendous amount of energy for what appears to the outside world as only an incremental improvement.

• Push yourself—take on emotional, leadership, business and physical challenges that stretch your endurance, intellect, relational skills, flexibility and strength. In other words, take a chance—but take smart chances. Don't agree to take on a project at work that is critical unless you feel pretty sure you have the necessary support around you to pull it off. Make sure it is well known that you are not entirely sure if you can pull it off before accepting it. Kurt Hahn used expeditions to catalyze teams and teach the importance of human relationships in Outward Bound. The ultimate goal was the same, to build confidence by helping people stretch and push themselves.

• Attach yourself to projects at work and in life that make a difference. In addition to doing the tasks and functions of your job that are expected and required, make the time to also work on projects and initiatives that are outside your traditional job function. Companies are led and run by leaders who don't just do their jobs; they do what needs to be done in the best interest of the entire enterprise. Hahn referred to this antidote as "Projects" to teach craftsmanship and the importance of interdependence.

• Adopt a mindset of service. What would the world be like if we all adopted a mindset that said, "My purpose in life is to make a difference for others"? Service to others teaches us humility on the one hand and pride in accomplishment on the other. In addition, adopting a service mindset gives us a vehicle to practice the first three bullets, above, if doing so at work seems too risky.

Expand Your Comfort Zone Through Intentional Experiences

This popular expression is more difficult to put into action than people realize. In order for us to gain confidence in the experiences we are having we have to be able to pay attention to what those experiences are. Have you ever done a really high stress/high adventure activity like rock climbing, skydiving or bungee jumping? If you have, reflect on what you remember about your very first attempt. If you are like most people, you remember only vague generalities about the experience and none of the details. The reason is, when we are really afraid, we either shut down completely or we go into autopilot, completing the motions of the exercise with no conscious or cognitive awareness of what we are doing. That is why a good rock climbing or sky diving instructor will ask you "How are you feeling?" during those high stress moments. They are attempting to help you connect what you are in the middle of doing with how you feel about it. If you can remember the feeling when you were on the edge of your comfort zone, the next time you are in a similar predicament you are more likely to draw strength from the moment.

Our "comfort zone" is the invisible zone within each of us that defines what is familiar or non-threatening and what is unfamiliar or threatening. We expand our comfort zones by having—and noticing—meaningful and unfamiliar experiences that allow us to stretch. We expand our comfort zones through successive approximations.

Toastmasters is an international club for people who want to learn to speak in public. The club has chapters all over the world. Toastmasters uses public speaking as an intentional method to help people overcome their fears, and they do it with great intention. Their vision has very little to do with public speaking and everything to do with providing experiences that help their members notice when they are stretching their comfort zones. The vision statement on the club's website says, "Toastmasters International empowers people to achieve their full potential and realize their dreams. Through our member clubs, people throughout the world can improve their communication and leadership skills, and find the courage to change."[3] The aim of the club is about much more than becoming a proficient public speaker. Toastmasters uses public speaking to help people find their potential. The organization's goals are only slightly different than Outward Bound's, the difference is the method.

What to Do:

Take a rock-climbing course, join Toastmasters, volunteer to lead a project that will stretch your talents. Whatever you choose to do, make sure to pay attention to how you cope with your discomfort or fear in the process.

Do Battle with Your Fears

> *You say you see no hope, you say you see no reason*
> *We should dream that the world would ever change*
> *You're saying love is foolish to believe*
> *'Cause there'll always be some crazy with an Army or a Knife*
> *To wake you from your day dream, put the fear back in your life...*
> *— David Wilcox, "Show the Way"*[4]

Fear is a natural element of life, and many of our fears serve us well. Neurobiologists tell us that a substantial portion of our brains is devoted to keeping us alive, and knowing what to be afraid of is a critical element to survival. However, having a brain that has a high sensitivity to identifying threats can be as much of a disadvantage to us as an advantage. Current research on how our brains are wired reveals an interesting characteristic: we have the same physiological response to a real fear, say someone pulling a gun on us, as we do to a perceived fear like receiving a voicemail or email message from our boss that says "I need to see you right now!" In both cases, studies show that our pulse rates go up, our pupils constrict, we breathe faster and if the threat is perceived as big enough, our brains tell our adrenal glands to give us a small burst of adrenaline in case we need to run like hell. The difference is, one event is life threatening while the other is not.

It is this autonomic response that wreaks havoc on our ability to develop confidence. We react as if flubbing our lines during a speech is going to be as painful as getting eaten by a lion, and when we do flub our lines, we hold on to it and flog ourselves for our stupidity. Then, the next time we are asked to give a speech, we reflect back on our last experience and decide that we would rather face a lion in a cage than have to try again. We have a totally rational response to an irrational fear. The rational response is, "Why would I subject myself to another painful and embarrassing event again for no reason?" But the irrational fear is based on the notion that flubbing lines really matters. So what if we flub our lines again? Will doing so result in loss of life or limb? Of course not. Will we lose our jobs if we appear nervous when it is time to give a big presentation or speech? Unlikely, unless you're an actor on Broadway. If the theory of successive approximations holds true, the best response is to try again and again until the discomfort and fear is replaced with confidence and skill.

When we are living in our fears, we are literally fighting for our lives, even when our lives are not at stake.

What to Do:

The first step to overcoming fear is to notice it. In their book *Play to Win: Choosing Growth Over Fear In Work And Life*, Hersch and Larry Wilson categorize emotionally based fears into four distinct groups, which they call the "Four Fatal Fears."[5] As discussed, these fears aren't literally life threatening, but they might as well be. Our responses to them usually don't serve us or the situation. The next time you notice your confidence is shaken by something and fear is creeping in, try and identify which one of these fears may be at play:

- Fear of Failure – No one wants to fail, but when we fear failure, we aren't thinking of doing our best. When we are in this fear, we are thinking defensively about how not to get found out, or how not to lose any more than we already have, or how badly it may feel if we try and don't succeed. Each of us wants to feel and be successful in whatever we are doing. Fear of failure sometimes prevents us from even trying.

•   Fear of Emotional Discomfort – This fear shows up most frequently as avoidance. If we know we need to have a difficult conversation with someone but rationalize lots of reasons why now is not the right time, we may be in this fear. The antithesis of this fear, of course, is a desire to feel emotionally comfortable, yet by not confronting the issue that needs to be addressed, we hinder our ability to feel true emotional comfort.

•   Fear of Rejection – Humans are pack animals. We need human networks to connect with. When we are afraid of being left out or excluded, it taps into our primal sense of safety and security. Kids (or adults) who succumb to peer pressure are doing battle with this fear and responding to their need to be accepted. Succumbing to this fear almost always results in us not being true to ourselves, or others.

•   Fear of Being Wrong – No one likes to be wrong, because it conflicts with our sense of intellectual or instinctual capability. When we are feeling this fear, we often fight to be right, even if doing so alienates those around us. But think about it: being wrong isn't so bad. Most of us are wrong about one thing or another on a pretty frequent basis. Not admitting to being wrong, however, causes a lot of problems.

Once we have identified what fear is showing up, we can start challenging our irrational beliefs and eliminating them. By doing so we develop a rational response to rational or real events, not irrational ones.

It's when the stakes are at their highest that we are sometimes in our most unaware states. This makes responding appropriately to our fears difficult. It is a lot easier to notice our fears and cope with them before, say, a Toastmasters speech than when we are standing at the door of an airplane at 14,000 feet getting ready to jump out. When high-stakes situations happen, sometimes the best we can do is to reflect on our response to the situation after the fact. Taking the time to notice emotionally based fears is the first step in the battle. As Jon Howard says…"I try to use fear as an ally instead of as an adversary."

Learn More About Your Strengths

As this section demonstrates, confidence can be built through a mindset of service to others as much as it can be built through experience or education. For example, Doug Acksel serves as the Director of Operations for a subsidiary of a worldwide biotechnology company. The company employs many scientists and engineers with advanced degrees. Yet Doug has risen to a very senior position in the organization without an advanced degree.

Doug's decision to not pursue graduate work was not a matter of aptitude, just interest. In spite of his technical expertise, Doug sought opportunities to blend his love of science with his interest in people. Doug graduated from Purdue University with a B.S. in Chemical Engineering. Following graduation, he says, "I didn't know exactly where I would end up, but I knew it would have to be more than just technical in nature. I liked people! I knew I could find a way to make my abilities and interests overlap if I stayed with it."

Doug got his first job in the bioprocessing industry working in process development. As his career progressed, Doug naturally gravitated towards jobs that allowed him to work with, and lead, people. "Eventually I discovered that what was *really* fun was finding a problem, then challenging people to work on solving it. My technical expertise became less and less critical in my jobs and my ability to work with people from all parts of the organization became more and more important. I may never have discovered how much fun it was to work with and lead a team had I not had some level of technical expertise, but once I realized my real skills were in other areas—like managing and leading—I started to gain real confidence in being a leader. One thing fed the other: confidence in my technical expertise fed me opportunities to lead and manage."

About ten years into his career, Doug had an epiphany of sorts that helped him apply his confidence to something he thought made a real difference in the world. "I remember being really busy, and really tired, and asking myself, 'Am I going to measure my life by how much product was made?'"

Doug's company subscribes to the "triple bottom line" philosophy of business. The triple bottom line is a measure of organizational success that measures financial profits as one third of a company's success. The other two thirds—which are seen as being equally important—are the measures of the company's environmental and social responsibility including, for example, developing and adding value to the lives of its employees. "When I came to work here, I knew I was where I was meant to be. My job today has little to do with engineering and everything to do with organizational development and building effective, innovative teams for the sake of the business and, most importantly, for the team members."

Doug's technical confidence allowed him to pursue some other unidentified way of making a difference. And the better he got at making a difference (in supporting the careers and lives of his colleagues) the more confidence he had in doing more of the same in roles that continually expanded his skills, talents and interests.

What to Do:

To build more confidence, there have to be successful experiences to draw on. To generate successful experiences, we should attempt to do things in our areas of strength. Doug Acksel sees his real strengths as leading people in an environment where he can use and apply his technical aptitude. Doug defines his purpose as "providing a healthy working culture for colleagues". He maintains skill levels in the engineering elements of his job, but he dedicates as much of his time as possible to the development and use of his people skills. Doug sees these skills as both his strengths and where he can make the biggest difference in his company.

How should you go about discovering your strengths? In general, the method you are going to most believe in is the best method to use. These methods tend to work well for our clients:

> •   Conduct a formal or informal "Strengths 360"- a 360 degree review in which the people above, below and beside you are asked to evaluate you using the exact same set of questions. A Strengths 360 is merely a review in which questions are asked to help you get a fix on what your colleagues, employees and manager see as your strengths. You can create

your own questionnaire, hire a performance management firm to provide you with a customized 360 or use an on-line survey. Each approach has some drawbacks and positives. The most important element of conducting a Strengths 360 is to make sure the people you use for feedback feel comfortable and are able to tell the whole truth without fear of retribution or bias. For this reason, it is good to involve a coach or a qualified supervisor to help you monitor and interpret the results.

• Interview Your Supervisor, Customers and Employees - Similar to a Strengths 360 review, a less formal, but more time consuming method of better understanding your strengths is to interview the people around you who work with you enough to tell you what they see as your strengths. Like a 360, using a standardized series of questions really helps so you can identify trends in the comments of the interviewees. But remember, one of our four basic emotionally based fears is the fear of emotional discomfort, so finding interviewees who are comfortable being candid and will therefore be willing to give you accurate information is key. A big advantage of the interview approach is, if it is done well, interviewing can build stronger relationships with those people who are being interviewed.

• Take a Professional Profiling Test – Take the Strength-finder Profile in *Now, Discover Your Strengths* or any of the personality or style instruments on the market. Consulting firms, adult learning companies and psychological profiling research programs offer a wide range of statistically validated tests that measure everything from the degree of creativity you display in solving problems to identifying the leadership strengths you are more likely to display given your style or personality. Which test is the one you should take? The one whose findings you will have the most confidence in.

• Record Your Biggest Career Successes and Notice the Trends – On the left margin of a piece of paper, write down the major accomplishments of your career, one at a time. As you write down these major accomplishments, on the right margin of the paper, write down all of the smaller successes you created or were part of as a result of that one major accomplishment. Now go back to the left margin and write down another major accomplishment, followed by the smaller accomplishments that were the result of the major accomplishment, and so on. Now look at the list, and pretend the list belongs to someone else. Pretend it represents the accomplishments of someone you were considering hiring. Based on what you see on the paper, what are their strengths? Make note of them.

Build on People's Strengths

Marcus Buckingham (with Curt Coffman) in his book *First, Break All the Rules* and then with Donald O. Clifton a book they coauthored, *Now, Discover Your Strengths* uncovers how the world's best managers manage their people.[6] Buckingham's findings fly in the face of what most managers do: focus on the negative. Instead of focusing on the less desirable behaviors or sub-standard skills of employees, say Buckingham and Clifton, find what your employees are good at and find ways to accentuate those skills. Focus on those behaviors that are critical to the success of the job.

What to Do:

Buckingham's and Clifton's book does not suggest ignoring employee's weaknesses, but their research shows that successful employees and managers get further—much further—by focusing on capabilities instead of "pathologies" or weaknesses.

FOR SENIOR LEADERS AND COACHES

If You Want Your People to Make a Difference, Make a Difference!

If you want employees to have the confidence to make a difference, help them understand how their work and the business they are involved in makes a difference. This requires you to do more than just coach your employees; you have to think about how your business matters. It is surprising to me how few senior leaders have even thought about how their business makes a difference in the world, but as soon as I ask them, most of them can identify ways that it does.

What to Do:

Learn to tell the story of what your business does, not with marketing jargon, but with the language of purpose and service.

- How does your business make the world a better place?
- Who directly benefits from your business?
- Who indirectly benefits from your business?
- What would your community or the world be like without your business?
- What is the highest, best purpose of your business in terms of fulfilling human needs?
- What makes you excited about your business in terms of the services or products it provides?

Employees know the world has complex, hard-to-solve problems. They know the world needs help. Show them how what you do and what they do helps make the world a better place.

Are You Teaching Drown Proofing or Drowning? Delegate, Don't Abdicate.

Freddie LaNue taught drown proofing to Peace Corps volunteers in stages. First he taught what he referred to as the "keyhole" stroke, then he taught them how to move through the water with minimal or no use of their hands and feet. Then—and only then—he tied them up and threw them in the water.

Abdication of a task is giving up on it and turning it over to someone else. If you abdicate a task, you abandon it. Delegation is asking someone to literally be your delegate to the task, your representative. When you delegate, you have to maintain a vested interest in the completion of the task. Delegating tasks that stretch their abilities is a great way to help aspiring leaders build confidence and capability. Knowing what to delegate, when to delegate and how to follow up on delegated tasks is a skill that senior managers and leaders almost uniformly lack. They confuse delegation with abdication. They lack the patience to teach the basics before tying aspiring leaders up and throwing them in the water, metaphorically speaking.

What to Do:

The confusion between delegation and abdication causes enormous issues in business. Mistaken expectations on both the parts of the senior leader and the person they are delegating to create breakdowns in trust, hurt feelings, frustration, and bruised egos. The problem is that most leaders don't acknowledge that they need to learn how to delegate. As a management skill, delegating is a fine art; it's an advanced skill that deserves a lot more attention than it gets. Courses in effective delegation abound. Take one.

The Pitfalls of Sink or Swim

How many times have you said, or heard someone else say: "It's sink or swim in this job. That's how I learned and that's how they'll learn. They just have to jump in and learn along the way." Although the metaphor of throwing someone in the water to teach them to swim sounds expeditious, teaching aspiring leaders how to lead by giving them tasks that are over their heads and not helping them is akin to watching a drowning.

Yes, all of us learned much of what we know about how to lead by actually doing it, not by watching it. And yes, we generally learned the most when the stakes were high. But your job as the coach of a senior leader is not to find a near-impossible task for an aspiring leader to attempt so they can learn to swim in the deep end of the pool. If you're thinking this way, you're creating far more problems than you are solving.

This inefficient approach is really just "facilitated sink or swim." In this approach, you set up a situation in which whomever you are trying to coach or teach has a major trial to overcome. You pick the trial, you set up the circumstances and, frequently, you dictate the definition of "success" or "failure." The problem with facilitated sink or swim learning scenarios is that they aren't real. If you control the choice of the task and the conditions, the person you are trying to help does not have the control they need to learn what is truly valuable about the experience. Think about it: your biggest learning experiences were in "sink or swim" scenarios of your own choosing, not your boss's. And this element—the element of choice—is what separates what you can do for those you are trying to coach from what they need to do for themselves.

What to Do:

Assume that whomever you are trying to coach will create enough of their own sink or swim scenarios. Your job should be to teach them how to think through the completion of a new or unfamiliar task by delegating it, not abdicating it.

Resist Creating Clones

Another problem senior leaders have to overcome as they delegate is the temptation to focus on style rather than results. Style—the method, mindset, strategy and tactics for accomplishing a task—varies substantially from person to person. Results—achieving the goal—usually have less variability. When you delegate a task, determine how much of what you want the person to learn is about style and how much of what you want them to learn is about results. If the style with which an aspiring leader attempts a task is important, then tell them what your intentions in making the assignment are. Is it an exercise in learning style, producing results, or both? Be clear when you begin.

If you are a successful senior leader, then you have developed a style for addressing business issues that works for you and you probably have a lot of confidence in that style. But it's important to remember that you learned that style on your own. The ability to help people find their own best style is a real gift that comes through practice and effort over a long period of time. Doing this is much, much more difficult than simply preaching about the virtues and benefits of your own personal style, but it is also much more effective.

What to Do:

Don't try and teach someone how to do a task your way. Teach them how to do it their way. Instead of rattling on and on about how you would do something, watch how the person you have delegated a task to completes it. Take note of what they did that worked for them. When they hit a setback due to their approach, take note and tell them what you noticed did not work as well. Observe their style and report back to them on what you noticed worked and what you noticed didn't work. This approach works much better than trying to turn them into a clone of you.

Become Attached to the Process, Not the Outcome

Coaching an aspiring leader can be an exhilarating and rewarding process. It can also be a frustrating one. What worked for you when you were developing your confidence may or may not work for anyone else. Each aspiring leader has his or her own comfort zone and areas that need development, and each person is different. A trap coaches frequently fall into is becoming attached to the learning outcomes of whomever they are coaching. Coaches, as others, like to see results. They also like to be right. But many managers get attached to being right instead of helping people make their own discoveries.

Maggie was an exceptionally well-educated, highly experienced marketing VP for a large professional services firm. She was as articulate and thorough in her communication skills—both written and verbal—as any member of the executive team, yet she believed that her communication skills were lacking. To compensate for what she felt was the inability to clearly state what she was thinking, Maggie had developed a habit of saying what she thought, then restating the same idea a second time in a different way, then restating the same idea again a third time to make sure whoever was listening got it. The result was that she was seen as being long- winded and redundant by her peers, some of her key customers, and the people who worked for her. At her request—and the ardent support of her fellow team members in the executive team—she and I began a systematic assault on her lack of confidence.

First, I asked Maggie to keep a running list of every negative, self-critical observation she had about her ability to communicate whenever she noticed one. Instead of arguing with Maggie, and trying to convince her she was wrong, I accepted her observations as valid and true. This alone was a big departure from how others had tried to help her. Her boss and several of her colleagues had attempted to argue her out of what she believed to be true about herself by using logic, or coercion, but that approach had not worked.

They were using a rational process to solve an irrational problem.

Next, Maggie started uncovering layer after layer of what was at the root of her behavior. Before long, she found a theme to her long windedness. Maggie discovered she was particularly redundant when she picked up nonverbally that people didn't believe or agree with what she was saying. The story Maggie told herself, we discovered, was that "I have to convince people that my ideas are valid—especially when I am not sure that they are. I have to sell people who look or act skeptically on my ideas before they say anything critical or negative about them." Underneath this belief, Maggie discovered one of her four fatal fears at work: Maggie needed to be right.

Now that we knew Maggie's long windedness was at least partially driven by the need to be right, we could discuss what being right actually won her. "I am surrounded by these really smart people who always seem so sure about the direction the business is going. Most of the time, I am not nearly as sure about what I think as they seem to be about what they think," she said. "In such a fast company, I'm afraid I'll be seen as stupid if I'm not at least as self-assured."

We had uncovered another irrational belief that drove her behavior: not wanting to be rejected or excluded because she wasn't as smart. I asked: "So what if you aren't as sure? Are you positive you'll be excluded or not listened to if you don't state your opinions with conviction?"

"Absolutely," Maggie replied.

"From what your colleagues are saying, they are already excluding you and not listening to you because you are so long winded and you say the same thing over again. Isn't that true?" I asked.

Maggie was getting frustrated. "Look, I've got to have respect, and getting it isn't easy!"

"So you think the way you are doing it works?"

Maggie was very attached to why she needed to continue to do exactly what she had been doing. Based on what I had seen and heard, I knew she was dead wrong. I felt like doing what everyone had already done with her, which was to try and argue with her, try and convince her that she really didn't need to be right all of the time, that it was hurting rather than helping her ability to communicate and her job performance. But when someone is stuck in what they believe, arguing with them sometimes just motivates them to dig in deeper.

Maggie was telling herself a story, and that story was driving her behavior.

After several more rounds that usually ended with me saying "…and is that working for you?" I got Maggie to agree to try an experiment that was outside her comfort zone. Instead of speaking up forcefully in executive team meetings, we agreed that she would bite her tongue and, if a question was directed her way, she would respond with "I don't know, let me think about it." Then, after she had really had time to think about whatever her suggestion or answer was, she would give it once and only once. Then, we agreed, she would finish her statement or explanation with a question: "Does that make sense?" and invite questions on what she had said. Maggie was to ignore what she read as the non-verbal, skeptical cues from the other people in the room. Finally, she agreed to observe the quality of those conversations and see if anything was different.

Holding up to her end of the agreement took a super-human effort on Maggie's part. But she noticed a marked difference in the quality of the conversations. Instead of hearing her point of view and moving off the subject, Maggie noticed that her colleagues started asking her more questions about what she had said. Before long, Maggie's opinions about a variety of subjects were being sought out in meetings and she ceased to feel she had to elbow her way into the conversations. After some noticeable improvement, Maggie was better able to see that her need to be right interfered with her relationships with colleagues and co-workers. But she would not have seen how her fear played out if I had become attached to getting results, or if I had become attached to being right. If I had taken this route, I would have continually engaged in an argument with her about *me* being right.

We become so attached to our point of view—like Maggie was—that we cease to help others and end up only disagreeing with them. People who lack confidence in an obvious area of strength are attachment magnets. When they say things like "I'm not very good at my job," a coach who is not very attachment savvy may think that the best course of action is to explain to them how wrong they are.

What to Do:

In spite of the most masterful and patient attempts to help people see the irrationality of their own thinking, they usually have to figure it out in their own time. When we become attached to someone else's problem, we adopt the problem as our own, which rarely helps.

Your job is to present valuable learning and development opportunities, then leave the rest up to the aspiring leader.

Be Human, Not Perfect

You are just as valuable as a role model for what your weaknesses are as for what your strengths are. Aspiring leaders don't need to try to emulate a super human, they need to try and emulate a real human. So be one. Confidence is not built in the absence of fear; confidence is built as a result of overcoming fear. Help those you are coaching learn how to effectively do battle with their own insecurities.

What to Do:

Check your ego at the door when you are trying to help someone else develop greater confidence. They don't need to hear how fearless you are, they need to understand the tools and skills you use to fear less. Share with them your fears and insecurities. Talk about how you do battle with your own four fatal fears. Tell them what confidence gaps you have.

This type of self disclosure helps aspiring leaders realize they are not alone. Knowing when to self disclose, and how much, is a delicate and intuitive process. On the one hand, you want them to know you are a mere mortal. On the other hand, you don't want to turn your relationship into a mini support group. After all, this is work, not therapy. Use examples that are relevant to work. Discussions you can have that will add the most value include:

- A time when you were overconfident

- A time when, if you had trusted yourself, things would have turned out better

- A critical event or defining moment when you discovered a new strength

- A critical event or defining moment when you failed utterly and completely, and how you picked yourself back up in the aftermath

- The fears that you have to do battle with in the work you do

- The types of situations that bring out your best

- The types of situations that cause you to feel insecure

Am I suggesting that you be unconditionally supportive to those you coach, even when they let their insecurities interfere substantially with their work? Absolutely not. Heed a lesson covered in *Now, Discover Your Strengths*. Demand a lot from whomever you are coaching, but demand it in light of their imperfections and challenges, not instead of them. Focus on their strengths while helping them improve upon their weaknesses to the point that those weaknesses don't impede their performance. The steps that build confidence are universally applicable whether we're 6 or 60: Acknowledge setbacks without dwelling on them. Find ways to become average at that which you are below average. And for those areas in which you are brilliant or very good, make them your life's work.

FOR BOTH ASPIRING LEADERS AND SENIOR LEADERS

Learn to generalize experiences to build confidence. What does learning how to rappel off of a cliff have to do with developing confidence in a board room? How does being "drown-proofed" make someone a better Peace Corps volunteer? How does having an undergraduate degree in chemistry help someone become a leader of people who all have more education than they do?

Experience is a great teacher when we know how to generalize that experience into other situations and apply what we learned to other contexts. What makes Outward Bound special is not much different than what makes the first year of law school special. Both teach students that they are capable of more than they ever thought possible. Outward Bound forges confidence through trials of adversity that are physical and adventurous. First year law programs are designed to do the same using high workloads and intellectual challenge. When we feel more confident in a specific area, that confidence can improve our performance in other areas. When this happens, we have "generalized" the experience.

Occasionally an exercise in developing confidence turns into a real-life situation. When we respond well to these situations, we become even more confident and able to generalize our experience to other contexts. The mountains of North Carolina are notorious for the frequency and severity of lightning storms in the summer. As a precaution, the North Carolina Outward Bound School teaches the "lightning drill"—a method of establishing a safe position insulated from the ground that is also relatively safe to lightning strikes—to each student soon after they arrive. The School also teaches CPR and basic first aid to each new student during their Main expedition. In a now-famous incident, a ground lightning strike known as an "eddy current" hit two of NCOBS instructors who were leading a group of students on a backpacking trip. Using the skills they had learned only days before, the students resuscitated them. We use generalization to link events or pieces of data. Then once we have generalized two or more things, we draw conclusions based on what we see. Teachers evaluate students based on test scores, classroom participation and assignment completion to develop a generalized view of that student's capability. Investors pour over profit trends, quarterly earnings projections and corporate press releases to determine the generalized trend of a company before deciding how or when to invest in it. Generalizing is what we do.

How could the students who were involved in resuscitating their instructors on the NCOBS course generalize their experience to their work-a-day worlds? How would you generalize the experience? First, it is a fair assumption that the students left that experience with significantly more confidence in the value of CPR to save lives:

> **Generalization #1.** Since they had just learned the lifesaving techniques they employed, it is also a fair assumption that they have more confidence in their ability to apply what they learn quickly and effectively.

> **Generalization #2.** Effectively applying a new skill in such dramatic circumstances helped the students gain a deeper appreciation for the importance of service to others and preparedness in emergency situations.

Without interviewing the students individually to see what else they held on to and applied, any generalizations beyond these two would be speculative. They may have learned and generalized their ability to respond effectively in stressful situations. They may have learned the value of teamwork through the experience. To know how this experience had affected the way they viewed the world, we would need to ask. At least for a time, it's a good bet that such an important and dramatic experience was generalized by everyone involved.

Outward Bound Advertisement

What to Do:

Organizational behavior expert David Kolb developed an experiential learning model to describe the process of how we naturally tend to generalize experience. After any concrete experience, Kolb states, there is a period of reflection and observation about the experience, followed by a phase of forming abstract concepts about the meaning of the experience, followed by a period of testing newly acquired learning in other, similar situations.[7] Taking the time to reflect on what is being learned, and creating tests to see if what we learned in one situation can apply to another, is a critical exercise for aspiring leaders and their coaches to do together. My favorite way to help people learn to learn through generalization is doing what I call: "Catching them in the act of being themselves." When someone you are working with does something bold, or wonderful or inspiring, tell them. When you notice someone taking a risk, particularly if it is an emotional risk, in an effort to solve a problem or rectify a situation, notice it with them. Compliments that are hollow or unfounded break down trust. Compliments and acknowledgements help people recognize their own strengths, which in turn helps them generalize from experience, which ultimately helps them build confidence in themselves.

COURAGE THROUGH SERVICE

Add Value...

- Find something that needs to be done that others don't want to do and do it.
- Be brave enough to say what needs to be said when everyone else is afraid to, especially about your own strengths and shortcomings.
- Apply your strengths and innate talents to making work and life better. Find where your talents are needed and apply them.

Inspire Others...

- Fearlessly pursue your own self- improvement.
- Find your "edge" of learning and skill development and push it emotionally, professionally, physically and spiritually.
- Notice what brings up fear in you. Don't deny it—understand it.
- Develop a vision of the future that is optimistic and realistic. Shoot for it and enlist the help of others in doing the same.

Change the World...

- Consider part of your life's purpose as serving those whose lives you touch.
- Look for opportunities to do community service where you live. Find that which needs attention and pay attention to it.
- Mentor a young person (they are usually more comfortable with your help if you just treat them like friends instead of like children you are trying to help).
- Counter the voices in our society that preach fear, blame and reprisal. Practice hope, accountability and service.

Section Four
Perspective

THIS SECTION IN BRIEF:

Systems are entities, or things. They are sustained by the ability of their parts to interact in a way that contributes to the system's overall performance. By this definition, the engines in our automobiles are systems. Human bodies are systems. So are our families. And most businesses and organizations are systems—if the business includes an aggregation of ideas, actions, or people that interact. This section first defines what "systems" are, then talks about how leaders can orchestrate change within them.

Systems leaders have to learn to use both hard data and intuition to affect change in a system. Usually they have less, rather than more, data than they need and they have to rely on what the military experts refer to as coup d'oeil, or incisive intuition, to determine how to make an impact on big, complicated systems.

Seeing systems is a crucial skill of successful leaders. Leaders who recognize systems are able to transcend their work-a-day perspective in order to see the bigger picture. They understand that everything is connected to something, and that everything in a system is influenced by everything else.

Leaders who are effective in seeing and influencing systems have another more subtle skill: they suspend their own biases about what they are seeing. They are aware of their "windows on the world" and understand how important being open-minded is. For more information turn to page 179.

PART ONE
SEEING IS BELIEVING

About the connection between the environment and world economies, co-authors Amory Lovins, Paul Hawken, and Hunter Lovins wrote, "The economy is the wholly owned subsidiary of the environment."[1] Everything we use, breathe, eat, drink, turn on, boot up, wear, install, twist, pull, read, write with, build with, drive, fly, and even throw away is provided to us, free of charge by the big blue ball: Planet Earth. We rely entirely on the use of what the Lovins and Hawken call "ecosystems services," the services and raw materials provided to humankind free of charge, day-in and day-out. In their book Natural Capitalism they describe a business model that combines the principles of capitalism with the principles of sustainability. The result incorporates the use, re-use and restoration of the capital reserves that power humankind, all of which are provided by nature.

For many who read the preceding paragraph—that nature provides all the raw materials that go into stuff used by humankind—the concept is implicit to you. In other words, you understood the concept before you read it. It is a primary piece of knowledge that is just *there*. You may not have even known you knew it, but having read about it, you became conscious of it, and were able to say to yourself, "Yeah, that makes sense." If you said this, or something like it, you are thinking like a systems thinker.

To understand the implications of the Lovins' and Hawken's statement, you have to understand at least two enormous systems and their interplay: the natural systems that are Planet Earth and the technological systems of humans. If the concept that humankind is totally reliant on the services provided by nature is true—shouldn't that little piece of knowledge determine how we treat each other and the planet? You bet. Does it? You decide.

If you are at all like me, a significant barrier to engaging in environmentalism is not apathy, but the same thing that prevents us from attempting to influence any large, complex system: the enormity of the issues and the difficulty in cutting them into bite- sized, actionable pieces. For example, the EPA recently completed a study warning that America's coastlines cannot fully support marine life and human activity given the pressures placed on marine life by human activity.[2] "O.K.," you may say. "I get it, we're hurting the environment, but what should I do about it?"

What has been missing for many of us has been a framework, a way of looking at the environment and man's effect on it that helps us understand how our behaviors overlap with nature's ability to handle those behaviors. That framework was eventually provided by Dr. Karl-Henrik Robèrt and the educational movement he helped to start called The Natural Step.

Karl-Henrik Robèrt is a Swedish pediatric oncologist—a physician who specializes in treating cancers in children. Early in his career, Dr. Robèrt (pronounced *Rober*) became aware of a staggering indicator of humankind's effects on the environment, a dramatic increase in cancers in children over the past 50 years. He immersed himself in the problem, talking to experts and learning everything he could from all sides of the issue. Eventually, Dr. Robèrt became aware of the lack of action around critical environmental concerns because of contention over the details. While everyone agreed there was a problem generated by humankind's influence on the environment, he found debate about the extent, exact cause, and long-term effects of the crisis, drags public action to a standstill. Equipped with a mountain of data on environmental problems worldwide, Robèrt set out to define the root causes of the problem in a way that would engage everyone in finding solutions instead of causing petty arguments over the details. Referring to the inability of the environmental community to agree on the important things instead of arguing over details, Robèrt uses a simple metaphor to define the problem:

> In the midst of all this chatter about the leaves, very few of us have been paying attention to the environment's trunk and branches. They are deteriorating as a result of processes about which there is little or no controversy; and the thousands of individual problems that are the subject of so much debate

are, in fact, manifestations of systemic errors that are undermining the foundations of human society. There has been a basic scientific agreement about the causes of that deterioration for nearly half a century, and it should be possible to anchor key decisions affecting society in that scientific consensus. We must learn to deal with environmental problems at the systemic level; if we heal the trunk and the branches, the benefits for the leaves will follow naturally.[3]

Once he felt like he had an adequate grasp on the list of problems associated with the earth's environmental crisis, Robèrt and his colleague, physicist John Holmberg, wrote a white paper that detailed his understanding of the root causes of the crisis and established a consensus process for revising it that involved scientists on all sides of the problem. Eventually, they had a document with which everyone who had read it agreed. The principles they established became the *Systems Conditions* of an international movement called The Natural Step. The Natural Step and its *Systems Conditions* became the blueprint and declaration for sustainability worldwide. Since the consensus process, the Natural Step has established offices in eight countries and has worked with many of the largest and most influential companies in the world to adopt its principles. Organizations like Cargill Dow, Bank of America, CH2M Hill, IDEO, IKEA, Home Depot, Interface, McDonald's Corporation, Panasonic/Matsutisha, Nike, Starbucks, Toyota Australia and the United States Marine Corps Base Camp Le Jeune have integrated the principles of the Natural Step into their core business functions. The Bank of America, for example, implemented a supplier scorecard based on the systems conditions which significantly influenced the environmental practices of its entire supply chain. In addition, the Bank has taken a number of steps in its own internal operating functions including education of bank employees on the Systems Conditions and changing their facilities management approaches to reflect a more sustainable approach.

The Natural Step helps bridge the gap in understanding between two different but mutually influencing systems, humankind and nature. Gregory Bateson, noted philosopher, anthropologist, photographer, naturalist, and poet, as well as the husband and collaborator of Margaret Mead, artfully described the clash of these two systems thus: "The major problems in the world are the result of the difference between how nature works and the way people think." Dr. Robèrt was able to see and explain the deleterious effects on Earth's systems by manmade systems. Even more importantly, he was able to suggest a systemic solution and he arrived at that solution by involving a third system; the system of academicians, doctors and researchers who had divergent opinions about the leaves on the trees, so to speak, without having attended to the trunk and branches. Robèrt's systems skills helped him develop a mechanism, The Natural Step, to influence the collective thinking and intelligence of his colleagues on the issue.

SEEING THAT WHICH ISN'T VISIBLE

> *"All there is to thinking is seeing something noticeable which makes you see something you weren't noticing which makes you see something that isn't even visible."*
> —Norman Maclean, A River Runs Through It

In 1968, a monumental systems event occurred for just about anyone on the planet who had access to a television or newspaper. The event was the Apollo 8 mission, the first mission in which a manned spacecraft circled the moon. Those of us watching held our collective breaths during the spacecraft's first orbit around the moon on Christmas Eve, 1968. After a few suspense filled minutes, the ship came out from behind the moon. At that instant something no one had anticipated happened—the crew experienced "earthrise." They took pictures of their home, Planet Earth, which appeared as a beautiful blue sphere illuminated by the sun, coming into view over the landscape of the moon. The earth looked like a suspended orb, beautiful in the void of space 385,000 kilometers away, fragile, warm and whole. The picture taken by the astronauts at that moment changed our views about the sacredness and beauty of our home. The picture became a symbol of the cultural revolution taking place in the United States. From the cover of the first Whole Earth Catalogue to an icon of the environmental movement, the view of the earth as seen from the moon transformed our thinking. For the first time, we could see how slender and fragile our atmosphere was: a thin, vibrant veil that sustains life for the entire planet.

The Cold War was at its zenith, yet we were able to see a planet without borders. In the aftermath of the Kent State tragedies and the assassinations of Robert Kennedy and Martin Luther King Jr., the United States was in a period of deep unrest and almost existential doubt about the efficacy of democracy. The picture of the planet Earth acted as a unifying experience that changed our perspective from one of fear and uncertainty to one of vision and beauty. It was a picture of connectedness instead of dividedness. And it could not have come at a more crucial time.

When we are in close proximity to something, we notice its detail. When we stand back, or in the case of the Apollo 8 astronauts, way, way, back, we are more able to see the whole system. We saw where we lived, and it was beautiful. Our perspective changed.

Austrian Biologist Ludwig von Bertalanffy's definition of systems is elegant and simple: "A system is an entity which maintains its existence through the mutual interaction of its parts." Earthrise on the Apollo 8 mission changed our view of earth. Instead of a mass of rock and water, the earth looked like a living system. When viewed at that great distance, it appeared strikingly similar to a cell.

Coming from a completely different viewpoint but with the same realization, Lewis Thomas in *The Life of a Cell* wrote:

> *I have been trying to think of the earth as a kind of organism, but it is no go. I cannot think of it this way. It is too big, too complex, with too many working parts lacking visible connections. The other night, driving through a hilly, wooded part of southern New England, I wondered about this. If not like an organism, what is it most like? Then, satisfactorily, for that moment, it came to me: it (the earth) is most like a cell.*

When something is seen as a whole, we can more accurately understand the inter-relatedness of all its pieces and we can see how its features are similar to other structures. This is *Perspective*.

Any aggregation of functions, actions, ideas or people can eventually become a system. Most businesses and organizations are systems. But not all businesses are systems, and not being a system may or may not help make the business successful. Small professional service firms like an architectural firm or a legal practice with individual partners who bill for their individual time but don't share resources may be highly successful without taking on many of the characteristics of a system. Sales organizations that promote competition between sales people are systems, but if they promote competition above collaboration, they have fewer of the attributes of a complete system.

Systems aren't just groups of people working in interconnected ways. Systems are also models, ways of thinking and policies, procedures and cultural norms. Countries, for example, have a system of governance which in turn is usually driven by local or municipal systems which of course are affected primarily by the belief systems extant in that community. Aircraft have separate safety systems which are one of the many subsets of the operating system of the airplane. Even learning can be described by systems such as the Montessori or Waldorf system. Want to learn to play the violin? Try the Suzuki System.

"Seeing systems" refers to the ability to see the patterns, trends, connections and threads that create interdependencies among the parts within a system. But seeing systems is only the tip of the iceberg; understanding how to influence them positively is just as important. Leaders who possess this insight are able to determine where in the system to insert a new idea to achieve a change.

CAPTAINS AND CEO'S

The ability to sail a ship from point A to point B is a good example of the skill of seeing systems. Sailing ships are self-contained systems. A specific set of skills is required to make the ship "go" or move through the water and there is a different set of skills needed to know how to navigate. Sailing ships are propelled forward by a complex but predictable interplay of wind and sails. Setting a sail at a given angle to the wind relative to the direction the ship is pointed will produce predictable results. The interplay of ropes, sails, masts, booms, the vessel's hull, etc. comprise a mutually beneficial and interconnected system unto itself. Learning this interplay is one of the first skills any sailor learns. The captain of a ship who understands this interaction is managing a relatively simple system.

As we stand further and further back to look at the global skills of a sailor, the analogy starts to get more interesting. Sailing ships don't generally go directly to any point, unless the wind is unusually favorable. For example, if you want to get your ship to some port that is due east of your current location, but the wind is coming *from* the east, there is no configuration of sail and hull position that allows you to sail directly into the wind. If you tried, the ship would either sit dead in the water or, if you were really unlucky, it might manage to actually go backwards. To sail into the wind, sailors have to "tack" back and forth towards their destination in a series of zigzag maneuvers at an angle to the wind, timing one of their tacks to intersect their ultimate destination. Sailors who can both maneuver their vessels and *navigate* to a destination are operating the system at a higher level of complexity. They are managing two or more systems in series: the sailing vessel itself as well as the navigational skills and the tides, winds and currents.

The progression goes on: upward and outward in both complexity and volatility. Sailors who can manage at a very high level of complexity are the ones who captain the tall ships that make trans-oceanic crossings on a time table as a business. They have to manage a number of interrelated systems *and* be able to think, work and communicate in abstract terms in order to set long-range goals. It's not a coincidence that one of the most frequently used similes for being a CEO is being the "Captain of the Ship".

	Tallship Captain	CEO or Manager
Management Responsibilities	The Ship	The Business
	The Command Structure	The Sr. Team or Management Team
	Daily Navigation	Tracking and Monitoring Priorities and Delegated Tasks
System or System to Manage	The Weather, Winds, Tides, Time, Vessel, Crew, Sails, Etc.	The Business Environment: Customers, Competitors, Suppliers, Partners, Markets, Etc.
	The Crew	The Employees
	Navigating to the next buoy or landmark	Setting financial targets and quarterly goals
	Navigating to the next port	Long range vision and strategy

Captains and CEO's

CONNECTED COMPETENCIES

Being able to think, work and communicate in abstract terms are not the only competencies connected with seeing and influencing systems. Others include:

- Seeing the whole picture and prioritizing accordingly
- Utilizing good problem solving skills
- Utilizing existing capabilities and systems
- Developing systemic solutions to local problems
- Identifying when and where change is needed
- Acting decisively when necessary
- Possessing good problem solving skills
- Seeing downstream effects of current decisions and actions
- Promoting collaboration
- Using intuition appropriately
- Working effectively across functions
- Creating novel solutions

The shoulder trait between Perspective and Passion and Timing is Innovation. Developing solutions to difficult problems takes an ability to see the big picture and a passionate desire to do the work necessary to stick with it until a solution is found. For more on developing Innovation in yourself or others, refer to The Practice in this section or in the section on Passion and Timing.

INTUITION AND SYSTEMS

No institution has spent more energy understanding the various dimensions of leadership than the military, and indeed the military has extensively studied intuition going back as far as the early 1800's. While studying the characteristics that made Napoleon Bonaparte an exceptional military leader, military historian Carl von Clausewitz invented a term to describe the ability of military commanders who were able to develop successful battle strategies based on limited and broad information. He called it "coup d'oeil" (pronounced "coo-doil"). Some military leaders, Clausewitz posited, had the inborn ability to develop a plan to win the battle based less on information and more on intuition. Leaders who possess this insight have coup d'oeil; they can take sketchy—frequently incomplete—information, combine it with their experience and intuition and successfully influence the system.

Since the early 1800's, more modern language has evolved to describe coup d'oeil. Today we call it "gut instinct," or "perception," or "a hunch" or just "feeling." Whatever the term, coup d'oeil is an elusive but critical element of what makes a leader effective at influencing systems. There is one exception to Clausewitz's explanation; coup d'oeil can be developed. The skill is not relegated just to those who are born with it. Evidence of this is that the United States Military teaches "battlefield awareness" to its rising leaders and in fact incorporates the concept of coup d'oeil into elements of its leadership development curriculum.[4]

Malcolm Gladwell in his fabulous book *Blink* describes what he calls "thin slicing," yet another way to talk about making decisions based on limited experience or information. In Gladwell's words, thin slicing is "the ability of our unconscious to find patterns in situations and people based on very narrow 'slices' of experience."[5] Gladwell suggests that we all thin slice to make decisions and some of us are better at it than others. He also suggests that the quality of the decisions we make when we use thin slicing is sometimes as good as if we took the additional time to ponder and consider a decision longer. The problem with thin slicing, like intuition, is that we each have biases and pre-determined judgments that both assist and interfere with the quality of our decision making. Leaders who see and intervene in systems thin slice effectively, but more importantly, they know when *not* to thin slice, when more information is both justified and required. Their intuition tells them when to use their intuition and when not to.

PART TWO
THE INSIGHT OF PERSPECTIVE
IN ACTION

WHY SEEING AND INFLUENCING SYSTEMS MATTERS

It's unlikely you will ever hear an announcement or read a press release about a newly appointed CEO—or one who has recently been canned—that mentions anything about their ability to lead and influence systems. Yet, in a four year study performed by LeadershipIQ.com, researchers found that 31% of CEOs get fired for mismanaging change, 28% for ignoring customers, 27% for tolerating low performers, 23% for denying reality and 22% for too much talk and not enough action. With the possible exception of ignoring customers, which is closely tied to the insight of *Connection*, the other factors are directly connected to the insight of *Perspective*. Managing change is all about the ability to see patterns and predict patterns and re-orient business objectives to changes. Low performers are typically tolerated by leaders who do not understand the effect that those performers are having on the system, which is why they tolerate them. If they had either a realistic view of the system—or of the performer—they would be more inclined to make a change. Systems leaders have an acute sense of current reality, but they don't get wrapped up in it. They stay focused on the *causes* of existing reality, not the momentary dramas created by it.

Enduring leaders who have this insight transcend their work-a-day perspective of the world in order to see the bigger picture. And they do it in a way that adds enormous value to their work. Michael Gerber, founder and chairman of E-Myth Worldwide, author, and expert on entrepreneurship and business feels that systems skills are highest among all the traits successful entrepreneurs need to have.[6] Systems leaders try to attach meaning to everything they see and if they can't attach a meaning to something, they investigate it until they can. Virtually every story recorded in business journals, books, periodicals and even in folk legends having to do with transformation or successful leadership involves an element of systems leadership—or failure.

How to Identify Systems Leaders

A great deal of what leaders who embody this insight do occurs between their ears, so knowing how to identify systems leaders is difficult. Whether they are conscious of it or not, all good systems leaders do the following:

- They stay open minded to ideas and input as long as possible, making their decisions just in time
- They frequently discuss events and occurrences as related to each other instead of as isolated events
- They offer solutions that address root causes instead of fixing symptoms
- They seek out data from divergent viewpoints so they can view an issue from all sides
- When they discuss a decision they are considering making, they typically share the thinking that led to that decision.

Finding Systems Leaders

Systems leaders are the ones who show-up at the scene of an accident and know instinctively what to do to help. They are the engineers who become inventors, and the inventors who become business owners or CEO's. They are the accountants who may be only moderately good at accounting, but great at finance. They are machine or production line operators who know how to keep things running even when a critical piece of machinery goes down. They are high school principals or superintendents who have happy teachers and successful students. They are air traffic controllers, orchestra conductors, auto mechanics, office managers, and county engineers. Being a good systems leader is less a matter of position than of mindset, and good ones show up everywhere.

Seeing systems is helpful—but knowing how to influence them is just as important and more difficult. The insight of *Perspective* is about seeing systems and then having the judgment and skill to know how, where, and when to influence them.

PERSPECTIVE AND OUR WINDOW ON THE WORLD

Systems leaders have the ability to collect information, separate the important from the unimportant, and assemble it in a way that is understandable and actionable. Leaders who possess this insight learn to think more openly and can attach multiple interpretations to the same data set depending on their view of the system. They look at trends, patterns and symptoms that show up as a bunch of apparently unrelated bits of information and find the pattern or trend that may indicate a systemic issue or situation. They don't just identify the situation or remedy the symptom—they find the source.

How do they do that? In short, they have flexible schemata. Translation: their window on the world allows them to view things more openly and more flexibly.

Each of us has a unique worldview—our "window on the world."[7] Our windows on the world are not only the result of how our brains are hard-wired, but also how our brains are conditioned to respond to various events. This conditioning includes, quite literally, everything. From the moment we were born, our brains start sorting information and looking for where to store it.[8] How we were nursed, when we were weaned, what our infancy was like in terms of parental attention and contact, the behaviors our parents tolerated or disciplined, childhood traumas and memorable childhood experiences, the culture in which we grew up—everything that went into what we noticed, felt, observed or heard—plays into who we are and how we behave. So much information comes at us at an early age, we develop a sorting mechanism—psychologists call it a schema or schemata (plural). Schemata are the buckets into which we sort and store information. Asleep yet? If you are, it is because some schema operating in your brain is telling you something to the effect that "psychological mumbo jumbo is boring and not valuable" so you sort the information you just read and file it in your "don't need to know or remember" pile, all thanks to your schema. Put more understandably, your window on the world tells you that what you are reading is not valuable, so you don't store the information. Your schemas are your windows on the world, and they strongly influence your perception about people, events, information, dynamics and systems.

If the above scenario applies to you, go back and read what you just read, again. You'll need it.

Our windows on the world help us. Without them (and without schemata) we would have a heck of a time sorting the thousands of experiences we have each day and determining the value of each experience. But our windows also interfere with our ability to see things as they truly are. To better understand how our windows on the world work, let's go for a hypothetical run in your hypothetical neighborhood as part of your hypothetical average day.

It's 6:00 a.m. and the alarm starts blaring loudly, signaling you that it's time to get up. You believe that sticking to a schedule is an important characteristic for someone who wants to be successful, which is why you set the alarm (a schema about success and structure is at work here). This hour is earlier than you would like to get up, but you like to get a workout in before going to work (another schema about your body, physical conditioning and perhaps routine supports this behavior). You get dressed and go for a run. On the run, you encounter an unfamiliar German Shepherd staring at you, 100 yards up the road. Instead of continuing to zone-out and immerse yourself in your thoughts as you've been doing, you check in and pay close attention to this new, unfamiliar animal. Your eyes fix on the dog (the result of a schema that says "beware of big dogs"). When you get within 30 yards of it, the dog takes off at a gallop—right at you....no barking, no growling, but ears back—like a dog that is either trying to show that it is submissive or angry. You stop in your tracks to wait and see what happens. Your logical brain tells you that hostile or aggressive dogs don't roam free in your neighborhood (another schema about the type of neighborhood you live in). But your instincts tell you to protect yourself (yet another schema about how to behave around dogs). The dog is very close now, only 20 feet away. You are pretty sure that this dog does not belong in your neighborhood (based on your schema) and that he means to harm you, so you yell at it in your most assertive voice: "STOP!" (a defensive response dictated by your schema). When you do, in an instant the dog plants its front feet, drops its haunches and comes to a complete stop and drops into a submissive posture—ears back, tail wagging and panting. You take a step towards the dog, and it lies down, looking straight at you, tail wagging furiously now as if to say, "will you play with me?" After petting the dog and resuming your run, you say to yourself, "what a nice dog, I am so silly, she only wanted to be petted because she was lonely and looking for someone to pay attention to her." And you file this new information in the "things I think are threats but aren't" schema.

Our windows on the world tend to filter information for us. In many cases, our windows do this before we have even had a conscious thought. Leaders who are trying to figure out how to influence systems learn to understand—and then suspend—their schemas so that they don't interfere with their ability to see the system as it more truly is, instead of through their inaccurate and often outdated windows.

Leaders who are experienced at seeing and intervening in systems are better at knowing where and how to *steer the ship* that is their business because they are able to see the important information inputs, suspend their perceptions and emotions, weigh the data in order of importance and priority, identify important patterns within the information and then apply all of this information into the strategy and tactics of running their business. Just as important, experienced systems leaders have learned when it is important to drill-down into a specific issue, when not to, and when to disregard or dismiss errant information. They filter and accumulate relevant data and then observe the data before making a decision about what it means.

Learning to work and think systemically improves with time and experience. It is not surprising that some of the best CEO's go through several failed business ventures, bankruptcies or at least several unsuccessful turns at the helm before finding their systems leadership skills. Experience is a great teacher—provided we know we are having an experience we need to learn from. Seeing symptoms of system failure in retrospect can reveal what we *should* have seen, if we are awake and aware enough to know what to look for.

INFLUENCING SYSTEMS

To effectively influence systems you need to understand their essential characteristics:

- Adaptability: The ways systems adapt, morph and change
- Information and Knowledge Transfer: How information and knowledge move in systems
- Velocity: The speed and focus of a system to achieve results
- Gravity: The attractive influence that engages customers, employees, suppliers and markets
- Mass: The breadth and reach of a system

ADAPTABILITY OF SYSTEMS

The theory of evolution is predicated on a relationship between adaptation and the environment. As the environment changes, those organisms built to adapt to it survive. Those that are not adaptable, and those whose structure or design is too different from the current demands of the environment, don't make it.

Likewise, the adaptability of systems helps them cope with the inevitable changes that take place in the environment. Adaptability is tied to three factors: size, health and diversity.

What size should a system be in order to survive? It depends.

Given one large and one small organization doing the same type of work, which one is more likely to be responsive to a client's needs? If the health of both organizations is roughly equal, the smaller one will be. The smaller organization uses less energy to simply exist, so it's better able to change course, just as a healthy 5'11", 170 pound individual is likely more nimble than, say someone who is 6'2" and 250 pounds. But which one is more likely to be able to survive a crisis or produce more predictable results? The larger one. Unless they are leveraged to the hilt, larger organizations have access to more capital and human resources, making them more able to shift resources to where they are needed when changes are needed. Smaller organizations have fewer resources, therefore less adaptability, in the face of a crisis. The lack of adaptability in small organizations is particularly true if that crisis requires redeploying or reorganizing resources to address the crisis.

One example of the difference in adaptability between large and small organizational systems is Microsoft and Red Hat. As most people know, Microsoft has risen to become one of the largest most powerful companies on the planet. With around 55,000 employees and annual revenues in excess of $40 billion, Microsoft is the dominant player in software for both personal and enterprise computing.[9] It advertises that the key advantages of its operating systems is ease of management, ease of deployment and its stability as the world leader of server and personal computing operating systems. Microsoft programs are "closed source" programs that allow for some customization by users but rely on the technical prowess of Microsoft's program engineers to create and manage solutions for its customers. Compared to Microsoft, Red Hat is a tiny (just over 1,000 employees, and approximately $196 million in revenues[10]) company that takes a completely opposite approach to developing, selling and improving technology for its customers. Red Hat is the world's largest distributor of Linux based operating systems, an "open source" programming language that is both visible and public, allowing for maximum customization by programmers and customers. In fact, Red Hat facilitates the ongoing work of its open source network to improve and refine its products.

Both companies claim the higher ground in server operating systems, enterprise-wide software solutions and virus protection. And both probably should, but the higher grounds they hold are completely different. Microsoft works to "own" the customer, providing services and products along with automatic upgrades and improvements downloaded over the internet at regular intervals. Their updating scheme is possible because they invest huge resources in "owning" product fixes and solutions as well. The result is a product that is deployed and implemented easily with moderate technical expertise required by the end user. Red Hat's approach is to leverage the wisdom and collective knowledge of its end users—plus the considerable wisdom of its software engineers—to make improvements which then get incorporated into new product launches. Instead of owning the customer, they own the process for improvement. Red Hat systems are highly customizable, but doing so requires significant expertise and knowledge.

Microsoft sells ease of use. The Microsoft brand's dominance in the marketplace helps support its claims and appearance of reliability. Red Hat sells choice, adaptability and networking. The company's size—or lack thereof—actually supports its value proposition of being intimate and accessible to its clients. Adaptation takes energy, a lot of it. And the bigger the change, the higher the energetic demands to make the change stick. In nature, this expenditure of energy is expressed in terms of multiple attempts to create an organism suited for the new or changed environment. At Red Hat, their investment in adaptation gives them the ability to turn on a dime.

Systems insure adaptability by preparing for the unknown needs of the future. And the best preparation is having an abundance of diversity. Nature insures the preservation of balance and continued evolution in her systems through *bio*-diversity. Likewise, human generated systems insure their adaptability by diversifying. Diverse products and services protect them against fickle markets. Doing business in diverse geographies improves market share. Hiring employees of diverse cultures, genders, ages and lifestyles helps generate innovation and creates a vibrant culture.

Systems need diversity to be adaptable, and when they have it, they have a competitive advantage that is hard to match. But diversity in nature or in business takes effort. Developing a new product line or entering a new market requires an investment of energy and money. Embracing new or diverse ideas from employees takes patience and the ability to assimilate new perspectives. Becoming aware of our ingrained cultural biases takes a willingness to learn and let go. The investment pays huge dividends, especially when being adaptable is called for. But *diversity* takes on many shapes, as we shall see when we discuss Red Hat's and Microsoft's different (but equally effective) approaches to business diversification and adaptability.

INFORMATION AND KNOWLEDGE TRANSFER

Healthy systems, just like a healthy body, are nourished by healthy blood (knowledge). Knowledge carries energy and information to the cells (people and operating units) of the system while taking out non- value added service or procedures and unhealthy, inaccurate or false assumptions and data. Knowledge transfer helps systems discern between useful information and merely interesting information. Most importantly, knowledge transfer helps reduce redundancy. When a solution to a problem has been discovered somewhere else in the system, knowledge transfer retains the solution. It puts the solution in the organization's memory and keeps it available for the system, which saves the system enormous amounts of energy and time. Instead of having to recreate the same solution for the same problem in different parts of the system, knowledge transfer makes each solution accessible to the whole.

Companies tend to focus on the technologies that drive knowledge transfer. Technologies that enhance or facilitate the speed of learning in an organization are important. But more important is the openness of an organization to new and innovative information. A lot of information dies in the intellectual pipeline of companies because new solutions to problems are inhibited or stopped altogether.

VELOCITY

Bill Gates, in his book *Business @ the Speed of Thought* wrote:

> *If the 1980s were about quality and the 1990s were about re-engineering, then the 2000s will be about velocity. About how quickly the nature of business will change. About how quickly business itself will be transacted.*

Velocity, literally, is speed divided by time. In organizations, velocity can feel like a lot of change and organizational learning, as long as this change and learning is focused in a specific direction. A competitive strategy of many businesses is to be fast, meaning responsive, to changes in market conditions, but speed without direction is chaos. The velocity with which business is transacted varies from system to system and knowing what generates and sustains velocity is a critical skill of leaders who know how to influence systems.

The concept of velocity in business is brand new, and business leaders and theorists have various models and constructs to describe its characteristics. Thus far, everyone seems to agree on many of the elements that make up velocity. They are:

- Focus and decisiveness – Learning to pay attention to what is important and track it relentlessly while tuning out the extraneous.

• Health – Knowing and tracking the indicators of what makes a particular business healthy or unhealthy. Knowing the indicators isn't enough. Leaders who want to develop velocity have to feed their systems with those essential nutrients that breed and develop health without sacrificing velocity.

• Investment in – and attention to – information technology. Before a leader can sort and prioritize information, they have to make sure they have access to the right information. Businesses who are trying to build velocity don't wait for new information to cross in front of them. They devote enormous resources to prospecting for, and collecting, analyzing and broadcasting what they are learning.

• Experienced innovation – Doing new things based on solid experience. Companies building velocity innovate constantly, but they do so with careful consideration. There are few "experiments" and lots of trials.

• Synergistic technology partnerships – In order to be focused, businesses that are building velocity have to find business partners whose value proposition is synergistic, but not competitive to their own. Nowhere does this strategy show up more than in the high tech sector. Companies with expertise or capability in infrastructure select partners who have innovative operating systems. Companies who excel in design and integration partner with those who have access to markets.

• Build a strategy based in part on "Adjacency" – To create synergistic technology partners, businesses have to be acutely aware of the businesses, markets, products and value propositions that are similar to—but different to the point of not being competitive with—their own. Adjacency in marketing and synergy is a key leverage point for building velocity.

- A "truth telling" culture – When all of the above doesn't work, companies who are building velocity tell the truth about the results they are achieving and change course as quickly as information and redirection will allow.

No better example of a company with a successful strategy to build velocity exists than Red Hat. In spite of their diminutive size compared to Microsoft, they see themselves as the veritable David determined to do battle—and win—against Microsoft's Goliath. Red Hat focuses on building loyalty and engagement within the open source community at potential short term expense of profit or more directly competitive lines of service to Microsoft. To demonstrate their commitment to the creative genius of the open source community, Red Hat established the Fedora Project, an initiative devoted to the dissemination and development of open source programming. The relationship with the open source community allows Red Hat to turn on a dime. When new developments or innovations are discovered, the open source strategy allows them to be applied almost instantly. Red Hat's direction is focused and clear—build a community that values innovation and then service that community impeccably.

Influencing systems with a lot of velocity can be like trying to jump on a moving train. Leaders in these types of systems tend to generate more success through incremental adjustments to existing plans than by radically reworking things. Red Hat's experience bears this out. As audacious and bold as Red Hat's culture is, each product or partnership adoption has been carefully unfurled and nurtured.

GRAVITY

The sun has more mass than any planet in our solar system, thus each planet is attracted to it through the invisible force of gravity that it exerts on them. Gravity isn't a static force, because it changes depending on the mass of the objects involved and their proximity to each other. Gravity is fluid, dynamic and invisible, and it is what binds the universe together.

In organizational systems, gravity manifests itself in a myriad of ways, from attracting new customers and employees to generating a unique and favored position in a market or niche.

A human or organizational analogy to the notion of gravity would be that icon of American convenience and retail genius, Wal-Mart. By combining low prices with lots of variety and convenient access to virtually every customer in the U.S., Wal-Mart has built a self-sustaining model of growth through gravity. They demand the lowest prices their suppliers provide to any other of their customers, which ensures they will be priced competitively for identical goods. Low price is a major draw for most retail customers, but so is selection, so Wal-Mart ensures it has a good selection of products within the same line to keep customers shopping for more. Their variety strategy attracts clients and suppliers. Since the suppliers can now provide inexpensive goods across a wide range of products, doing business with Wal-Mart becomes even more attractive. Even though suppliers don't make as much per unit as they might selling through a smaller retailer, the sheer volume of Wal-Mart's business more than makes up for the smaller margins it pays its suppliers. By its sheer volume of business, Wal-Mart pushes many retail manufacturers who would prefer not to do business with it into a game of play or die. Become part of the whole, resistance is futile. A growing number of manufacturers and businesses are dependent on Wal-Mart for their livelihood. Wal-Mart is a system with enormous gravity in the retail market.

Systems can have gravity and make a significant impact without being huge, if the statement they make in the marketplace is huge. The end result is the same, a system that is known or recognized for its impact or presence. An example of a system that has made a significant impact although it is comparatively small is Patagonia, a direct mail clothing manufacturer and marketing enterprise based in Ventura, California. Coincidentally, Patagonia is the polar opposite of Wal-Mart, as we shall see.

Yvon Chouinard, the founder of Patagonia, started his career as a rock climber and a blacksmith who sold climbing tools to his friends out of the back of his truck. By 1970, Chouinard Equipment Ltd. was the largest climbing equipment supplier in the U.S. (it would later become Black Diamond, a provider of premium climbing products and backcountry skis). Chouinard then turned his attention to what climbers and outdoor enthusiasts were wearing, particularly during activities like fly fishing, skiing, surfing and casual wear. Chouinard was frustrated with the lack of clothing on the market that would hold-up under regular outdoor use, so he set about creating apparel the same way he created climbing hardware—assuming the clothing was not up to the task and redesigning it. Patagonia was born.

It is doubtful that anyone reading this book has not heard of Patagonia, yet the company's gross revenues in 2004 were a comparatively small $200m.[11] Chouinard is widely regarded as a pioneer, and Patagonia is certainly a respected brand in the marketplace—not bad for a self-taught blacksmith who would rather call himself a surfer than a businessman.[12]

It follows that Yvon Chouinard would be an avid environmentalist given the types of activities he and his customers pursue. In the mid-90's, Patagonia commissioned an independent environmental impact study of the four primary fibers used in Patagonia products in order to develop a strategy to reduce the company's impact on the environment. Surprisingly, the biggest offender was not petroleum based polyester or nylon. Over 25% of the pesticides made in the world are made to manage cotton. Cotton, Chouinard found—grown from the soil of the earth—was the "villain."[13] By 1996, all Patagonia cotton products were made from 100% organic cotton, and have been ever since. Chouinard saw the system supporting the textile industry and its effects on the environment's systems, and then he found a way to intervene. Patagonia continues to speak out against non-sustainable cotton farming methods specifically and non-sustainable agricultural processes in general. Patagonia's "pull" towards environmental stewardship exerted enormous influence on the apparel market. Other larger apparel companies have followed Patagonia's lead at least in part by offering and marketing apparel made of organically grown cotton.

Patagonia never set out to be the biggest, only to "Do well by doing good" and by doing so, Chouinard and his employees created a company that has tremendous gravity. Patagonia's mass is relatively small, but because of the fit of its values and ways of doing business, it serves as a great model for other socially responsible businesses.

Influencing systems with a lot of gravity requires a tremendous amount of tenacity and energy; they don't move easily, unless a keen systems leader knows exactly where and when to push. Companies with a lot of gravity tend to develop cultures that take themselves pretty seriously and feel understandably good about the degree of popularity or acceptance they create. The downfall is, they become resistant to change. "Hey it's working pretty well as it is, why change it?" becomes the mantra of many leaders in high gravity organizations. Successfully influencing high gravity systems is best performed through smaller demonstrations of what is possible that are separate from the core functions of the business. High gravity systems are typically more open to new influences by off line experiments that are incorporated into the system once they have been perfected. Wal-Mart, for example, experimented with the superstore concept (stores that are roughly double the size of a traditional Wal-Mart that sell groceries in addition to the normal product vocabulary of Wal-Mart) before deciding to build superstores in certain markets. Patagonia did exhaustive research on every element of switching to all organic cotton before committing, but once the company did commit to making the shift, they did it as quickly as supplier and manufacturing capability would allow.

MASS

Mass is size: the combination of volume and weight. Mass is the stuff that generates more velocity. Gross revenues compared to others in the same market are an indicator of the mass of a company, but there are better, more accurate gauges that measure it, too. Employee head count, or geographic distribution, or the size of the market owned by the company are all indicators of mass. Mass can also be the depth of inventory or the number of suppliers who can provide the same service or product. In human generated systems, mass comes at the expense of flexibility, but not adaptability. As the example of Wal-Mart and Microsoft discussed above proves, mass helps to drive down cost per revenue unit generated. Organizations with mass can do business in more locations, or in more markets, or both.

By now, your insight when it comes to the topic of *Perspective* has probably improved. Let's test that theory. Take the Perspective Quiz on page 176.

REINFORCING AND BALANCING LOOPS

Now that we understand a bit more about the nature of systems, we can talk about what happens to systems when they are altered. The results are surprising.

Systems, like everything in nature, are constantly working to equalize themselves; when too much energy collects in one place, nature attempts to balance the system by redistributing and re-dispersing it. When animal populations exceed the carrying capacity of the land they live on, animals starve or fall prey to predators more easily, death rates go up and the population goes down until it again stabilizes. Markets become saturated with a

By now, the physics of systems and the concepts of velocity, gravity, and mass are becoming obvious. Instead of explaining more, put your understanding of systems to work in the following exercise (pick one):

1) Volume or collective purchasing power - the ability to get discounted rates from suppliers - is easier to accomplish in systems that have:
    A) Gravity?
    B) Mass?
    C) Velocity?

2) If systems with a lot of mass have a more difficult time being flexible, how do they compensate when they need to be flexible?
    A) By eliminating the competition?
    B) By segregating operating units so they are smaller?
    C) By building more mass?
    D) A and B
    E) A and C

3) A system with a lot of velocity is likely to have more...
    A) Gravity?
    B) Mass?
    C) Both?
    D) Neither?

4) A system with more gravity is likely to have more...
    A) Mass?
    B) Velocity?
    C) Both?
    D) Neither?

5) If Patagonia has mass (compared to other, larger companies) would it be in...
    A) Its retail presence in multiple geopgraphies?
    B) Its influence on the clothing industry for its environmental example?
    C) The competitiveness of its pricing?

Answers: #1: b; #2: e; #3: a; #4: c; #5: b

The Perspective Quiz

product or service, cost competition increases as demand decreases, non-competitive suppliers leave the market or go out of business and the system's overall balance is again restored. Understanding how these loops play themselves out in systems is crucial for leaders who are attempting to influence them.

This balancing process is also expressed in the first law of thermodynamics which most of us learned early in school: "for every action, there is an equal and opposite reaction." Systems theorists call this phenomenon *balancing and reinforcing loops*. This concept is not new, at least not to philosophers over the past 2000 or more years. These familiar symbols are variations of the idea that every action generates an opposite reaction:

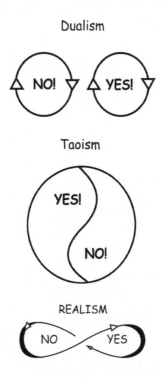

The Symbols of Systems Over Time

Variations of these symbols go back as far as the written record of humanity. Man, it appears, has always been capable of seeing the connectedness of everything. But learning to actually do something about what he sees has taken much, much longer.

For every virtuous (reinforcing) action that occurs, a balancing (or unintended) action springs forth. Understanding this phenomenon and accepting it as a certainty is something that takes some getting used to. Think of the implications:

- Your gain may be someone else's loss.
- For every decision you make, there will be a cascade of unintended reactions to that decision.
- For every action you take, there will be a cascade of unintended reactions that surface as a result of that action.
- For every step forward, there is resistance to that step.
- The amount of energy spent trying to bring order to a system is always counterbalanced somewhere, somehow, by the amount of energy expended to pull it apart or dissolve that order.

And so on....

Are these statements true? Absolutely! But some of you reading this may notice your resistance to accept the statements as true. For every statement of fact, there is a counter-balancing energy at work that challenges the certainty of that statement.

In human systems, this self-equalizing process takes on countless forms. It can be seen in the behaviors of groups of people who push back against the flow of the system. When properly channeled, these individuals contribute just as much to the system as those who comply with every requirement within it, but they are frequently labeled as "trouble makers" because they aren't willing to go along with whatever the majority thinking is.

In organizations the question is not if balancing and virtuous loops exist, but *where*. Successful products and services attract imitators and competitors. Ideas that sweep through a team or organization attract those who prefer to "fight the tide" and consider alternative points of view. Healthy organizations sometimes attract unhealthy employees who are hoping that by being in a healthy system their own personal health will be restored.

By now, enough of the fundamentals of systems have been discussed theoretically to allow us to dive in to how to intervene in them practically. Again, *seeing* systems is just the tip of the iceberg; knowing how to effectively influence them takes practice, and lots of it.

PART THREE
THE PRACTICE

FOR ASPIRING LEADERS

Practice Seeing Systems Everywhere

For managers who are paid to manage tasks and solve problems, the hardest part of learning to develop their systems skills is that there is little time in the course of a normal work day to take a step back and actually look at the patterns of problems they are asked to address. Ironically, the people who most need to develop their systems thinking skills are hung up by the inaccurate perception that they were hired merely to *do*, not to *think*. So the first thing to learn is to not use your job description as an excuse for not learning this insight, one that is critical to your own growth. Maintaining a dual focus: one that is fixed on the specific tasks and areas of operation you are responsible for while at the same time scanning the landscape of the organization to understand the mutual interactions of the departments or functions of the whole system is tough, but doable. Even with a dual focus, if you ask your brain to keep track of both, it will. Don't make excuses for why you can't see the big picture, just work on it. It is unlikely your manager is going to start doing a better job filling you in on what's happening globally unless you show her how to do so. And how do you do that? Learn to ask very good questions based on your own observations.

What to Do:

To further develop the insight of *Seeing and Influencing Systems,* use the day-to-day happenings in your normal line of work and start examining them.

At home:

- Play "current events coup d'oeil." Pick a story in the evening news or newspaper and see how far back you can trace the root systems issue that underlies the story. Many of the issues that make the news are symptoms of huge systems problems.

- What are the themes and issues that are recurring in your community? Find those themes and boil them down to the systems issues causing them. Does your community need new roads? Why aren't funds available to build them? What priorities are taking the place of road repair? If road repair were a priority, what other issues would be neglected? What "windows on the world" are at work among the community's leaders?

At work, pick a system, any system:

- Where and what are the sticking points?

- What creates velocity and gravity in the system? How can more of either be produced?

- What policy, practice, habit, method or procedure constantly produces less than great results or drags down the entire system?

- What are the trends and patterns of what generates great success in your business?

Listen More/Talk Less

The skill of truly listening and watching is a constant theme throughout this book; aspiring leaders usually do exactly the wrong thing to get ahead: they talk too much. Don't. Listen and watch. Eventually, new patterns will emerge. Being perceptive and having great coup d'oeil happens best when a leader disciplines him or herself to listen and observe.

Time after time in my coaching relationships with aspiring leaders, I notice that their ability to listen is underdeveloped even though they see themselves as being very good listeners. In most cases my assessment is corroborated by the viewpoints of those around them. Many leaders suffer from an inaccurate window on the world that tells them "a leader should be articulate and charismatic." I think this belief has the effect of interfering with their ability to listen. Remarkably, in the research of core competencies for this book only 4 references to public speaking or verbal communication were listed as important. In the same sample group, there were 15 direct or indirect references to the importance of a leader's ability to listen.

We develop our ability to listen effectively in spite of our culture and educational system, not because of it. There are plenty of public speaking courses for us to take beginning in high school, yet very few school curricula have a course to help us improve our listening skills. Our society elevates those who have great public speaking skills, yet there is no obvious metric to acknowledge someone's ability to listen. You might have a problem listening if you:

- find that everyone always defers to your opinion or asks what you think instead of sharing what they think

- interrupt people when they are speaking

- find your attention wandering when someone else is speaking

- find yourself planning your response to what someone is saying while they are still saying it

- feel like you know what someone is saying before they finish saying it (it doesn't matter if you know, they still need to say it)

- find that people you work with tend to use a loud voice, repeat instructions to you for no apparent reason or follow up what they tell you with a letter or email confirming what they have already told you

- notice that you are not included in a meeting or conversation that you feel you should be included in, or are not being promoted or acknowledged by your supervisor.

What to Do:

Of course, the best way to access your listening skills is to ask those with whom you work what they think about your ability to listen—provided of course that you *listen* to their answers.

Challenge Your Schemata

It is very difficult to solve a problem when you are working within the mind-set that created it. Even if YOU didn't create the problem or systems issue that needs attention and you are merely part of the system, you have naturally developed a window on the world (a schema) that makes seeing the real issues more complicated. The first—and most difficult—action to take is to try and continue to perform the tasks of your job while at the same time removing yourself from the mindsets, habits and assumptions that drive your actions so you can better see the system.

What to Do:

This is an exercise that reveals both our own personal underlying beliefs that guide our thinking about the issues and a clear picture of the system at work.[14] To begin, pick a systems issue that warrants attention. At the top of a piece of paper, write down the systems issue. This will become the issue you apply all of your thinking towards in the rest of the exercise. Next, divide the rest of the paper into three columns. In the left hand column, write down the evidence or facts that show what you are studying is actually an issue. In the center column write down what you believe to be true about why what is happening is happening—this should reveal your window on the world. For the right hand column, become a scientist and write down only real facts that you have observed, what you know to be unequivocally true. Surface as many major dynamics as you can, then review the list. What you may notice as you review the list is that what you have done is to identify things that are universally, unquestionably true from things that are fabricated or only partially true. You may need to talk to some of the people who are involved in the situation to see if what you are thinking they think is in fact accurate.

Know When You are Going with Your Gut

Malcolm Gladwell's *Blink* pushes the issue of thin slicing—making decisions or judgments based on partial exposure to information—to the limit. Gladwell argues that thin slicing, also known as rapid cognition, is at play in almost every human reaction. Gladwell's research shows that thin slicing is just about as accurate as taking a longer, more measured approach to decision making. Thin slicing has its drawbacks, most notably that the practice can be the result of laziness instead of need. If a rapid decision or judgment is needed about a systemic issue, by all means make it. But if it is not, don't rush a decision when expediency has no value. More information may confirm what your rapid cognition told you, or it may show you that you were pointed 180 degrees in the wrong direction.

Every successful leader I have worked with has developed a keen sense for when to move quickly and when to collect more information and proceed cautiously. In most cases, their cautious and plodding approach to some issues is seen as overly cautious or even obstructionist to the needs of the business. They often catch a lot of heat and criticism for not moving as quickly as those around them think they should, but there is almost always a method to their approach. They all have a mantra of some sort that boils down to "All decisions have their time," and they don't rush that time.

What to Do:

Make a conscious decision about when to jump into a problem and solve it expediently and when to take your time, collect more information and solve it more slowly. Waiting or moving more slowly can take Herculean discipline, particularly since expediency is so highly valued in many businesses today. From an early age, we are taught to admire the decisiveness and quick reactions with which leaders solve problems and confront crises (yet another schema). But what is important to do is to learn when thin slicing is called for versus when we are simply thin slicing because it's convenient.

Influencing Velocity and Gravity

Once you can see what generates velocity and gravity in a system, consider what might create more of either of them and what the net effect of doing so might be, then experiment. In terms of velocity, systems tend to have an abundance of either speed or focus, but rarely both. The characteristics of these traits make them very, very difficult to develop in unison. Speedy systems tend to foster high energy cultures that tend to have the organizational equivalent of Attention Deficit Disorder; they value speed and love to bounce from one project or initiative to the next, often sacrificing results for agility. On the other hand, organizations with great focus tend to bring analysis of that focus to every activity they pursue, which of course slows them down substantially. This hyper-focus is particularly true in mission-driven, non-profit organizations that run most decisions through a very narrow mission filter which—although it keeps them headed in the right direction—impedes their ability to actually *achieve* that mission.

Gravity can be created by great velocity, so to build the attractive influence of any system, try improving its velocity, then learn how to explain it; doing so will create more gravity. Alternatively, slowing down velocity can create some gravity as well. Popular or previously sited examples of the interaction between velocity and gravity include:

Wal-Mart's pricing focus and constantly changing inventory (based on careful trend analysis) creates the system's velocity. Low prices and having the right products on the shelves at the right time create the system's gravity.

Patagonia's focus on functional designs and limited product vocabulary coupled with their attention to trends in their markets (outdoor enthusiasts) gives them velocity. Their multi-channel marketing approach, coupled with their stance on the environment, gives them gravity. Patagonia was also willing to sacrifice some cost savings in the form of non-organic cotton (velocity) for altruistic purposes that actually increased its visibility in the marketplace (gravity).

Fewer than 3,000 Lamborghini sports cars are crafted each year, yet almost everyone knows the name. Enormous gravity, no velocity (unless you actually get to drive a Lamborghini!).

Toyota manufactures cars based on four basic chassis and five basic body types, demonstrating its focus. Toyota makes cars for about 19% of the world's car driving public, making it the most popular brand in the industry (mass). The now famous Toyota production system created a product of exceedingly high quality at a reasonable cost which in turn created enormous mass and velocity with Toyota. The velocity allowed the company to develop equally impressive gravity.

The Practice

To generate velocity, look for ways to clarify focus and accelerate decision making. Activities that increase velocity include:

- Streamline decision making, learning or communication processes. Simplify decision making wherever possible by reducing the number of people who need to have input. Create options for employees to advance their own learning and understanding about key business processes independently. Make important information accessible to everyone.

- Create communication activities that reinforce the direction and focus of the organization. Employee newsletters or regularly scheduled employee meetings are examples of these types of activities.

- Push decisions down and out in the organization. Systems leaders have an acute sense of what decisions they need to make and which decisions are better made by those who work for them. They empower those around them to make key decisions. By increasing the quality and frequency of decision making in the organization, they increase its velocity.

The primary method of increasing gravity—attractiveness—is to increase interest in the initiative, product, or service you are trying to bring attention to. Tell the story of the initiatives under way to increase gravity. Build interest in what is happening, but don't push people to participate. Gravity is generated through interest, not coercion.

FOR SENIOR LEADERS AND MENTORS

Resist the Urge to Solve, Question

What to Do:

When aspiring leaders come to you to discuss their growth in this area, don't tell them your answers to systems problems, help them find the answers on their own by asking pointed questions that stimulate their thinking. Remember, a systems issue may have multiple solutions, so offering your solution doesn't help them develop ways of solving problems for themselves; it just helps them understand how you would do it.

Better yet, identify an appropriate systems issue that you are working to solve and share your thinking on it with them. Ask them to act as your coach. See what they come up with.

Encourage Aspiring Leaders to Build Gravity, Respect Velocity and not worry about Mass

In our society, speed (and therefore velocity) is sexier today than ever before. Building velocity is a dangerous, subtle business. It is easy to go fast, but to go fast with focus—that's a skill. And to set a pace in business that is sustainable is not only a good idea, it's a survival imperative. It doesn't matter if you can exceed customer expectations in January if you disappoint them in August. The quickest way to go out of business is to have one element of the business outpace the other elements. Nowhere is this more true than in high tech businesses that struggle to keep up with their own data and knowledge acquisitions. According to Baroudi Bloor International, an international research and analysis firm that studies technology business trends, fifty percent of companies that lose their data (through server crashes, poor archiving, or no formal mechanism to retain knowledge) go out of business immediately and ninety percent don't survive more than two years.[15] Why? Because their speed to market outpaced the natural constraints of the system that supports their ability to serve clients. If you ask an aspiring leader to work on an initiative to increase velocity and they are new to the practice, set clear expectations and success goals. Discuss the risks of too much velocity and help them develop tools to watch for overshooting capability. Mass is the byproduct of velocity and/or gravity; attending to them will increase mass (but be careful what you ask for)!

What to Do:

Many aspiring leaders get hooked on the notion of adding value by showing how fast they can accomplish something. Instead, encourage them to look for ways to increase gravity with an existing initiative. Socializing an initiative and gaining employee buy-in is the work of leaders. You can find someone who wants to move faster at any coffee shop at 6:00 in the morning.

Practice Being More Consciously Competent

If you are a senior leader with a successful track record managing your part of the business, chances are you know how to look at the big picture and think systemically. I have rarely met a successful senior leader, particularly a founding senior leader, who wasn't aware of the trends and opportunities that existed in the marketplace and found a way to capitalize on them. The problem is, most of you have no idea how you do it, so it's difficult to pass on how you think to others.

What to Do:

The first thing you can do to help the rest of us—and your business—is to try and become *consciously competent*, versus *unconsciously competent*, in how you do what you do so you can effectively mentor others. To become an effective coach and mentor, work to be clear in the following areas:

- **Take time to consider how you do what you do:** Intervening effectively in systems is not easy—if it was, more people would be good at it. Make time to think together with whoever you are coaching or mentoring. Explain your thinking to whom you are mentoring so he or she can see how your mind works its way around problems. For those of you who need more structure to insure quality communication happens, conduct pre- and post- action reviews on any action designed to create a systemic change. These meetings help insure mentees are learning from their experience.

- **Clarify accountability:** One of the most frequently committed errors among leaders is that they delegate responsibility to someone, then take over for whomever has been delegated responsibility when things aren't going well. Define who is accountable for solutions to various problems, then stick to your agreements. Although taking over a task that was originally delegated is sometimes necessary, be sure to explain to the employee why you are taking over for them. If they were not quick enough diagnosing problems, tell them. If their technical expertise was not up to the challenge at hand, tell them. They can't learn if you don't.

- **Perfect your delegation skills:** Delegating is different from abdicating or surrendering a task. If you delegate a task or a problem—you have by definition agreed to assume management responsibility for the execution of that task. Stay involved in how your delegated tasks and projects are coming along. Offer support where and when you can, but don't expect a mentee to be successful in a delegated task if you're not willing to stay involved.

- **Provide enough information:** Mentors and coaches of systems leaders—especially the ones who do what they do from instinct and are unconsciously competent—pick up their cues to identify underlying issues from lots of sources. Some of these cues are instinctual. When they work as a mentor or a coach, they mistakenly think their job is to act as a filter—removing information they consider unnecessary. By doing this, they rob their mentees of one of the critical experiences needed to develop systems talent—the ability to decide which information is useful and which is not.

- **Embrace "and/both" thinking:** Underlying systemic problems usually have more than one point of leverage that, if addressed effectively, will change the system in a desired way. What you observe as a solution to an underlying systems problem may be a right answer, but guard against thinking it is the ONLY right answer. When having problem solving discussions about system issues with your mentees, listen to their perspective and point of view devoid of judgment or a pre-determined opinion. They may have an equally valid solution that is the polar opposite of yours.

FOR BOTH ASPIRING LEADERS AND MENTORS

Look for Global Solutions for Local Problems

Again, look for solutions to the underlying issues, not just the issue of the day. This kind of thinking and creative problem solving is summed up succinctly in this well-known parable:

> *"Give a man a fish and you feed him for a day.*
> *Teach him to fish and feed him for a lifetime."*

Don't settle for a solution to a symptom (feeding a man for a day). Look for the cause of the symptom and solve THAT problem.

Solving local problems with global solutions is not easy. In fact, it is so difficult, most leaders avoid doing it. They dwell endlessly in the quagmire of symptoms and minutia—never solving the root cause. Karl-Henrik Robèrt identified the local problem of childhood cancers and developed a high level, global solution: an approach to move towards sustainability.

Finding global solutions to local problems is the ultimate expression of a systems leader. In organizations, what leaders need to look for are issues underlying the undesired behavior.

What to Do:

Choose a behavior problem in your organization. Find what you think is the underlying issue and test your theory by applying change to the system. If, for example, you believe the underlying issue of not following procedures is that the procedure has some flaw in it, make the change necessary to the procedure and then watch what happens. Listen and look for a change in behaviors.

Choose one thing at a time. Systems theory holds that when you find the biggest, thorniest underlying issue and address it successfully, that one change will affect everything else in the system positively.

Look for Upstream Solutions to Downstream Problems

Looking for global solutions to local problems can be likened to the example of Apollo 8 and the perspective that the images of earth as seen from the far side of the moon gave us. Those images and the entire mission changed our perspective. To influence systems, however, *Perspective* alone is not enough; it has to be coupled with a temporal approach. Work on seeing the big picture (finding global solutions to local problems) and develop a sequence to intervene.

For four years, Doug Harper was the director of manufacturing for World's Finest Chocolate Company's Canadian operation, the North American leader in the manufacture of fundraising chocolate.[16] Doug came to WFC with a wealth of manufacturing experience, but no experience whatsoever in chocolate making. In fact, he has held senior management positions for several best-in-class manufacturing organizations. He has been successful in virtually every role he has held in spite of the fact that when he takes a new job, he has no knowledge of the product or processes of the company.

Doug's expertise lies in a more fruitful area: he is a fabulous systems leader and a genuine leader of people.

When Doug took the reigns of World's Finest's production in the summer of 2000, the efficiency of the plant was only incrementally better than it had been in the late 60's. Rework and rejections of huge volumes of WFC product were normal. Profits were abysmal. Customers were loyal more through not having a suitable alternative than from being satisfied with the levels of service of the company. Morale of the manufacturing workforce was low and a fatalistic "this is how it has always been and will always be" attitude pervaded the plant.

Almost from the very first day Doug showed up at World's Finest, he knew he was going to implement "Lean Thinking," or Lean. Instead of tying up capital and resources in the traditional "batch and cue" method of manufacturing, Lean works off of the principle of value streaming or "just in time" production.[17] Lean manufacturing by nature requires a system that is flexible and adaptable, which requires employees who possess those same traits. Lean pushes decision making down and out in the system and requires employees to work together as teams to find solutions to problems that are generating waste. In Doug's words, "I knew WFC would need to move to Lean, but the culture wasn't right to implement it when I got there. People were too used to waiting on "superiors" to make decisions for them instead of taking the initiative to solve the problems they were more than capable of solving themselves. They were afraid to take a chance. We had a culture that didn't encourage risk taking."

Doug knew that the *downstream solution* to many of WFC's manufacturing woes could be solved by Lean. But he needed to address an *upstream problem* before implementing Lean: the culture of the employees in manufacturing. Over the course of the next year, Doug took on a number of culture change initiatives that prepared WFC to move to Lean. Remarkably, throughout that first year, he never even mentioned Lean to most of the employees. "When the culture was ready, implementing Lean wasn't just easy, the employees were crying out for something to do with their new team skills. They were bored and wanted me to up the ante, so we implemented Lean. I didn't so much lead the lean initiative as much as just hang on while the employees took it and ran with it. It was amazing—but it was pretty predictable. When you get the culture right, the rest follows," Doug said.

Doug's story is a textbook example of a systems leader having the foresight and restraint to solve an upstream problem before addressing a downstream solution. His experience and knowledge of Lean led him to hold off on its implementation until a critical precursor to implementing it—a different organizational culture—was in place.

What to Do:

Intervening in systems is an art that is informed by your intuition and your knowledge. Pick a point of leverage to begin your intervention that is upstream of the eventual solution so that when you implement that solution, all of the upstream interfering factors have been take care of.

Put Balancing and Positive Loops to Work

Another important tool for influencing systems is understanding how the phenomenon of balancing and positive loops plays itself out. Before systems leaders start influencing a system, they spend time studying and considering the consequences of each intervention before beginning it. They understand that by putting into motion a reinforcing—or positive—loop of new actions or behaviors, they are creating a balancing—or negative—loop. As we've discussed, this is not a possibility, it is inevitability, and accounting for it is critical to the success of any systems intervention.

In the above example of Doug Harper's amazingly successful approach to implementing Lean, the reinforcing loop he put into motion was the development of a new, more autonomous and independently thinking culture. Doug considered what might happen as a result: "I knew everyone was hungry for the new culture, but I also knew not everyone would know how to play by the new rules in it. Sure enough, a few folks didn't learn how to behave in it and they ended up leaving, but a majority of the employees worked into the new culture perfectly—they were hungry for it. "

Doug knew that the kind of systemic change he was pushing had the potential of creating a balancing loop of negativity and fear among his colleagues, so he worked to prevent that loop from interfering. He also knew that not all of the employees would make the transition to the new culture and he focused a lot of his attention on them—trying to keep them positively engaged and ultimately willing to ask them to leave if they could not make the transition.

What to Do:

When you make a change in a system, do your best to anticipate the unintended consequences of that change and plan contingencies for them.

Leading Measures, Lagging Indicators

For every leading measurement or change you create, be ready for a lagging indicator or symptom of whether or not it is working. Another movement is afoot in corporations around the world today called "The Balanced Score Card." The Balanced Score Card (BSC) is a management system that encourages businesses to measure their success and performance in much wider terms than short term profitability. In addition to measuring profits, the BSC system encourages businesses to develop metrics to measure three additional aspects: Learning and Growth, The Customer Perspective, and Business Processes. A maxim of the BSC is: "Not everything that is measured matters, and not everything that matters can be measured."

Measurements with respect to the BSC come in two forms: leading measures and lagging indicators. In every system, there are obvious, immediate indicators of its effectiveness. But there are also less obvious, longer-term indicators that do the same thing. Leading measures are the "drivers" in a system; they are the immediate effects of the performance of the system. Lag indicators show us the consequences of our actions over the long term. Systems leaders need to take both into account when determining where and when to influence a system.

Examples of the Leading Measures/Lagging Indicators concept include:

When a business downsizes to improve cash flow, the immediate (leading) measurement is improved cash flow. One long-term (lagging) indicator may be loss of capability or market share, which of course further inhibits its cash flow. Another lag indicator may be improved investor confidence.

If a service firm increases the case load on each of its employees, the leading measurement will almost certainly be increased volume capability. But what will the lagging indicator of customer confidence tell us?

Simply Paying Attention Leads to Results

And finally, for reasons we don't yet fully understand, the very act of observing a system and considering ways to influence it, changes it. Physicists call this phenomenon the "Heisenberg Uncertainty Principle" but don't let the fact that the phenomenon has a name fool you—it's still a mystery to most of us.

What to Do:

Pay attention. The plain truth is that when we turn our attention to a systems problem we alter the problem ever so slightly. The more attention we put towards the problem, the more impact we have on it.

PERSPECTIVE

Add Value...

- Stay aware of how your job fits into the overall plan of your department, unit, team or company. Find ways to improve your work in relation to what the system needs, not just what you need.
- Look for upstream solutions to chronic, difficult problems.
- Let your intuition guide you, but substantiate it with facts whenever you can.

Inspire Others...

- Notice your connection to everything and revel in the knowledge that you're part of many interesting systems. Which ones would you like to have more impact on? Don't think small—if you can see it, you're half way there!
- One of the most effective coaching skills a leader can have is the ability to explain to others how their work fits in to the grand scheme. Learn to explain how everything and everyone fits together. Doing so generates clarity and a heightened sense of purpose.

Change the World...

- The most important, urgent issues facing humankind are big hairy systems issues. Stay informed about what they are, especially those issues for which you have passion.
- Once you've found the issues you most want to make an impact on, start a campaign to do so (intervening in big hairy systemic issues is a lot more like a campaign than a one time event).
- Vote!

SECTION FIVE
PASSION AND TIMING

THIS SECTION IN BRIEF:

Enduring leaders are inspiring, motivating, hard working people who give their jobs their all. They are able to do this because they are working at something they feel passionate about. Passion is the emotion that drives enduring leaders to excel, achieve and produce. Passion is LOVE, and how a leader expresses their passion depends on what it is, exactly, about their work that they love.

Passion and Timing make up the combustion engine that puts the other four insights to work. Being a great leader is hard work, and this insight is what makes it possible for you to work hard and work long—the other insights are what help you work well.

Enduring leaders feel passion and are aware of timing; everyone else just sees results. Passion and Timing is what motivates and inspires employees and customers. Employees love working with leaders who have it; they see a role model for getting work done while having fun, and they imitate it.

Timing and passion originate from opposite places: passion comes from a deep personal desire; timing is an acquired skill that comes from interacting with the world. All of the insights discussed in this book are a journey unto themselves, not a destination, and this principle is never more true than with Passion and Timing. The pursuit of passion inevitably takes us on a quest for meaning and an answer to the question: "Why am I here?" Our sense of timing helps us on the quest for meaning. It is both a compass and a regulator, helping us find our direction without running out of steam. In this section, we will learn about how passion may eventually turn into our life's calling, and how the ordinary or mundane may eventually turn into our passion. Jump to page 229 to learn how to develop more passion and better timing.

PART ONE
PEOPLE, PERFORMANCE AND PRIDE

"Passion makes the world go round.
Love just makes it a safer place."
—Ice T[1]

As far back as six years of age, Tracy Forrest can remember going to work with his father. His dad was a cabinet maker and mill worker who usually worked on Saturdays, so if Tracy wanted to be with his dad, he had to go to work. When he could, he helped his father work on projects. From making sawhorses on jobsites to pouring driveways, Tracy's connection with his father was through work and, specifically, building things.

A quiet, somewhat shy boy, Tracy developed skill and confidence working with his hands. He found he was good at solving mechanical problems and fixing things. The first magazine he remembers reading was *Mechanics Illustrated*. Tracy would spend hours studying the articles that came with plans on how to build something, from storage sheds to house additions: he was fascinated with building. For fun, he started riding motocross, which naturally led to a need to work on motorcycles. He became an adept mechanic in addition to what he was learning about trim carpentry from his dad.

As his school career progressed, Tracy grew less and less interested in the required courses, but showed an intense interest in courses that he thought would be useful to his building, mechanical, and design interests. By 17, Tracy had had enough with school and he struck out on his own, hitch-hiking all over the country until he found himself once again working with his dad, who by this time had relocated to Orlando, Florida to work on a huge new project called Disney World. Tracy got a job working for Disney as a framer and started attending night school to get a degree in engineering. At Disney, Tracy liked the work of building, but, in his words:

> *I didn't make for a very good hourly employee. It didn't matter whether I was more or less productive than the people around me, I got paid the same, even when I could build faster and better than someone else. There was no encouragement or reward for performance.*

At night school, Tracy struggled to understand why, if he wanted to be an engineer, he had to take two semesters worth of English composition. These courses held no interest and made little sense to him given his plans and goals. He could learn what he needed on his own and start applying it more quickly. He rationalized his decision to drop out of night school with the knowledge that a good carpenter could earn more than most engineers. Tracy's aptitude for construction, coupled with a tremendous boom in residential home building as Disney World opened, led him to start his own framing subcontracting company. By 22, as Tracy tells it,

> *I discovered that I could make a lot more money doing piece work (work where workers are paid based on how many 'pieces' of work they produce, not on an hourly rate) than doing hourly work and there was more residential piecework in Florida than anyone could keep up with. It was great. I was a 22 year old kid running a small crew of framers. I'd get paid $30,000 cash for a week's worth of work. I would pay my crew and still have a $20,000 wad in my pocket left over. I bought so many different cars during that time with cash, the guy at the Chevy dealership just kept my deposit check in his desk drawer for the next vehicle I was likely to buy.*

Then, the oil and gas crisis of the early 70's happened. The bottom fell out of tourism, Disney World's attendance went down and construction plummeted. Banks stopped paying developers, developers stopped paying construction companies, and construction companies stopped paying piecework crews like Tracy's. People who owed him money could not pay their debts, which meant he could not pay his. The most stinging of his problems was his inability to pay his crews for the work they had done. He sold his Corvette to make payroll, but it only postponed the problem. Sixty days later, Tracy's lavish, flush-with-cash lifestyle was gone. He was out of business, flat broke. He made ends meet by taking odd jobs as a truck driver and working once again as a carpenter. Over thirty years later, Tracy still identifies going out of business as the biggest failure of his life.

According to Tracy, the sting of that experience stays with him. "I wanted people to be able to trust me and I wanted to be seen as reliable and dependable. The construction business has a lot of shifty characters; I wanted people to see me as above that, different." As the market slowly started to improve, he resolved to save enough money to weather a short term crisis like the gas crisis. Having more cash reserves, he reasoned, would help him be more dependable and less susceptible to periodic fluctuations. To make it easier to find work if the market changed, Tracy studied for his Florida General Contractor's license and soon took the test, which he easily passed. Now as a licensed General Contractor he could do any kind of work he wanted to—all he had to do was convince people to hire him as their General Contractor.

Tracy was determined to be successful and independent. He worked diligently to achieve both. He started reading biographies of successful people to try and pick up ideas on how he could accelerate and further his own success. He had learned enough about engineering that he could read just about any set of plans and calculate loads as well as most journeymen engineers. He kept a sharp eye out for talented workers and when he found them, he attracted them with more money and the promise of good work. Tracy's impeccable organization and attention to detail impressed clients, and the business grew. As Tracy put it: "since then… my fear of failure has been part of my success. I convinced myself that failure was not an option."

Over the next 30 years, Tracy Forrest built one of the most successful and profitable construction companies in the country. Winter Park Construction (WPC) grew to become the premier contractor for timeshare, multifamily and resort condominium construction in central Florida and one of the top 300 construction firms in the nation. WPC's success is the result of some basic but disciplined leadership principles that Tracy stayed with:

- Build a culture of trust and respect. WPC's mantra is "People, Performance and Pride." If the employees feel respected and respect each other, clients will notice it, and feel more trusted and respected as well. Today, over 70% of WPC's work is negotiated with clients instead of competitively bid— the result of the trust and respect their clients have for them. Trust and respect is also critical to the culture of learning and continuous improvement at WPC. Few professions create as many mavericks and lone wolfs as construction, yet, WPC has developed a culture where asking for help and admitting when one needs support is not only acceptable, it is preferred.

• Work hard, really hard, and when it's time to stop working, play hard, too. There are just over 130 employees at WPC, a very small employee head count for a company that produces close to $200 million of work annually. Employees are given the resources and training to be very productive which keeps payroll down and profits (which translate to bonuses and benefits) up. When it's time to stop working, WPC sponsors an average of 10 annual employee events each year to show its appreciation for the employee's hard work and dedication. These informal appreciation events have another effect: to help create the camaraderie and teamwork so critical to WPC's culture and success.

• Be aggressive, but be careful. Don't recklessly jump into new markets or types of construction, particularly if it means having to learn a whole new product type, but be ready to do whatever is needed for clients. Tracy's mechanical and technical interests led him to invest in information technology resources way before it was popular to do so. WPC was the first construction company in the world with its own web domain and probably one of the early adopters of desktop computers and the internet. Today, most jobsites have wireless connectivity so visitors or staff can stay connected to the company's vast information assets wherever they are. Being careful sometimes frustrates hungry, less experienced staff. When Tracy turned down an opportunity to branch into new markets to keep up with competitors in those markets, some of his senior managers got frustrated. Tracy felt, "Why go out of town to lose money when we can do it right here in our own back yard?" But when a loyal and valued client asked WPC to get involved with a construction project in Las Vegas, the answer was obvious—go where loyal clients take us.

• Be patient when the stakes are high and move quickly when there is a lot of money on the table. Tracy flatly refuses to make major investment or expansion decisions quickly. For example, his concern about over-expanding the company's head count too quickly led him to take 6 months to approve the addition of one part time payroll clerk. His experience during the gas crisis taught him the pain and anguish of letting good people go, so he scrutinizes the recommendations of department heads when they want to hire new people. Each hiring decision reflects Tracy's determination not to become a company that fires and hires a lot of people based on short term blips or changes in market conditions. Conversely, once WPC has been awarded a construction contract, it puts a lot of effort into completing the work as quickly as quality and the client will allow. WPC has a full time scheduler who works with every project team to drive out as much "waste" or idle time as possible from every construction schedule.

The culture of WPC brims with pride and quality, largely due to Tracy's hard work and disciplined approach as he built the company. Ambition, fear of failure and a strong desire to build a company that would survive beyond his reign were the motivators that helped Tracy achieve his success. Tracy is a classic example of a passionate, driven leader who knows how to temper his passion with a keen sense of timing.

THE COMBINATION OF PASSION AND TIMING

Imagine spending each day doing something that consumes you, fills you up or calls you. Imagine finishing that day, even if it is a 14 hour day, with energy to spare. That's passion. Now, imagine being able to maintain that passion over months, years, decades. That's the result of effective timing.

There is no *enduring* in *enduring leader* without timing.

A leader with a keen sense of timing but no will to work hard is merely patient. A leader who is passionate but has poor timing is just energetic. Timing without passion is merely diplomacy.

Passion is the fire that drives leaders towards achievement. Timing is the discipline to know when to let the fire rage and when to keep it smoldering. When the two are hooked together, they qualify as an insight of enduring leaders. *Passion and Timing* are mutually reinforcing and mutually limiting; each one makes the other stronger.

Most of us have worked with someone whose energy and enthusiasm for their work was over the top. When they are able to focus and control their enthusiasm, the result is a very effective employee. However, if they can't curb their enthusiasm when restraint is called for, or if they have no ability to pace themselves, their performance is inconsistent. When faced with a critical decision, a passionate leader who uses timing to help guide his actions will restrain themselves even when every fiber in his being says "Act Now!" and consider alternative options. Timing helps passionate people express and pace themselves effectively.

CONNECTED COMPETENCIES

"Passion" isn't a term we are used to hearing very often to describe leaders. But passion is the basis for a lot of words we are used to hearing such as "motivating," "inspiring," "committed," and even "loyal." Passion is the base emotion from which these other feelings emerge. Passionate leaders who have good timing bring out these feelings in the people around them.

The terms and competencies most frequently connected with *Passion and Timing* include

- Holds self and others accountable
- Recognizes the efforts and effectiveness of others
- Sets ambitious goals for the business
- Continuously seeks self-improvement
- Fosters a sense of urgency
- Appropriately challenges others
- Demonstrates an intense desire to succeed

- Does whatever it takes to keep the customer happy
- Expects excellence from self and others

Leaders who have this insight hunger to succeed. They are driven by a zeal that usually exceeds the expectations of their supervisors. Because they see their ability to be successful as a key element of their self-esteem, passionate people are highly accountable and generally pretty good at helping others become more accountable. Passionate people are goal setters; they have a plan to express their passion. Leaders who possess this insight but lack the insight of self-awareness and personal mastery tend to expect too much of others.

Since they are driven by a desire to do their best, the high standards passionate leaders set push them to seek self-improvement. If leaders lack the other element of this insight, timing, they are prone to burn-out; pushing themselves too hard for too long in work, in their personal lives and in their quest for self-improvement.

Since they are enthusiastic about their life's work, passionate leaders with good timing tend to be good coaches. Employees who work for a passionate leader tend to be more interested in their work and more motivated to do a good job. If the leader is passionate *and* has a sense of timing, employees see a role model for getting work done and having fun, and they imitate it. Leaders who don't have passion for their work can be very successful under most circumstances, but when extra work is required, dispassionate leaders struggle to keep up.

The shoulder trait between Passion and Timing and Connection is Purpose. In this section, we will discuss defining and developing our Purpose. In the section on Connection, there is a lengthy discussion about how to apply, refine and communicate our Purpose through personal mastery and self-awareness. Refer to the exercises in both of these sections under The Practice.

MAKING PASSION HAPPEN

Passion is a privilege. Passion is discovered from the inside out. It springs forth from an awareness of how we feel and think about our lives and our work. To be able to pursue our passion, we have to take care of more basic needs such as job security, health and strong relationships. Not everyone is so lucky. We still live in a world where the only thing some people can afford to be passionate about is where their next meal is coming from. Why then are humans motivated to get beyond a hand-to-mouth existence? Why do people crave deeper meaning in their lives? Why can't we just be satisfied with three square meals a day, a roof over our heads and a place to sleep? To better understand this, we need to pay homage to Dr. Abraham Maslow and his study of the sources of human motivation, which is frequently referred to as the "Hierarchy of Needs."

Abraham Maslow rose to prominence as one of the great psychologists of the 20th Century at a time when research about the origins of human motivation was peaking. At various points in his career, Maslow worked with some of the most noted intellectuals of the era. His colleagues and collaborators included psychologists Alfred Alder and Karen Horney and psychotherapist Erich Fromm—all of whom were deeply involved in the study and early exploration of the origins of personality.

Maslow's research eventually led him into a study of the sources of human motivation. He theorized that the ability to work and function at our highest levels of capability and motivation is a developmental process. Before each of us can pursue those activities that engage our intellectual and spiritual selves, basic needs have to be fulfilled. Maslow developed a model to describe his theory that was improved and augmented over a 20 year time span. Eventually, the model became one of the most widely recognized psychological models used in understanding motivation and behavior in humans. If you run a Google search on "Business+Maslow's Hierarchy of Needs," over 110,000 references pop-up; not bad for a poor boy from Brooklyn!

What makes Maslow's model so popular and so appropriate is the simple and obvious ways it describes what motivates people. Maslow believed that taking care of basic physiological needs is a prerequisite to being able to work on more abstract or intellectual needs that require self-reflection. In other words, if you're hungry, cold or physically threatened, it's hard to spend much energy thinking about the meaning of life. At the base of Maslow's hierarchy are what he called "Basic Physiologic Needs"—food, shelter and warmth. Once these most basic human needs have been fulfilled, it is possible for people to think about and work on the next level in the hierarchy, or what Maslow calls "Safety"—establishing stability and freedom from fear in the environment. Next on the hierarchy is the ability to work on developing relationships and personal connections with others or what Maslow refers to as "Belonging and Love." Having meaningful relationships and feeling a sense of belonging helps us ascend to the next level, which is the development of "Self-Esteem" through the pursuit of activities that require mastery and foster a sense of accomplishment. Finally, according to Maslow, the most rare "Need" we humans ever get to focus on is the pursuit of "Self-Fulfillment," or the search for meaning and purpose

Need

Motivation to Satisfy Need

need for self actualization — Challenging Projects. Opportunities for Innovation and Creativity. Learning at a High Level.

need for self esteem — Important Projects. Recognition of Strength, Intelligence, Prestige, and Status.

social needs - belonging — Acceptance, Group Membership. Association with Successful Team. Love and Affection.

need for safety and security — Physical, Safety. Economic Security. Freedom from Threats. Comfort, Peace.

physical survival needs — Water, Food, Sleep, Warmth, Health, Excercise, and Sex.

Maslow's Hierarchy of Needs

Maslow was a big believer and early advocate of the human potential movement—a collective of scientists and students of human behavior that believed humans are capable of far more than they typically achieve. Human potentialists believe people are held back by human emotions such as defensiveness and fear. The impact of the human potential movement and Maslow's view of human potential has been—and is—huge. Instead of assuming employees are not giving their jobs their all because they are unwilling, Maslow's theory says that their lack of performance is more likely tied to a need lower in the hierarchy that is not being met. When those physical and emotional needs are adequately taken care of in the context of work, an employee is more likely to be able to throw themselves into their work with a higher level of commitment and motivation.

It is not too much of a stretch to see why people who understand Maslow's hierarchy also see developing and maintaining a healthy organizational culture as a key element in motivating employees. A positive culture removes physiological fear, increases belongingness and promotes independent action. A negative culture breeds fear and generates instability.

Maslow believed that the ultimate source of happiness in each person is to pursue activities that fully engage them intellectually and spiritually and to not do so was an invitation to an unsatisfied life. As Maslow put it, "If you deliberately plan on being less than you are capable of being, then I warn you that you'll be unhappy for the rest of your life."

Once we have fulfilled all of our basic needs, Maslow believed our focus shifts from taking care of ourselves to seeing how we can make an impact on the world around us. He described this state as "self-actualization" and he frequently referred to Eleanor Roosevelt and other well known humanitarians of the time as examples of self-actualized people. What drives each of us to expend the energy to climb Maslow's hierarchy? Why aren't we just satisfied with having our basic needs attended to? Maslow felt that the motivating force underneath all of this hard work was the desire in each person to somehow influence the world around them. In other words, our willingness to work hard comes from a desire to have an impact. Maslow's theory describes why people perform at their best and are happiest when they feel they are doing something that makes a contribution and has meaning beyond their own needs or circumstances. If belonging, feeling important and having meaning are important to happiness, then it follows that great work environments are places where people can do that which brings them a sense of accomplishment, feelings of belongingness and a sense of self importance. Just as surely as Tracy Forrest built buildings, he built a company culture that satisfied those needs. Enduring leaders build cultures where people can express themselves through work in ways that feel full of purpose and meaning.

People LOVE feeling like they make a difference in the world and one of the best places to do that is at work.

THE ART OF TIMING

We don't discover our sense of timing, we learn it. We learn it over time and we learn it from the outside in, because timing is developed by interacting with the world. To accommodate the social or cultural standards we were raised in, we learn it is better to repress urges and not respond impulsively.

This type of behavioral shift is the result of developing better timing. Our timing training begins at a very early age and hopefully continues throughout our lives. Toddlers and preschoolers get constant training on their timing under the guise of "learning manners" or "waiting your turn" or "being patient." Developing a sense of timing is part of our social and behavioral conditioning.

No matter what age we are, when we make poor timing decisions, the world usually gives us feedback, and if we listen to the feedback, our sense of timing improves. The feedback we receive when we make good timing decisions is often more subtle than the feedback we receive when we make poor timing decisions, but the feedback is there nonetheless. Frequently a timing error is at the core of a poor judgment. For example, have you ever told someone what you really think when what they wanted to hear was that you agreed with them? Or, have you ever poured your heart and soul into a project at work only to discover the project was not where your boss wanted you to put your talent and energy? Can you think of a time when you overextended yourself to achieve a deadline, only to discover that the deadline didn't really matter or, equally bad, when you took it easy and missed a deadline because you didn't understand how important making it was to your boss or a customer?

Timing is an art that can be learned and improved upon indefinitely. Enduring leaders see their sense of timing as critical to their overall success, so they actively collect feedback on their approach and style. Then they work to accurately and honestly interpret what they are hearing and sensing.

INDICATORS THAT YOUR SENSE OF TIMING IS WORKING/NOT WORKING FOR YOU INCLUDE:

Feedback: In discussions, you are able to make your point in a way that provokes thinking and interest from those to whom you are speaking.

Possible Interpretations:
- You have chosen a good time to bring up a specific subject.
- You are very articulate.

- You make room for—and show genuine interest in—
  the opinions of others.

Feedback: Before a presentation or an important meeting, your colleagues spend an inordinate amount of time prepping you for what to say and what NOT to say.

Possible Interpretation: Your colleagues either don't think you are prepared, or they don't trust your judgment and it may be an issue of your sense of timing, or both.

Feedback: You are building trust and openness in an important relationship.

Possible Interpretation: They perceive you as sensitive and open to their feelings, opinions and perspectives.

Feedback: You are NOT invited to a meeting that involves discussion about something you should be included in because of your expertise on the subject.

Possible Interpretations:
- Maybe they just wanted to give you a break because you're busy!
- Your passion and energy about the subject is so high that you don't make much room for the opinions of others.

Feedback: A project team you are working on is doing well. You and the team have been able to identify issues before they became a crisis.

Possible Interpretation: You offer and seek out solutions to project related issues in time. You stay ahead of the learning curve on projects where learning is required so that you can add value to the project team. You manage your time well and you are responsible with how much of someone else's time you take.

Feedback: In groups, people report liking the way you lead a project.

Possible Interpretations:

- You exert your influence and leadership only when doing so adds value to the group's work.
- Working with you is fun and a rich learning experience!
- You achieved great results, whatever the cost.

Feedback: People don't seek you out for assistance, guidance and support even though you offer it frequently.

Possible Interpretations:

- You are not perceived as being open or very good at coaching or assisting others.
- You are perceived as being too busy or overextended.
- Your enthusiasm and passion leads you to micromanage projects instead of helping them do it themselves.

PART TWO
PASSION AND TIMING IN ACTION

PASSION IS BIGGER THAN "THE JOB"

Passion comes from a deep instinctual alignment of our hopes, dreams, interests and aptitudes. When we are lucky enough to find or create a job where these elements are all in place, watch out! Great things are likely to occur. When work becomes an opportunity for a person to use their talents and skills to the utmost doing something they really enjoy doing they are working at the top of Maslow's hierarchy. For these people, "work" just isn't work any more; it is an extension of their ability to express themselves in the world.

Passion loves company and it grows stronger when it is shared by teams and groups. If Tracy Forrest wanted to be successful on his own, he would have picked a profession that did not involve so many people. But Tracy's definition of success was broader; he needed to feel like he was doing something for and with other people. This is frequently the case. Artists who are passionate about a certain style of art tend to seek each other out. Clubs and professional associations are often the result of people wanting to discuss or learn more about their collective passion. We look for kindred spirits whose passions align with our own. Tracy *loves* building things, and nothing makes him happier than being around people who share that interest and skill. In any work environment, when enough people work together who share a common, passionate interest in something, the group starts generating more energy than it uses. This is how positive organizational cultures are born.

Imagine an organization where every single person was performing a job that was close to their passion. There is plenty of evidence to show that the most successful businesses do just that; they find people who are passionate about a cause or area of expertise and then let them pursue it.

TIMING: MAKING PASSION PAY OFF

If passion is the fuel that propels leaders to excel, then their sense of timing is the rudder that directs and focuses their efforts. Is having a keen sense of timing actually a form of intelligence? Absolutely. Timing comes from intuition and intuition comes from experience and knowing how to accurately interpret what is happening around us. Leaders who have the insight of *Passion and Timing* don't burn out at their jobs because they know when to work really hard and when to back off and recharge their batteries. They know when they need to jump into a problem and when to act more as an interested observer and let the process unfold without their intervention.

The leaders who have an abundance of temporal intelligence exhibit their skill as much through what they *don't* do as what they *do* do. For example, all of them have a seemingly unlimited supply of patience and they resist pressure to make a decision until they feel completely comfortable with it irrespective of what others think. They are equally likely to fixate on a problem or task and pursue it tirelessly. Both behaviors are driven by an innate sense of when to strike and when to wait. Leaders who have a lot of temporal intelligence rely extensively on their experience to distinguish between action and inaction or between restraint and pursuit.

Enduring leaders have to develop great timing for events that they have control over, but they also have to develop their timing for events that are completely outside of their control. Enduring leaders who have great temporal intelligence respond equally well to both types of events, but they usually gain the most notoriety and attention when they respond to the unexpected. Whether the event was planned or random, enduring leaders leverage timing to:

- Know when to confront a situation or let it brew
- Decide when to go public with important information related to their business
- Help them decide who to partner with, and when

- Make the most (or least) of an event that is outside of their control
- Launch a new approach, strategy or initiative
- Postpone a decision when more information is needed or the timing just isn't right

ANTICIPATE THE FUTURE

As he built WPC into one of the largest and most successful construction companies in the nation, Tracy Forrest learned a lot about timing from his experiences, and he applied that knowledge. Construction is a cyclical industry whose cycles are driven by a number of factors including the state of the national and regional economy, materials pricing, tourism (especially in Central Florida), interest rates, gas prices, international trade and labor. "It's dangerous to be greedy in construction," Tracy says. "Owners will show up with deals of all shapes and sizes. Sometimes the deals appear to be too good to be true, and they usually are. Every time we have built a project where we lost money, there were signs (that things were not going to turn out well) but we proceeded anyway and got burned in the end. That's why we work to develop relationships with clients over the long term. It's tempting to go after high margin work with unknown owners, but almost every time we jump into a project with people we don't know, the unexpected happens and it usually gets paid for by us." Tracy remembers just about every project where WPC lost money so he can learn from the experience. Temporal intelligence is built by learning through experience.

Like every company in the United States, the tragedies of 9/11 deeply affected WPC's business. Timeshare resorts and vacation condominiums appeal strongly to tourists as prospective owners when they visit Disney and the Orlando attractions. No one wanted to travel by plane after 9/11, so the reduction in visitors had a significant impact on WPC's timeshare clients who put a hold on plans for any additional expansion after 9/11. The immediate response to this for many contractors and subcontractors was to reduce overhead and "thin the ranks." Tracy's instincts about timing told him that the 9/11 downturn was not the time to reduce headcount—business would rebound or a new market or direction for success would emerge if he waited.[2]

To keep everyone on the payroll and busy as the market softened, WPC doubled up staff on most of its projects. Job sites that were normally staffed with a superintendent and a few assistants suddenly had three superintendents and seven assistants working together. Clients didn't pay a penny extra for the additional staff on projects, Tracy did. In spite of the doubling-up strategy, anxiety about the market and the future of WPC grew. Tracy and his Senior Team called everyone from the company together for what they called a "Town Hall Meeting" where they explained how they viewed the future, specifically, the future for WPC's employees. As Tracy's brother, Jeff, explained during the meeting, "Everyone needs to go to work knowing and trusting that, if you are adding value to the project you are involved in, WPC will make it. We're not interested in taking this great machine apart because the market has gone soft. We'll do our part to keep everyone together, but please do your part, make us look great with the subs and clients you work with." Tracy and his team reasoned that it would be more costly to let people go and later replace them with people of equal skill and character than it would be to take the short term loss and keep them employed with WPC.

In the months after 9/11, the multi-family apartment and resort condominium market bounced back. Not reducing headcount gave WPC the necessary staff to respond to the multi-family upturn. Tracy stayed the course. WPC's results have continued to improve both in terms of annual revenues and net profits. More importantly, Tracy's loyalty and commitment to the employees during hard times won their loyalty and respect 100 times over. Enduring leaders make the most of events out of their control through their experience and sense of timing.

ORDINARY PEOPLE, EXTRAORDINARY RESULTS

When people are given the chance to work in an area that brings out their best, extraordinary things can happen. Being *inspired* to work in a way that transcends the job is not the privileged territory reserved only for senior leaders. Some of the most inspired people in organizations are frequently the ones closest to the product, service or client. But sometimes what motivates and drives an employee has to do with things *other* than the job description. Some employees develop great working relationships with the people on their shift and become passionate about their friendships. Others are trying to pay for a child to go to college, so they become passionate about their jobs as a vehicle for achieving that goal. Regardless, tapping into an employee's passion helps them bring forth their best.

On a break from some training I was doing for Herman Miller, a premier manufacturer of office furniture, I approached two employees who appeared to be doing the same job across from each other in an assembly area. I had seen each of them over the preceding three days as I entered the plant on the way to the training room and they always seemed to be having a lot of fun as I walked by. Their work appeared to be fairly redundant yet they seemed to always be happy with what they were doing—happier than I would have been if I had been in their shoes. Yet, their attitudes were contagious. I was curious what made them so cheerful so I finally asked "what do you like about this job?" The first associate's eyes lit up as she grew excited and ebullient. She went into an animated five minute monologue about how the chairs she was making were helping to keep the backs and spinal cords of "all those poor people who have to work in offices day in and day out" healthy. She was certain that her job was bringing more comfort, and less pain, to office workers all over the world. When I asked the second associate what she liked about her job, she pointed across the assembly area to the first associate and said, "Her!" They had exactly the same job description, or so I assume, but their motivations for doing the job were different.

You might ask, "If motivation is as personal as passion, isn't it up to the employees to find their own motivation instead of it being up to the leader?" The answer is, both are correct: employees have to find their own internal fire for showing up at work each day AND leaders can help by creating a work environment where people see their job—however menial or small—as an important element of the team's effort... The parable of the three bricklayers describes this idea:

> *A man walking through the city came upon three bricklayers who were hard at work. He approached the first one and asked "What are you building?" and the bricklayer replied "I am building a wall, of course!" Not satisfied with the answer, the man approached the second bricklayer and again asked "What are you building?" The bricklayer proudly replied "I am building a huge building that will have spires that reach 200 feet into the air!" Still not satisfied with the answer, he approached the third brick layer and asked "What are you building?" to which*

the third bricklayer looked skyward and replied "I am building a church where people from all over this city can come together and share their faith".

Leaders who possess the trait of passion believe they are doing something much grander than laying one brick on top of another, even if that is their job day in and day out. They have found inspiration in their work and it drives them. And what's more, they are able to help others find their own motivation—the connection between what we do and what is important to us. By doing so, enduring leaders help employees achieve Maslow's "self actualization." The woman at Herman Miller who shows up every day feeling like she is making a difference for others IS making a difference, in ways that are both obvious and subtle. Every day, ordinary people—people like you and I—create extraordinary results not because we are smart or talented, but because we feel strongly about the work that we do. That passion for work motivates and inspires us to create extraordinary results.

SEIZE THE OPPORTUNITY!

In the summer of 2004, four hurricanes hit the state of Florida within five weeks. Two of them traversed the state from west to east in a highly unlikely pattern that affected parts of the state that up to then had been thought to be out of range for hurricanes. The eyes of the two hurricanes managed to pass within 15 miles of downtown Orlando. Screening from most screened enclosures—a popular feature on many houses in central Florida—had been ripped from the frames that held it and blew away. The employees and clients of WPC were strongly affected by the first hurricane, Charley, as it leveled trees, flattened houses, tossed cars and boats around like toys and left over 4 million people without power. By the time the second hurricane, Francis, arrived, they had had enough. The houses of two WPC employees were almost destroyed and several of their cars were flattened. On top of the personal discomfort and inconvenience employees felt during the hurricanes, everyone was concerned about the damage on WPC's projects and the impact on clients and subcontractors. In spite of insurances covering damages on jobsites, the long term effects of the hurricanes posed serious problems to business and profitability.

Although in his mind he was just doing what needed to be done, Tracy's response to the storms was classic Maslow. He attended to the employee's and client's basic needs and showed them the same sense of loyalty and self-less commitment so many of them had shown the company over the years. Tracy demonstrated a core principle of good leadership: take care of the people, the rest will follow. Tracy and the WPC management team set up an emergency response center of sorts at WPC's corporate offices. As the first hurricane passed, they systematically made contact with every WPC employee to make sure they were OK and to make sure they didn't need any immediate emergency assistance. Teams of WPC employees did the same for clients; those whose property was not affected went to job sites to assess damage, work on restoring power and begin cleaning up. Aside from emergency assistance, the biggest need seemed to be for tree and brush removal on streets where high winds had toppled literally hundreds of thousands of trees. Tree removal required chainsaws and folks capable of using them. Tracy dispatched a team of employees to first buy as many chainsaws as needed, then the chainsaws and operators dispersed to the houses of WPC employees most in need of help. They also rendered assistance to many of WPC's clients and even went so far as to send crews to help at their homes. By the time the second hurricane hit, all of the WPC teams who had been diverted to help their fellow employees were back on the job, fixing the damage to projects. Thankfully, the second storm brought more water than wind, so damages were less severe. Why didn't Tracy put more focus on getting people to deal with the damage to the business's damaged projects? He didn't have to. The employees took care of the clients. "We have 130-some odd people out there right now concerned for their families, houses, neighbors—even their jobs. I can't ask them to worry about our projects until they feel taken care of" as Tracy put it. The upshot: 130 employees once again got the message (and support) that showed them they were cared for, and 20 new, but heavily used chainsaws.

Caring about people is a characteristic behavior and a belief that threads it's way through all of the five insights of enduring leaders but it shows-up most strongly in *Passion and Timing*. If you don't care—really care—about the success and happiness of your employees, you don't need to read the rest of this book. Take it back and ask for a refund. Leading well is impossible if you don't care.

WORKING "ON PURPOSE"

As we've discussed, passion is a mindset, a feeling we get when our interests and abilities and the opportunity to express them converge. I believe that our passion is also connected to our quest to understand our role in the universe, and our role in the universe is frequently connected to our work. We humans love to search for deeper meaning to explain what happens in our lives, and since two thirds of our lives are spent working, it makes sense that we would also attempt to attach a deeper meaning to our work. The woman at Herman Miller was sure she was making a difference in the world by the way she built chairs. Like her, when we see our work as part of a grander plan that benefits the part of the world we touch, we become more connected to our sense of belonging. We become more aware of our purpose. When people feel as if they are working "on purpose" watch out, amazing things happen.

PURPOSE AND PRECESSION

Passion and Timing help us achieve our goals. Our passion is what motivates us and keeps us moving toward our goals. Developing our sense of timing helps us know when to pour on the juice and when to take it easy. Yet, we rarely hit the dead center of our goal. That is, we usually end in a place that is slightly different than where we intended. Or we arrive at our goals through a more indirect, circuitous turn of events. For example, a busy entrepreneur may have wanted to build more reflective thinking time into his days, but he ended up spending more time exercising because it helped him be reflective—he achieved his goal, but the end result looked slightly different than he had originally imagined. Others have wanted to get more involved in community activities to find themselves starting a business that serves the community. As a beneficial exercise, notice what goals you have set and where you ended up in relationship to those goals. It's critical for enduring leaders to have goals, but they also have to stay aware of where life, fate and coincidence or a higher power ends up taking them.

R. Buckminster Fuller, noted author, architect, mathematician, philosopher, inventor, designer of the geodesic dome and the man who coined the term "Spaceship Earth" took a geophysical principle called "precession" and applied it to this discussion in a way that helps to explain the phenomenon of purpose and passion from a human behavioral perspective.[3]

GRAVITY AND PRECESSION

Simply put, precession is the effect of bodies in motion on other bodies in motion. If you spin a top—or better yet, a bicycle tire on a rim—fast enough it will start to behave like a gyroscope, balancing on its axis. Then, if you exert pressure on the top of the axis by gently pulling it toward you, something unexpected happens: it doesn't move towards you at all. Instead, it moves at a right angle to the direction of the force. This phenomenon is called "precession," the movement of a spinning body at a right angle to the direction of force exerted on it.

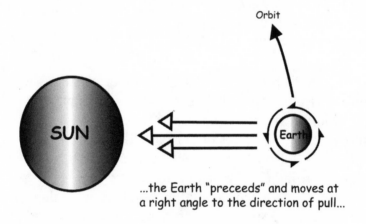

...the Earth "preceeds" and moves at a right angle to the direction of pull...

Precession

In the geophysical world, understanding precession is one of the keys to understanding why the earth moves around the sun instead of being drawn straight toward it and why the earth wobbles on its axis, which in turn is critical for understanding why the star's positions change ever so slightly when viewed from the earth.

Precession literally describes a side effect of exerting force on a body in motion; force in one direction moves things sideways to the direction of pull. Dr. Fuller theorized that precession is a way to explain the interplay between what we do for work, where we are heading in life, and how things tend to turn out.[4]

Now let's take this idea and superimpose it on some of the personalities we discussed so far. Tracy Forrest's "goal" was to be successful, or after his failure in 1974 during the gas crisis, to not be a failure. Tracy's goal of not being a failure contradicts the pie-in-the-sky image many of us have of leaders. We often believe they only focus on success, as if thinking about avoiding something is a poor strategy for achievement. Tracy built a successful company driven at least in part by his passion to not fail and his ability to make key changes to the business when timing was right. His "work" was starting and running a construction company. But the side effect of his passion was the discovery of something much more powerful than not failing, as he put it: "One day, I was working on payroll or insurance or something having to do with the number of employees WPC had and I remember thinking, I've created a monster! All these people are counting on me and the company to make a living!" In Tracy's words, "We have to make decisions (about the strategy and management of the company) that answer one simple question: what's the best thing to do for our clients and the 130 employees, the 400 family members and the thousands of subcontractors who count on us for their livelihood now, tomorrow and 10 years from now?" In spite of his success, and the sustained success of WPC, Tracy is still driven by a sense of responsibility to everyone whose lives are directly affected by the actions of his company. His work is construction; his goal and passion is success, but his purpose is the people of WPC.

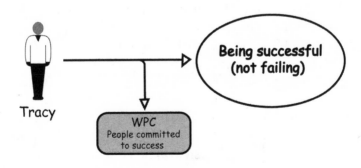

Tracy Forrest and WPC

Here's the point: *Passion and Timing* make for a powerful elixir that helps to reveal our purpose. When we are fortunate enough to live and work in a job we are passionate about, we create interesting and sometimes wonderful side effects—from a vibrant and successful company that has an energy and culture all its own to a global movement to save us from ourselves—the work we do not only *can* but *will* produce unexpected side benefits. Buckminster Fuller's theory of precession offers another important insight: For precession to work, bodies have to be moving. Precession doesn't happen if one is standing still or not going anywhere. You've got to keep moving. Passionate people are always on the way to somewhere. Passion and purpose are a journey, not a destination.

PASSION AND CONTINUITY

Passion takes energy, and energy requires fuel. Leaders are fueled by a variety of things, but one source they all seem to share is when they see passion spread and permeate their group, department, committee or organization. Passionate leaders are great recruiters. They love nothing more than showing a group of bricklayers that their jobs are much more than just laying bricks.

Passion is as strong as any corporate strategy for achieving great results. As consultant and author Richard Chang puts it:

> *The most practical and enduring lesson I have learned over twenty-five years of helping to improve individual and organizational performance is that passion is the single most powerful competitive advantage an organization can claim in building its success. Many organizations possess the same technology, resources, equipment, and expertise in their employees, but it is the organization that runs on passion that prevails.*[5]

The "snowball effect" of passion inside an organization is something both to be cautious of and work towards. As we've seen, pursuing a goal with passion creates unexpected side benefits. When enough people are motivated and driven by the same variety of passion, the group or organization develops its own momentum, which changes the leader's job from motivating the group to monitoring the group's progress as they motivate themselves. Watching a group that has achieved this level of capability is awesome.

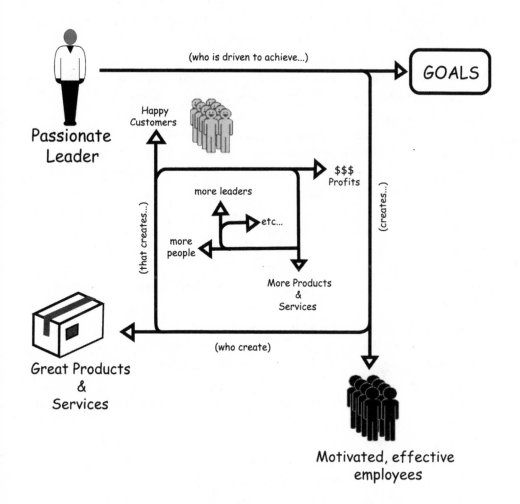

The Snowball Effect of Passion

Their common passion frequently creates a clarity and sense of purpose that improves other elements and behaviors within the team. Members of teams who have achieved a sense of mutual purpose and passion report that the work actually became easier, not harder, as a result of the team's combined energy.

Leaders can also fall into unrealistic expectations by thinking that they can predict exactly how their passion will effect those around them. This is an act of hubris that is driven by ego. For example, a leader who is passionate about helping the group succeed may work tirelessly to insure their success by excessively pitching in and helping out to model good behavior. But if people are overly awed or intimidated by the leader's energy level or competence, the side effect of her efforts may be that everyone around that leader becomes passive or afraid to match their energy for fear of appearing to compete. Instead of catching a contagious passion about work, the group begins to lack confidence and falls into a malaise of inaction.

Again, passion without timing is just energy, and it is timing that makes passion effective. The leader who is infusing passion into the group also has a responsibility to do so with restraint and a more global perspective about the ultimate goals of the business.

Even more dangerous is when the passion of the leader does not line up with any form of reality and they are good at recruiting others to their fantasy. Tragic examples of these kinds of passions include the cults of the Branch Davidians in Waco, Texas, with David Koresh or the mass suicide in Jonestown led by Jim Jones: passionate leaders whose passion was driven by control instead of something to better the world. A passionate leader who is driven by less honorable goals like ego or insecurity (needs that are pretty low on Maslow's hierarchy) is much more likely to attract followers whose needs and interests are similar. Insecurity begets insecurity just like inspiration begets inspiration. The results of leaders whose passion is to fulfill their own self-serving, unhealthy needs are more of the same and, as we have seen in recent corporate failures and scandals, the results are devastating.

Even in this day and age, there are businesses who manage to succeed in spite of how they treat their employees, not because of how they treat them.

Aside from the obvious moral issues, the problem with treating people poorly is that it breeds an operating model where the best employees eventually leave and the employees who stay are the ones who either aren't very good at their jobs or lack confidence in their ability to find another job. When employees don't feel important or, at the very least, respected, they eventually trust and respect the business less.

The other extreme is a business in which employees are inspired to do their work. The impact of a leader on the "inspiration index" of a business can be enormous. Their ability to inspire, motivate and create loyalty has less to do with their public speaking ability than their true, heartfelt caring for the people in the business. If a leader attends a public speaking course, they may return being able to articulate things more clearly or interestingly, but they won't be any more inspiring. Listen to someone who has truly found

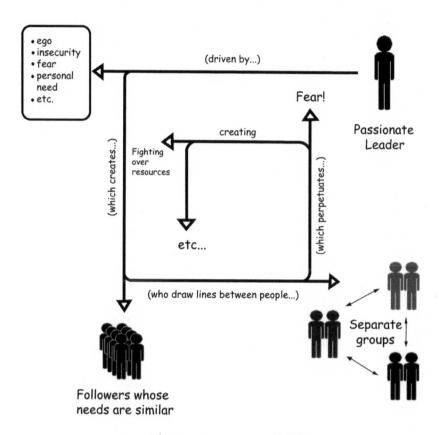

The Reverse Snowball Effect

their passion and energy. Vocabulary and rhetoric, compared to this leader's dynamic charisma, hardly matter at all.

Almost no one who works for him would say Tracy is an inspiring communicator or public speaker, including Tracy. He chooses his words very carefully in conversations and prefers to know what topics are going to be discussed before having a meeting with someone so he is prepared for it. However, among the employees of WPC, Tracy is a major source of inspiration. Of all his traits, the two that stand out the most for employees are Tracy's intelligence and his work ethic. The culture of WPC is full of Tracy stories: the time Tracy solved a problem no one else had a solution to, and his habit of shutting down the office in the evening long after everyone else has gone home. As the saying goes, words are cheap. Action says it all.

Passion is motivation in Technicolor.

PART THREE
THE PRACTICE

FOR ASPIRING LEADERS

Meet Your New Life Coach

Y ou are unlikely to achieve your potential until you are in a job you feel passionate about, so first things first: go to work in a job you can feel passionate about. This is a hard but very true reality of developing a career; the sooner you accept it, the sooner you'll start performing up to your true potential.

In his studies about life, purpose and meaning, coach, consultant and author Richard Leider did a survey of over 1,000 senior citizens who were successful in their jobs and asked them to look back over their lives and talk about what they have learned.[6] According to Leider, their answers are strikingly similar:

- They would have been more reflective – Instead of getting caught up in working and reacting, they would have spent more time questioning the meaning of their actions to make sure that what they were doing made sense to them, personally. This is timing.

- They would have taken more risks – In relationships, work, and life, they would have risked more. This is passion.

- They would have sought to better understand what gave them fulfillment, and pursued that more. Fulfillment is the application of talent to a cause that gives our lives a sense of purpose. And fulfillment is an iterative loop of work, noticing the purposes our work fulfills and the people our work touches and then re-directing our efforts given our new understanding.

What to Do:

For the purposes of this exercise, let's assume Leider's research is true for all of us. Assume that you are likely to have regrets when you reach your 80's about some of the choices you have made in life. Let's also assume there is a way of not having nearly as many regrets if you hire a good life coach. Your life coach happens to be a very wise and thoughtful 80 year old. Pretend you trust the advice you are about to receive from your life coach implicitly. As a professional, your life coach only has your best interests in mind. You are eager and willing to listen with an open mind and a courageous heart to whatever your life coach has to say.

Ready to listen?

Now it is time to have your first meeting with your coach. Before you begin, there is one more thing you need to know: Your life coach is you. The You of today is going to have a make-believe conversation with You of tomorrow—20, 30 or 50 years hence. The You of tomorrow has all the wisdom of experience in life that the You of today is missing. The You of the future—the 80 year old You—is going to tell you when and where you should take more time to be reflective. He or she is going to give you some pointers on what risks you should take, since risk taking appears to be one of the things that all of us should do more of to be fulfilled. Finally and most importantly, he or she is going to give you a little more insight into You. What *does* give you fulfillment? How could you lead a more fulfilled life?

What would the You of 20 years hence tell the You of today about the way you are making decisions in work and life? Listen to yourself carefully; the conversation should be enlightening.

Go on a Quest for the Holy Grail of Your Life

Chase passion as if it were the Holy Grail, for in truth it is. None of us will live forever, but research indicates that those of us who pursue our passion live happier, longer, more fulfilled lives. Of course, choose your time wisely: most of us have commitments that make chasing our passion without considering our responsibilities dangerous. On the other hand, don't fool yourself out of doing what makes you happy by convincing yourself you have to maintain the status quo for everyone else's benefit. If you want to truly make those around you happy, get happy. If you have to bide your time until the time is right, bide it, but not indefinitely. Take the risk, reflect on your choices, make sure you're headed in a direction that brings you joy, and go!

"But what if pursuing my passion doesn't pay as well?" you may ask.

Studies show that, after a minimum threshold has been achieved, happiness is not connected to your income. According to a number of studies of both the American workforce and the international public, there is very little, if any connection between income and happiness. Truly! Unless you live in poverty or below a minimum income standard, your happiness is no longer connected to your income.[7] Actually, the reverse is true: chasing a large salary without purpose has been found to be a life shortening event!

What to Do:

In thinking about changing your career or job, notice how attached you are to the status quo. Many people stay in jobs they hate simply because the idea of change is worse than whatever they are already doing. If you are making up lots of excuses why you can't change, notice that, too. To break out of this type of thinking, start asking yourself "what if" questions:

- "What if…I changed jobs or careers?" Would it be more of an inconvenience or would it truly be a risk?

- "What if…I found a job that brought me joy but paid less money; would it be worth it? Based on my history, is it likely that I will fail miserably if I try something new that I really love?" Probably not!

- "What if…I had to learn a whole new set of skills to do what I am really passionate about?" Isn't learning something I enjoy?

- "What if…I had to go find another job?" – Would that be awful or just tough on my pride?

- "What if…all of this made me miserable or didn't substantially change my life after all?" – How miserable or unfulfilled am I right now? How important is the prospect of being happier or more passionate worth to me?

Once you have completed the "what if" exercise, question the assumptions that led you to believe what you believe about change. Are your assumptions based on fact or are they a product of your own fears? If you are noticing that a lot of what keeps you from pursuing your passion has to do with your own fears, consider reading the section on "Courage through Service."

Find a Coach

Coaching has become a popular and effective means of discovering and pursuing your passion. Coaching is not therapy, at least not coaching that is well done. Whereas therapy focuses on our past and our pathologies, most effective coaches have been trained and know how to help us focus on our present and future opportunities. Some coaches have gone through very extensive training programs while others seem to be just as effective having received little or no formal training. The most important criteria may be a coach's ability to understand in practical terms the experience of the person they are coaching.

What to Do:

Seek out a coach. Do research, talk to friends and colleagues who have had successful coaching experiences and check references before beginning.

Another option for coaching is to ask a colleague or co-worker whose situation and life and work experience is different enough from yours to coach you. The coach should have a fresh, unbiased perspective on whatever the coaching topic is so they can help you uncover new ideas. In many forward thinking companies, more and more effort is being placed on developing internal coaches who can support the development of everyone around them. Collegial coaching relationships are often not as formal as profession-al coaching relationships, but they are every bit as expensive even though money may not be changing hands. If you ask a friend or colleague to coach you, make sure you're willing to invest time and energy into it as if you were paying for it. The time you will take away from daily duties of both you and your coach is every bit as costly as hiring a pro, so make the most of it either way.

Be Present. Notice the Side Effects Created by Working Towards Your Goals

If you are passionately pursuing your goals, you are creating ripples. Like a stone dropped into a pool of water, your passionate pursuit of your goals is having effects on the people around you. In fact, your hard work and com-mitment to what you're doing may be the spark that lights a fire in others. Like the two women who worked at Herman Miller, everyone finds their joy for work in different ways. Your joy (or lack thereof) will affect those around you.

What to Do:

Notice where those effects are helping the people or the organization, and notice where they are not. Apply your sense of timing to what you notice. Does someone who is being affected by your actions need more attention or reassurance? Are you keeping the people who matter the most in your life abreast of the changes you are experiencing inside of you? Are you over-whelming people around you and do you need to back off some?

Regardless of where your passion is taking you, don't get hung up on the end result. Of all the ideas and suggestions in this book, the most important and perhaps the hardest lesson to accept is the notion of not being attached to the outcome. In other words, follow your bliss, pursue your passion, and understand that the act of pursuing what is important to you in no way guarantees what the outcome will be. The outcome is out of your hands. It will happen on its own. Your job is to have a plan and a path, and then stay open to what unfolds. Passionate acts do not automatically lead to the results we expect. As a matter of fact, the phenomenon of precession proves that the outcomes of our efforts will almost certainly produce results we don't expect. Rely on whatever form of faith works for you, because not being attached to the outcome of our passion is truly an act of faith.

Keep Moving

Buckminster Fuller's model of precession is based on a simple premise: Movement begets direction. Columbus didn't discover the new world by plotting his entire course. No one knew the entire course. The new world had not been accurately mapped. Columbus had a special insight of his own; he was great at what navigators call "dead reckoning." He stayed on course as best as the events of time, weather and ocean currents would allow. As these events influenced his direction, he adjusted accordingly. The exact location where Columbus landed in the new world was the result of recalibrating his course every day based on his dead reckoning skill.

John McIntosh, CEO of NOOD (pronounced *Node*) Fashion in Dalton Georgia is a master at directing his passion towards goals. In high school, John played tackle for the Dalton High School Catamounts, one of the winningest programs in the country.

John had and still has what coaches call "heart." As an offensive guard playing for Ray Perkins at Alabama, (John was recruited by Bear Bryant who retired after his freshman year), John showed grit, determination and the same fanaticism for beating whoever was across from him that he showed when he started for Dalton his sophomore year. John's passion is the stuff of legend with his teammates and his family. "On game days," John's dad said, "if Johnny didn't run to the sidelines after pre-game warm-ups with tears in his eyes, we knew something was wrong—he wasn't psyched up enough." His passion for success drove him to prepare, practice, work out and prepare some more. "Early on, I learned to like hard work. I liked the idea that, no matter who was across from me, I had outworked him coming into the game, and there's no faking that."

A knee injury entering his junior year ended his dream to play pro ball, so John took his major in Public Relations and Marketing and went to work in the business that built Dalton, carpet. Over the course of the next 20 years, he built a career and reputation in the industry, rising to vice president of sales roles in some of the largest, most successful carpet companies in the world. At the core of his success was John's passion for people and his ability to connect with them. "I want my gravestone to say, 'he really helped people,' not 'he was a great carpet salesman,'" John once told me.

In his free time, John started working as an assistant coach for the Catamounts. Working with the team and reconnecting with kids opened his eyes to the scarcity of suitable role models available to teenagers. Listening to the kids on the team, he became deeply concerned about the poor examples so many professional and college athletes set for teens, and he realized that players who end up in trouble at those levels didn't get good council when they were teens. In his words: "We spend upwards of $1,000 per player giving them gear to protect them on the outside. How much do we spend protecting athletes on the inside? Zero!"

To combat the problem, John founded the *Why? Character* program, a program that teaches character development to student athletes. In his spare time, he is working to get the program adopted by high school athletics departments across the country. His years of leadership experience in big corporations have taught him that "winning" isn't the result of pursuing "winning," but rather the preparation of each team member to do and be their best. Although the Dalton Catamounts have been able to maintain a winning (more than 50% of all in-district games) record for the past 45 years, their performance had faded recently. In 2005, John was allowed to take the team through the *Why? Character* program, which had *nothing* to do with football and *everything* to do with self-improvement. That same year, the Catamounts got to the state championship quarterfinals for the first time in 4 years. Their slogan for the year: "Teamwork Makes the Dream Work."

John expresses his passion through his work and though a contribution to his community's youth. He literally teaches passion. In his words, "All we have to do is love them (the players) and teach them to love one another. The rest is gravy."

What to Do:

Set goals that align with your passion and pursue them relentlessly. Be ready for the unexpected to happen because it will. When the unexpected does happen, pay attention and learn from the event. Apply your sense of timing in how you respond to the event. The act of moving towards goals helps new opportunities and directions unfold. Don't get overly attached to the fulfillment of goals and don't try and plan your future before embarking on the journey towards your goals. Launch, take off, get moving! Rely on your dead reckoning to help you make mid-course adjustments as time and opportunity require.

FOR SENIOR LEADERS AND COACHES

Find Leaders Who Know When and How to Work Hard

The most obvious evidence of the insight of *Passion and Timing* in others is their work habits. People who are passionate about money or the status that their work affords will work long hours, but they generally can't sustain the pace over the long term. Hard work is driven and sustained by an internal desire to produce results irrespective of immediate gain. Leaders who are passionate about their role in an organization show up every day and give it their best all day regardless of who is watching or what others may think. They work hard because they are driven to, not because they have to, and if they have good temporal intelligence, they don't burn-out or become resentful about the hours they keep.

Hard work should not be measured by how long someone works in a week, or how late they leave work each day. Instead, effective businesses measure hard work by output. With the exception of professional services organizations like law firms, architectural or engineering practices, etc. employees aren't generally compensated by their hourly throughput. Yet virtually every office has at least an informal culture where there are unspoken do's and don'ts about when one leaves at the end of the day and even how long it is acceptable to get a drink at the water cooler.

Leaders who have good timing know when it is important to be present at the office or on the job. Leaders without a sense of timing may be passionate about their work, but they have a tendency to keep their own hours without thinking of the model they represent. Leaders who have *empty office syndrome* (never being in their office or available to employees) may be working 60 hours a week but they are nowhere to be seen during regular work hours.

What to Do:

Employees notice the work hours of their supervisors and leaders. The example you set sends a strong non- verbal message. Learn when and how to work hard. When your employees are working extra hours to complete a project or make a deadline, show up and lend a hand, even if your contribution to the team is minimal. Conversely, when someone is working harder than they need to (usually as a result of not understanding a timing issue of some sort) encourage them to take some time off.

Life and business are defined by the times when we see an opportunity and seize the moment. Look for those defining moments and seize them! Then look for feedback on your decision of when to work hard and how. Learn from your victories and failures and be ready for your fair share of both.

Build Employee Loyalty Through Managers and the Pursuit of Passion

You will get the most out of employees if you have them doing work that matters to them. Accept this as a certainty. The realities of business make building this connection between work and meaning very hard, but remember "work" is not just the task at hand, it's also the environment in which people are working. Pay as much attention to creating an environment physically and culturally that brings out the best in people as you do on tasks that you think will maximize productivity. Building culture is not an overnight process. It needs to happen in concert with building the business. The stronger the business becomes, the more opportunities everyone has to build the culture.

People work for people, not for companies. In your company, who are the managers that touch the most employees and how well developed is their level of passion and sense of timing? The people who supervise the most employees are the highest leverage asset a senior leader has to make a difference in employee loyalty.

What to Do:

Show this group how important and special they are in every intelligent way you can come up with, and tell them you expect them to repay the effort by passing it on to their employees. Don't coddle them; encourage them to fulfill their professional passion through the work they do.

The single hardest transition middle managers have to make is the leap from content expert to people expert. Managers are usually promoted because of their technical skill in a given area. They *are* the best at what they do, so they are promoted to help others learn from their example. The problem with this thinking is that sometimes, the people who are the best at what they do are the best because that's what they like to do. Newly promoted managers need to develop an interest in becoming as expert at supporting and developing employees as they were at their given technical skill. Leadership, *enduring leadership*, is the practice of helping employees find their own brilliance instead of admiring yours. Help those you coach make the transition from being experts to being leaders.

Lead Discussions about Motivation, Purpose, Trends and the Serendipity of Timing

You can have an enormous influence on the people around you by asking them questions that prompt reflection and consideration. You can also help them by paying close attention to what seems to be interesting or exciting to them, and letting them know what you are seeing.

What to Do:

Ask questions like, "You seem to really like this part of your job, Jim, does it have special significance to you?" may help people who have never thought about passion and leadership become more aware of it.

Other great questions to ask to help people find their own passion include:

- What parts of your job really excite you? What type of job in our company would make you really excited?

- What parts of your job do you feel you do better or as well as anyone you know?

- If you could focus on just one thing in your job that you feel really strongly about, what would it be?

- What do you do that adds value to you (versus the organization)?

- How can I help you do more of what you're really good at while making the parts of your job that are less interesting be less unpleasant to perform?

Work to Live or Live to Work?

It is important to remember that not everyone finds passion in the work that they do. Hopefully, most of us find passion somewhere in our lives. Compared to the vast majority of people in the workforce, being passionate about our work qualifies us as exceedingly lucky. Many, many people work so they can pursue their passion in their off time, or they may work at a job they don't enjoy to serve a purpose that has less to do with being passionate about work and more to do with fulfilling a practical financial need. Not everyone at WPC is passionate about their jobs, but they are passionate about doing a good job for the company. They gain satisfaction and purpose by working for a great company and they pursue their personal passions in their time off. Assuming everyone should find the same level of passion for their work as, say, a Tracy Forrest is a mistake.

I was working with a group of textile mill workers in Maine who were unhappy about some recent decisions management had made regarding shifts and work hours of the hourly employees. Management had decided to move most of the mill to what's called a four/ten schedule. Employees work their 40 hours a week in four ten-hour shifts instead of five eight-hour shifts. Their feelings about the event had snowballed and they were now airing out a long laundry list of everything they didn't like about the company. I knew that some of what they were saying about the company was true, but a lot of what they were saying was simply untrue and fueled by their anger and frustration. I finally got fed up with listening to the endless stream of complaints and said, "Look if it's so bad here, why don't you go somewhere else? Go work somewhere where you can feel passionate about the work that you do!" One of the workers looked at me quizzically and said, "Jim, we're mill workers, not social workers. We work to make a living, not because we think that working in a mill is the be-all/end-all. You must have us confused with the muckity mucks up there in the front office. We work for a living."

The mill worker had helped me uncover an unconscious and inaccurate assumption of mine. For some people, *a lot* of people, work is work. For others, work is a source of happiness, identity and purpose. This line of thinking seems obvious, but it isn't. Think about it for a moment: how many people do you know who say they are passionate about the work they do? I'm around a lot of very fulfilled and happy people who love what they do, but most of them would prefer to be doing something else if making a living was not a necessity. As with most things, the degree of satisfaction we have with our jobs is more of a continuum than an either/or proposition. When fate and opportunity align, we find ourselves in jobs we love. At other times, we have to settle for a job that affords us a living so we can pursue our personal passions, and still other times, work may be real drudgery. At still other times, we find ourselves working in a so-so job, but we love who we are working with and the connection we feel to the group we are working with. The point is be conscious of what you've settled for and know the ramifications of the decision on your health, your happiness and your sense of security.

One of the greatest sources of discontent among employees in corporations everywhere is the disconnect between what gives them job satisfaction and what their supervisors think gives them job satisfaction. Supervisors tend to rank things like high wages, job security, internal promotion and good working conditions among the top attributes for employees. Yet employees report that being included in decision making, being acknowledged for good work, and working in a company that accommodates work/life balance concerns are, for example, more important than high wages.

What to Do:

Don't assume you know what kind of work employees would like to be doing if they had a chance. Ask them. People sometimes need help finding or pursuing their dreams, and the most supportive thing you can do for them is to ask them what they want to do and then coach them on how they might be able to get there. Taking a genuine interest in the hopes and dreams of the people you work with lets them know they mean more to you than their work productivity. The mill workers who felt that their jobs were a means to an end responded really well to any change in process that allowed them to fulfill their work obligations more efficiently given their new work schedules. Once I changed my thinking about what was important to them (finishing work and getting home), they became very motivated to help find process improvements that benefited the business and them.

FOR BOTH ASPIRING LEADERS AND SENIOR LEADERS

Become a Time Master

Your passion is much more likely to serve you and the business if you are not in survival mode, so work not to be overwhelmed by too many conflicting demands in your job. The thing that most interferes with a leader's ability to be their best selves at work is time pressure, so work to remove it. Master time. There are lots of courses on how to eliminate the urgent but unimportant from your task list, or how to better organize your daily work habits, or how to set boundaries around your own work load. Determine what your weaknesses are and seek out help in fixing them. One caution: at the root of everyone's time management issues are undermining behaviors or "stinking thinking"—the messages we tell ourselves that keep us stuck doing whatever it is that we do that caused the time crunch in the first place. Simply changing work habits and skills won't reduce your stress level unless you also look at those unconscious, undermining behaviors.

What to Do:

Work on developing your timing, or temporal intelligence. Like all forms of intelligence, we are born with varying levels. We can increase our ability through practice and effort. Temporal intelligence is a skill and you can develop it if you work at it.

Enjoy the "Tension of Opposites" [8]

There is much to be learned when we face conflicting, equally important priorities. In fact, learning to manage these situations productively is one of the marks of an enduring leader. Pay close attention to the tension created between your passion and the necessary restraint you have to exercise in pursuit of your passion. Just because you are passionate about something doesn't mean it is the most important element of your job. Usually, the most important element of your job is producing results; how you do so is a matter of choice. Let your passion influence how to produce results, but make sure your sense of timing is guiding your behaviors and, at times, tempering your enthusiasm.

What to Do:

Be ready for the unexpected. Frequently your sense of timing and intuition about when to pour on your passion is most noticed during times of crisis or uncertainty. Don't focus on "perfect" timing. Focus on intelligent timing; as one senior leader said with regard to timing: "Perfection is a hobby we can't afford." When the right time presents itself, act. When the right time is not obvious, don't act. Listen to your intuition.

Pay Attention to the Side Effects of Your Passion

Your passion will spark excitement in unexpected ways and unexpected places. Assume this statement is true, then go out and prospect for the next generation of passionate leaders in your business. In virtually any job I have held as a leader, there were always two groups of potential leaders around me: those who had the position and authority given to them through their jobs to act like leaders, and those who just acted like leaders.

I have frequently found the best leaders—the ones with the most passion and a good sense of timing—are the ones who are leading every day without incentive or notice. They are just doing what they think needs to be done. When these leaders are given more authority, one of two things happens: they blow up or they bloom. The difference has almost always been determined by my successful or unsuccessful timing in how I brought them into the formal leadership circle of the business. When I rush them, they overstep their authority through lack of experience or their egos get in their way. When I take my time and work with the system, emerging leaders are more likely to blossom. On some rare occasions, leaders who are "leading in the wings" should be left there; that's where they are the most comfortable and the spotlight of formal leadership does not work for them.

What to Do:

How do you know who is who? Ask, watch, observe and encourage. Think like a gardener who is growing feeding and watering a garden in which lies great potential. Take your time and know that everyone comes into their own in their own time. Harvest the fruits of their development (by promoting them, changing their job assignment, or encouraging them to find a new path). Pay attention to those who are hungry and eager to move up, don't let them rot on the vine. Be ready to occasionally pull up a few weeds (typically when someone is miscast for a specific role, it is a management failure as much as it is their failure) and most importantly, tend to the garden every day. If you are a senior leader, one of your most important tasks is the development of the people who work for you. Don't make people development a task you attend to once a year during annual reviews. Make it a daily element of your work.

Passion and Timing

Add Value...

- If at all possible, do work that is important to you, personally—
you're likely to add more value to your job than to a job you only
feel so-so about.
- Work hard unless you're too tired or saving up for something big.
Hard work generates rewards in ways that exceed financial
remuneration such as heightened self-esteem from doing a job well,
pride of work and the feeling of satisfaction that comes from having
given a job your all.
- Manage your time well. It is one of your most precious treasures.

Inspire Others...

- Do the "what if" exercise with yourself and with others to reveal
what keeps you from doing that which you love.
- Go on a quest for your purpose in life. Share what you are learning
with others along the way.
- Catch someone in the act of being brilliant. Tell them you noticed.
- Take more risks. Doing so is good for you, and it helps propel
others to do the same.

Change the World...

- Extend your passion out into the world. Use it to make a positive
impact on others. It is one of your most valuable assets.
- Watch for those serendipitous events in which timing and your
passion line up. When the moment for action presents itself, seize it!
- Find ways to help remove want and suffering from the world.
Nothing spurs desperation like the feeling of having to literally
fight for survival.

SECTION SIX
CONNECTION

THIS SECTION IN BRIEF:

You could have remarkable Perspective. You may have Passion and Timing down cold or you may feel like you are well practiced in the other four insights. Yet without Connection, you won't be nearly as effective. Connection is the attractive influence that makes enduring leaders approachable, accessible and credible with their employees, their customers, and their business partners. It quite literally is what makes a leader "attractive" as a leader, even if they are hard-nosed, demanding and results-oriented. In fact, Connection, it has been proven, is the most important insight a leader needs to have.

Developing Connection involves a combination of looking inward and working outward. Connection involves practicing self-awareness, which helps leaders better understand and control their own behaviors. Practicing Connection also involves learning the discipline of personal mastery, which helps leaders consciously apply their awareness to how they interact with the world. Self-awareness isn't practiced in a vacuum; it requires interacting with the world and noticing what happens inside of us when we do. Once we notice, our personal mastery disciplines help us determine how to change or modify our behaviors so they are tailored to the situation.

Nothing attracts people like genuine openness and inquisitiveness, especially if it is motivated by caring. And caring about people, including ourselves, is at the heart of Connection. To jump to the practices of Connection go to page 277.

PART ONE
GOODNESS KNOWS

There is a reason why people who score higher in social skills, emotional intelligence or self-awareness scales out sell, out lead, out recruit and out perform their counterparts. That reason is *Connection*, a critical insight that represents the ability to work well with people, motivate them and maintain meaningful relationships.

What is remarkable about this insight isn't that it is so unique. It isn't. What is remarkable is that it matters so much. It is the keystone of the collective. While the other insights are vitally important to an enduring leader, they each rely upon *Connection* to get the message through.

To put it another way, the ability to connect is the spark that brings the other insights to life. It guides leaders as they select and mentor new employees. It informs their ability to empower and enable employees to produce their best. It keeps them open and receptive to feedback so they can learn from customers. It helps them be present and able to facilitate the projects and initiatives that help them generate great products and services.

Connection matters and enduring leaders know it. They view it as a vital part of their work and they spend time cultivating it. But for leaders who effectively practice this insight, connecting is not difficult; in fact, they enjoy practicing it. There are two related but distinct practices that help us build connection with others. One focuses on the journey inward towards a deeper level of understanding and acceptance of ourselves.

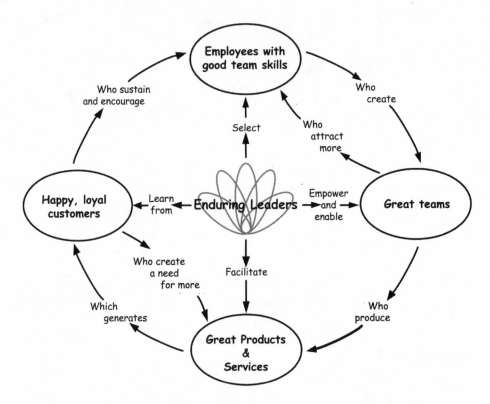

*Connection enables leaders to select, empower and learn from their
employees in a way that benefits everyone, including the organization*

This is the journey of self-awareness. The other focuses on how one handles his interactions with the world. This is the journey of personal mastery. Here are more complete definitions:

SELF-AWARENESS:

> *Self-Awareness is the practice of becoming aware of who we are
> on a number of levels: emotional, physical, and spiritual.*

What does self-awareness have to do with *Connection?* Awareness of one's emotional, physical, and spiritual self allows us to better manage our own emotions, opinions and behaviors. People who are self-aware are substantially more likely to understand their emotions, and emotional understanding is a critical first step for a leader to effectively connect with others.[1] Also, by knowing ourselves better, we become more able to genuinely assess the performance, temperament or needs of those around us. By being more accurate in our interpretations of others, we are more able to connect with them.

PERSONAL MASTERY:

> *Personal Mastery is the discipline of focusing one's energies, talents and interests on the pursuit of personal goals based on a realistic view of the world. Essential to personal mastery is keeping long and short-term goals in sight, controlling impulses, wellness, and having the ability to keep track of our plans and priorities.*

Being more self-aware is a great start, but personal mastery is what helps us decide what to do with our awareness. People who practice personal mastery have more control over their emotions, since this discipline gives them choices in how they respond to emotionally charged events. People with a high degree of personal mastery also tend to tell themselves the truth about the world and their role in it. The capacity to responsibly handle their emotions coupled with an ability to maintain a realistic world view makes it much easier for them to build *Connection* with people.

YOU CAN SUBCONTRACT THE MESSAGE, BUT NOT THE HEART

Sometimes events occur that just plain tick us off, and we are justified in our anger or indignation. Still, how we deal with our feelings is critical to our success. Tracy Forrest, the CEO of Winter Park Construction we heard about in Section Five, has built a successful construction company in one of the most litigious and hostile contractor markets in the country by knowing when to curb his temper, when to temper his message and by building great relationships with clients and employees.

Tracy understands and believes that business is all about people: motivating them, building relationships with them, developing trust and demonstrating loyalty. Although Tracy would identify himself as an introvert, people see him as generous, caring and friendly. They would also characterize him as tough, demanding, impatient, perfectionist, blunt and sometimes even rude. To Tracy's credit, he knows he can be perceived in all of these ways and he is neither defensive nor apologetic about it.

During some of WPC's most tumultuous growth years, Tracy had to make some very tough management changes and deal with a number of employee performance issues that required him to make difficult, sometimes unpopular decisions. He poked fun at himself by getting an "Attila the Hun" license plate and he passed out copies of Wess Robert's *Leadership Secrets of Attila the Hun* to reassure everyone that he was aware how tough he had been. When things began to settle down again, Tracy worked to restore any hurt feelings and to once again focus on relationships with and between employees. As WPC continued to grow, Tracy began to share more and more of the limelight with his senior team. He hired a copywriter to help improve the quality and readability of the written messages the company put out to clients and employees, including the company newsletter, appropriately titled *Building Blocks: Work-Play-Community*. To help improve relationships between everyone in the company Tracy engaged consultants and trainers to improve the company's teambuilding, conflict resolution and negotiating skills and he started running semi-annual Town Hall Meetings to increase connections throughout the company. Tracy intentionally became less and less visible as the face of the company delegating that job to his brother Jeff and the rest of the senior team.

I once asked him what he had most learned in the years following the "Attila the Hun" phase. "Perception is reality," he answered. "I was doing what needed to be done in the only way I knew how. I was worried about doing what was right for everyone in the company, but I knew some people didn't understand. Their perception was that I was a mean, hardnosed SOB and I couldn't argue with them. I always *knew* that our people were what make us special, but it has taken me time to learn to be warm and fuzzy. There are times when I still feel like him (Attila the Hun), but I keep that to myself. Perception is reality. Making decisions in business based on emotion doesn't work. I've learned to keep my mouth shut when I'm angry—usually—and I need to model that for everyone. Communicating better doesn't mean yelling louder when someone doesn't get it. As much as I wished that worked, it doesn't."

In spite of his diminished visibility, Tracy remained heavily involved in the behind the scenes decision making when it came to developing relationships. Tracy once reminded the senior team when they were talking about communicating an important change in the company, "We can subcontract for what we write, but not for what we do; we all need to be involved in sending the message that we care."

Like the enduring leader he is, Tracy does a lot more than just talk about caring for people. He models it in a way that fits his natural style. Never one to be overly effusive or visibly emotional, Tracy takes time to consider how he connects with people, and he does so very effectively. At WPC it is pretty common for an employee to get a book or audio tape having nothing to do with work in their "In" basket with a note that says, "Thought you might enjoy this…T." He takes the time to read every company newsletter and when an article appears from a staff member who isn't a regular contributor, he often sends them an email thanking them for contributing to it. In this day and age, most offices have an "Open Door" policy to the top executives in the business—WPC is no different. And like most offices, younger or more junior employees are often intimidated by Tracy and would prefer to avoid having to meet directly with him. When someone *does* step into his office to ask him a question or chat for a minute, Tracy makes a point to say "thanks for stopping by!" particularly if he senses that doing so was a stretch for them.

Tracy is not alone. Each leader selected for inclusion in this book has their own unique way of bringing this insight to life in their work. In *Part Two: This Insight in Action*, we will look at how each of them applies and practices building connections.

We will take another look at Karl-Henrik Robèrt, the Swedish pediatric oncologist who founded a non-profit organization dedicated to the dissemination and practice of the principles of sustainability called The Natural Step. Karl-Henrik's ability to build consensus around contentious environmental issues provides an excellent example of a leader who knows how to see and influence systems. Karl-Henrik's contribution to this section will be in his ability to acknowledge diverse opinions—even when those opinions are diametrically opposed to his own. I learned a lot about having difficult conversations with people from Karl-Henrik—I hope you will too.

Doug Harper, the Director of Operations of World's Finest Chocolate Company LTD, helped transform the operational element of his organization because of his skill as a systems leader. Doug has successfully learned to not let his self-doubt or lack of confidence interfere with his ability to support and lead others—and we will learn how he builds solid relationships in spite of his self-doubt.

Leaders who are self-aware and relate well to others are able to notice when their egos get hooked. They detach from the situation in a way that allows them to maintain objectivity and do what is best for the situation. Karen Garcia, a bureau chief at New Mexico's Mine Reclamation Bureau, is an example of a leader who is both comfortable and effective in leading through complexity and change, and one of the most visible applications of her use of this insight is her ability to separate the personal from the professional without becoming impersonal or unapproachable.

Jon Mark Howard, the President of Outward Bound Discovery, a national non-profit education program that builds confidence and capability in adjudicated and at-risk youth, provided us with an example of a leader who has the confidence to make a difference. Jon uses his humility and fearless self-examination as an important tool to guide his decision making and leadership of one of the U.S.'s largest, most renowned educational programs.

John McIntosh, CEO of NOOD Fashion, finds purpose and meaning through his job and as a volunteer coach and mentor for his home town high school football team. Whether it's selling carpet or developing character in high school athletes, John sees his *real* work as making a difference in the lives of the people in his sphere of influence. John's personal mastery habits help recharge his batteries so he can give to others.

Doug Acksel, the biotech company Director of Operations, engages and encourages people because of his unflagging confidence in them and his constant desire for self-improvement. We will examine his ability to use his connection to others as an essential tool in his work as a coach, mentor and leader.

THE ISSUE OF GOODNESS

Before we dive into how each of these leaders brings their personal practice of connecting with others to life, I feel compelled to cover the issue of character and integrity.

Imbedded in this insight is the belief that a leader cannot sustain connections with people without having character, a desire to somehow improve the lot of the world and/or humanity. Yet, you may ask, isn't it possible that many of the world's most successful leaders have embodied all of the five insights *and* ill intentions?

Take Kenneth Lay from Enron. You have to give him credit. Someone who gets a doctorate in economics, works as a federal energy regulator and becomes the undersecretary for the Department of the Interior knows a thing or two about connecting with people. Mr. Lay robbed a lot of people of their dreams, leveraging money that belonged to the employees, not him, to increase his personal wealth. Once Enron folded, we discovered that he had socked away four million dollars of employee and shareholder money two years before the company declared Chapter 11. Before he passed away in mid-2006, Mr. Lay and his wife were on track to receive $43,023 and $32,643, a month, respectively, for life!

More subtle still, there is the distinguished career of Philip A. Cooney. Cooney served as the chief of staff for the White House Council on Environmental Quality after having previously served as a lobbyist at the American Petroleum Institute. According to a report released by the New York Times, it appears that Mr. Cooney routinely doctored the language of reports on global warming submitted by government-sponsored scientists on climate research to soften their message and increase the level of doubt about their findings.[2] The original reports indicated that it's getting warmer, faster and faster and the source of the acceleration is, beyond doubt, an increase in atmospheric greenhouse gases produced by humans. Mr. Cooney gets credit for his ability to develop and maintain important connections with people. In spite of having a background in economics, not science, he landed one of the most prestigious and influential environmental positions in the nation editing scientific reports. Empowered to make an impact for the betterment of all mankind, Mr. Cooney chose his short term career interests over the greater good. His connection skills were so good that in the fall of 2005 he took a job with one of the companies that has influence over how much greenhouse gas we release into the environment, Exxon Mobil Corporation.[3]

Doesn't goodness count for something? Isn't there a reckoning for people who abuse their positions at the expense of others or of mankind?

The answer is "yes." Leaders who know how to fake a sincere interest in people may have a good opening act. They may even have a good enough act to withstand scrutiny for years, but their lack of interest in the human condition, their lack of empathy, eventually catches up with them.

Connecting with people and goodness, I believe, go hand-in-hand. The companies whose competencies I used for the research that was the foundation of this book all referred to integrity, honor, honesty and trustworthiness in their competency models. These attributes arise from the inside out, not the outside in, and the way they are developed begins with understanding one's self.

Without a doubt, the most dangerous leaders at work today are the ones who know just enough about connecting with people to have the appearance of having character, or integrity, or honor. They know how to maintain a facade of caring and support for their organizations and employees even when their primary interest is the aggregation of their own wealth and power. "Our job," a CEO once boasted to me, "is to pay everyone as little as possible, keep them as happy as possible and pray they never discover what a raw deal they are getting." They are so adept at the game of earnings re-statement and subterfuge that groups like the Securities and Exchange Commission and the Better Business Bureau cannot trace their trails. But again, their shelf life is limited. Either they get caught, they transform, or they get out of business before they get caught.

Coercion, brainwashing, extortion, emotional abuse and leveraging fear are not relational skills—they are manipulation skills. One does not have to be a manipulator of people's minds in order to be a successful leader. Capitalizing on fear and anxiety may require exceptional intuition about human behavior, but being able to do so does not make someone a leader. With only a few notable exceptions, leaders who have used their power for personal gain or who simply don't give a shit about people go down, and they go down hard.

"Goodness" is a desire to be successful within the rules and norms of society, not at the expense of that society. Goodness is charity and karma; the belief that making a positive impact on the world is worth doing even if the payoff is not obvious or apparent. Enduring leadership is a generative—versus subversive—process. Enduring leaders create results that exceed their individual skills or efforts. They generate the best thinking and actions of the people around them.

In the 18th Century, Christian theologian John Wesley said "Do all the good you can, in all the ways you can, to all the souls you can, in every place you can, at all the times you can, with all the zeal you can, as long as ever you can." For the human experiment to succeed, I believe this is the work that will be required of enduring leaders.

Bill George, the former CEO of Medtronic Corporation, in his book *Authentic Leadership – Rediscovering the Secrets to Creating Lasting Value* suggests that just throwing corporate scoundrels in jail isn't the answer. "We don't need new laws. *We need new leadership* to get us out of the current corporate crisis because you can't legislate integrity." George's example as the CEO of Medtronic is potent. Medtronic is the world's leading medical technology company; they make everything from pacemakers to dialysis machines. Under his leadership the company grew its market capitalization from $1.1 to $60 billion dollars, averaging 35% annual growth, and earned Fortune Magazine's endorsement as the #1 company for long term shareholder value. All the while, Medtronic has been rated as one of the 100 best companies to work for. George's claim is simple: companies that will dominate markets in the 21st Century will be those that have leaders who embrace purpose, values, self-discipline, heart and relationships.[4]

CEO's and leaders in corporations around the world face more pressure than ever to deliver shareholder value, and the temptation to do so in less than ethical ways is greater than ever. Yet, a growing number of leaders are choosing the road less traveled and are putting George's values ahead of practices that compromise values and relationships. The best legacy we can leave is one that comes from making a difference for the better in the lives of those we touch. Look around: we humans are capable of both unspeakable meanness and remarkable kindness. I choose to believe most of us are good by nature, that our true colors are the colors of goodness.

CONNECTED COMPETENCIES

It is remarkable that less that 10% of the competency inventories used in the research for this book had language even coming close to resembling "is self-aware," but over 70% listed language that referred to "relates well to others" or "controls emotions" or "manages emotional situations objectively." As I've discussed and will continue to emphasize, at the root of being able to manage or control these types of situations is self-awareness. In a study of 130 executives, for example, researchers from Walter V. Clark and Associates discovered that how well they handled their emotions directly correlated to how much people preferred to be around them.[5] Self-awareness is the precursor to Connection; the more we understand ourselves, the more able we are to control both our reactions and our assessment of the behavior of others, which in turn increases our ability to effectively connect. The list of competencies accumulated from clients includes:

- Holds self and others accountable
- Builds trustworthiness (or is trustworthy)
- Coaches and develops others
- Sees and promotes talents in self and others
- Understands own weaknesses and works/delegates around them
- Embraces diversity
- Makes decisions that are in the best interest of the business
- Demonstrates credibility and integrity
- Builds consensus when needed
- Develops people networks
- Confronts and works through conflict

Each of these competencies could easily be attached to one of the other insights, but at their core they are about *Connection.* To learn why, read on.

- ***Holds self and others accountable:*** The theme of accountability showed up again and again in the competency research, yet it is apparent that there are several slightly different definitions for the term. For the sake of clarification, the definition for accountability I will use is as follows: "The ability to accurately and honestly account for the results one is achieving." Accountability begins with self-awareness and is sustained through a willingness to constantly seek ways to improve, which is, of course, a skill of personal mastery. Accountability is achieved through personal mastery.

- ***Builds trustworthiness (or is trustworthy):*** "Trustworthiness" as a behavior is subjective and complex. One person may find a leader trustworthy while someone else may feel that same leader is not worthy of trust at all. And what, precisely, someone can be trusted for varies. If someone is steady as a rock and unflappable in the face of great change, are they more trustworthy than someone who has great passion for their job who shows up to work before everyone else and leaves after everyone has left? Ultimately, trustworthiness is more about a feeling than an action, and leaders who relate well with others and are self-aware are more likely to build that kind of trusting feeling.

•   *Sees and promotes talents in self and others:* Spotting the talents and coaching the skills in others begins with being able to objectively evaluate them. To refer back to the story about Michelangelo's David, coaching begins with removing our own "stuff" and understanding the effect that our mental models, biases and schemata play in our interactions with others. Evidence of the importance of self-awareness in coaching is found in the plethora of coaching certification and training programs for coaches and leaders. All them begin with understanding one's self in relation to the coaching offered to others—for good reason.

•   *Coaches and develops others*: Effective coaches don't have to be experts at achieving the goals their clients are working on, but they do need to be able to separate their problems from their clients' problems. For example, because you are unable to get along with everyone, are you unable to coach someone through a difficult relationship issue? No. The difference is more subtle. If you are adept at seeing your own relationship faults and working through them, you may be able to help your clients work through theirs. If, on the other hand, you continually see your relationship issues as someone else's problem, you are unlikely to be of much service to someone else as they try and work through a similar situation.

•   *Embraces diversity:* "Diversity" is listed by many companies in their desired skill set for leaders, including most of the companies whose leadership competency models were studied for this book. But what exactly does "diversity" mean in this context? In my experience, what companies actually desire are leaders who "embrace diversity." And to truly embrace diversity the leader must be willing to accept the possibility that their own biases and preconceptions about race, religion, lifestyle choice, rank and status, privilege, etc. may influence their decision making or the ways they interact with others. They have a desire to be inclusive in their thinking and interactions with people and they understand that difference is a strength, not a weakness. Leaders who embrace diversity are willing to look at their own biases and attempt to suspend them when dealing with people.[6]

• *Confronts and works through conflict:* Leaders who are reasonably self-aware are more comfortable with conflict than those who are not. They see conflict as a means towards an end, and since their ultimate interest is heightened awareness, they are more comfortable with going through conflict to get there.

FROM INTUITION TO INTENTION

Of all of the insights of enduring leaders, self-awareness has been the subject of the most research, writing and leadership training recently. Its popularity is not a fad or passing trend, but an encouraging reflection of the changing values of our society and the pressures on all of us to find connection in an increasingly global, disconnected world. Evidence of the popularity of the trend is the explosion of books, training programs, workshops and seminars on the subject of self-awareness, conducting difficult conversations, negotiation, personal mastery and self-improvement.

Self-awareness, the practice of learning about our selves for the purpose of self-improvement and self-discovery, like personal mastery, is a journey, not a destination. It is a practice that of late has taken on many new forms: from taking any one of hundreds of instruments, profiles or assessments that highlight one element or another of our personalities, social styles, brain dominance, work styles, and so on to meditation, yoga, a rigorous spiritual practice, peer groups, coaching circles and self-awareness training. The aim of practicing self-awareness is to move our ability to read interpersonal situations from our intuitive senses where our unconscious makes most of the decisions, to an intentional action where we have the option to consciously make a decision about how to respond. By converting more of our decision making to a higher level of consciousness, we are more able to control how we manage people and events, which of course enables us to improve our personal mastery.

In the last part of this section, The Practice, we will do a survey of the tools and practices that help us increase our self-awareness, but I won't recommend one over another. Internet service providers don't care which browser people use; they care that people are attracted to the web. Likewise, I am not interested in recommending a particular school of thought or approach that you should use to increase self-awareness or your connectedness with people; I'm just glad the trend exists! I am hopeful that it will yield benefits for everyone, everywhere. What I can recommend is this:

• Anyone who tells you "self-awareness" is something that can be mastered in anything shorter than a lifetime is full of beans.

• You can't practice self-awareness in a vacuum. You need to be interacting with people and it is helpful to work with someone who is also working on the same insight to compare notes with.

• Having a background in psychology doesn't make you any more likely to develop self-awareness or personal mastery than having a degree in finance.

• However we chase them, whatever tool, technique, habit or assessment we use, the pursuit of self-awareness and personal mastery is how we find goodness in ourselves, in others, and in the world.

TWO
THIS INSIGHT IN ACTION

WHY CONNECTION MATTERS

Inside every successful organization is a group of people who know how to work well together. And inside of many of them is an awareness of what they need to do—and not do—to make that team successful. Such is the value of knowing how to connect for an organization. Having this insight unleashes a cascade of wonderful events: being able to work effectively with others helps improve the functioning of the people and teams who are responsible for providing the products and services to customers, which impacts the success of their organizations.

As the keystone insight, *Connection* comes to life through the other insights, not instead of them. Leaders who have the insight of *Perspective*, for example, are able to see and influence systems, which allows them to lead change at a systemic level. The insight of *Connection* helps them to build support and generate influence. The insight of *Courage through Service* is exemplified by leaders who have the confidence to make a difference, but their *ability* to make a difference relies heavily on their ability to develop connections with employees.

MOVING FROM KNOWING TO UNDERSTANDING

> *"I hear, I know. I see, I remember. I do, I understand."*
> *- Confucius, 551-479 BC*

Before becoming effective in the practice of this insight, leaders have to make a leap of sorts in their perspective on what "connecting" means, and they certainly have to change their viewpoints on what self-awareness is. We tend to think of *knowing* as a linear process with a clear beginning, middle and end, as if the goal is to learn and eventually *know* the practices of connecting with people and self-awareness.

We are raised in a paradigm that learning creates knowing, and knowing is all we need. Further, we are brought up to believe that, by knowing enough of something, we become expert at it and that being an expert in something is a good thing. The problem with this line of thinking is that once we *know* something, we become closed off to learning about it because after all, we *know* all about it, what do we have to learn? In truth, we spend our whole lives learning—school just teaches us is *how* to learn. Beyond learning and knowing there is a deeper, more fulfilling level of growth that Confucius called *understanding*, and it occurs through experience.

Understanding is accepting the possibility that we don't *know* much at all, and the more we *understand*, the less we truly *know*. *Understanding* is a cyclic process without a clear beginning or end. The more we understand how the world works, the less we know about how it works. The more we understand about the magic of relationships and people, the less we know about how human interactions actually work. The trade off is that as we *understand* more, our view of the world expands, which opens up new levels of learning. Since understanding comes with experience, we have to accrue a lot of experiences before we make the leap. Making it isn't easy or particularly pleasant.

Tracy Forrest, CEO of Winter Park Construction:

> *There is a down side to understanding myself. Sometimes I don't like everything I see. Sometimes the person I am most afraid of is myself. I have failed before, I have many faults which I have to be aware of, but not overly focus on, sometimes our faults can be depressing, we and others remember our mistakes and faults, the successes are sometimes soon forgotten. I have to balance my self-awareness and know I have met the enemy and it is me.*

When we move from *knowing* to *understanding* we see our own naked frailty and imperfections which, oddly enough, can be quite liberating. Connecting with people begins by letting go of knowing and embracing understanding. When we *understand*, we become aware that life is complex and mysterious and that not knowing helps us more than it hurts us because it keeps us curious and interested in each other. We accept the reality that life and growth is a journey with no end and that the biggest mystery of all is ourselves. The leap from knowing to understanding is liberating for several reasons:

- Once we accept our frailties and imperfections, we can take the energy that we spent maintaining the image of who we think we were supposed to be and redirect it towards more genuine, fulfilling pursuits like discovering what really brings us joy and passion.

- We become a lot more interested in the questions that need to be asked to understand the world than we are in the answers, which in turn make us far more inquisitive about the world and less judgmental about everyone else.

- If we're really lucky, we learn to let ourselves off the hook. We stop looking at what we have done in life as a matter of right or wrong and accept that, however badly we fouled things up life goes on and punishing ourselves for what we've done indefinitely doesn't have any value. We forgive ourselves.

- And finally, by going through all of these realizations, we have greater capacity and energy for the things that matter most in life: friendship, love and meaning.

There is research that indicates *understanding* involves a lot more than just our brains.[7] Dr. Candace Pert is a well known neurobiologist, lecturer, researcher and author on the subject of the origins of human emotion. She believes our emotions are a bio-molecular process generated by our whole bodies, not just our brains. In other words, according to Dr. Pert, our mind is not our brain. Our brain—the gray matter inside our skulls—is part of a bigger process that collectively forms our *mind*. If Dr. Pert is right, and a lot of people in her field think she is, then we could say that *knowing* happens in our brains and *understanding* and emotion takes place on a molecular level throughout our bodies. As she puts it: "Body and mind are simultaneous. I like to speculate that the mind is the flow of information as it moves among the cells, organs, and systems of the body."[8]

It would make sense that *understanding* ourselves involves a lot more than just how our brains work, given the difficulty of the task and how our bodies react to some information and stimuli. Dr. Pert's theories are provocative in traditional western medicine, but the mind/body connection has long been an accepted truth in many other parts of the world going back thousands of years. What has been accepted in western medicine is the idea that for our *minds* to work well, our bodies have to work well, also.

FEARLESS SELF-EXAMINATION

Leaders who practice this insight have less to hide or protect than those who don't. They accept their imperfections and *humanness*, so having someone else critique their actions is not as painful or scary as those who are trying to hide those parts of themselves that they don't like. As the president of Outward Bound Discovery, Jon Howard gets to use his lack of *knowing* and his ability to seek understanding frequently, especially when the heat is on and when things aren't going well. When he faced a staffing crisis, his willingness to expand his understanding of both himself and the problem generated connections with staff who needed it, and a heightened level of personal understanding for him.

Finding and training instructors to work in Outward Bound was a piece of cake in the 60's, 70's and early 80's. Thanks to the growing interest in attending wilderness schools and outdoor leadership programs, outdoor skills and outdoor leadership was shifting from something people could practice on weekends to a legitimate profession. If someone were so inclined, they could make a living guiding people and groups on expeditions and wilderness river trips. Someone with average physical ability, a desire for adventure and reasonably good people skills could teach rock climbing or outdoor team-building, or work with adjudicated youth using the outdoors as a classroom like Outward Bound did. When the outdoor education boom began, there were more interested instructors than there were students, so programs like Outward Bound had their pick of qualified instructor candidates.

As the industry matured, the demand for instructors increased faster than the qualified applicant pool. International adventure travel programs gobbled up instructors as the adventure travel industry boomed. The commercial rafting industry became a major force for tourism and income in states with whitewater rivers. Climbing gyms sprung up around the country as alternatives to traditional weight lifting or conditioning programs. Outdoor education moved from a specialized recreational option for a few to a mainstream activity for the masses. While many of the more seasoned instructors gravitated to sexier, more lucrative jobs that allowed them to travel to exotic locations with highly motivated, educated clients, there was a bigger need than ever for instructors who were willing to work with teenage felons, kids on probation and "at risk" youth for close to minimum wage. No program has felt and seen this shift more dramatically than Outward Bound, and specifically, Outward Bound Discovery. Jon Howard and his staff found themselves having to cancel courses due to insufficient staffing. Morale was sagging. Funding was in jeopardy as a result of cancelled courses and some of the most experienced, senior staff started to leave out of sheer frustration and exhaustion.

Part of Jon's response was not to find fault with the situation, but to carefully and courageously examine his own leadership ability. "While I know that I didn't cause the situation, I have to ask myself —am I the right person to be leading us?" He solicited the help and feedback of trusted advisors and colleagues who were willing to look at what he could do differently as a leader given the staffing setback. Self-awareness and his *understanding* of himself allowed him to ask the really hard questions: "What do I not see about myself that may be contributing to the crisis?"

There is a great saying about not being able to see things about ourselves: "We're not sure who discovered water, but we're pretty sure it wasn't fish."[9] Leaders who have this insight build connections with others, but first, they examine who they are, where the blind spots are in their self-perception, and what they can do to increase their understanding of themselves. Jon's fearless examination of himself and the situation eventually helped him correct it, not because he was at fault, but because of the confidence and trust his approach built in those around him. Jon's request for help ended up engaging the smartest management minds in his circle to help address Discovery's staff recruiting crisis.[10] One way he continually refines his ability to act as a great servant leader is his willingness to invite critique and feedback from others, even when doing so may reveal an area of weakness or a need for self-improvement.

NOT "IF" BUT "HOW"

Leaders who connect well with others don't question whether their behaviors are affecting the people around them, they assume their behaviors are affecting others. The more they understand themselves, the more they can regulate their emotions and their interactions in a way that promotes relationships. Doug Acksel, the director of operations at a global biotech company calls himself a perfectionist. No matter how successful a project or task is, Doug can always see a way that it could have been done better. In his words, "I am known for over analyzing things. While most people go: 'ready-aim-fire,' I tend to be: 'ready-aim-aim-aim-fire.' Sometimes [that approach] works well, but sometimes it doesn't. I know I can drive people crazy or de-motivate them, so I have to be careful." He goes on: "My tendency for perfectionism could get in the way if I wasn't aware of it. I tell others I am a perfectionist and ask people to let me know when it gets in the way."

Imagine what a person like Doug would be like if he was completely unaware that he was a perfectionist? You probably don't have to imagine; you probably know one. If Doug or any one of us doesn't know how we are behaving, we don't have much of a choice about how we want to behave. Instead we just act out, and doing so drives the people around us crazy. Doug's self-awareness gives him a choice, and when he (or any of us) has a choice, we tend to make better long term decisions.

Doug also directs that same quest for perfection on himself as he strives to be a better person, leader and coach. "I look at my interactions with people and ask myself 'What is the impact I am having on others?' This has really changed my approach to people and life in general." Doug applies an important practice of this insight: he doesn't question if his behavior is having an impact on others, but *how*. "If you're aware of your weaknesses, and you look at the issue at hand as an opportunity to work in a coaching or a backup role," says Doug, "by doing this you're able to develop your organization. When I know my own weaknesses, I'm able to learn from the people who work for me."

Being aware that it is always possible to impact others with our behaviors is a great step in developing more productive and trusting relationships. Finding that awareness, those parts of our personalities that may drive others crazy, is a great first step in developing this understanding.

WHOSE JOB IS THIS, ANYWAY?

In both of the examples above, Jon Howard and Doug Acksel use their self-awareness to be fully accountable for how they lead, work and relate with others. Being personally accountable is an essential trait of an enduring leader, and it is an important aspect of both *Connection* and the insight of *Passion and Timing*. But accountability has its limits. It is just as important for a leader who has this insight to be able to separate what they can be accountable for, from what they can't be accountable for. When we take action to solve a problem that isn't ours, we tend to create interpersonal problems with the person we are trying to help. Learning to separate what we are responsible for from what everyone else is responsible for, or the ability to set boundaries, is a key element of this insight. Without the ability to set boundaries, it is impossible to generate healthy, productive connections. Karen Garcia, the bureau chief at New Mexico's Mine Reclamation Bureau, is a master at the insight of *Faith and Agility*. Karen routinely has to balance the priorities and perspectives of the mine operators, legislators, other regulatory agencies and environmental groups when she and her team work to enforce the regulations they are paid to uphold. Karen succeeds by using her intimate knowledge of the regulations to determine when to hold her ground and when to be flexible. Karen has to have solid boundaries about what her job is, exactly, and what it is not.

Being able to stand her ground when she disagrees with people or groups isn't Karen's only gift with regard to this insight; her other gift is her ability to not be aloof, or arrogant, or dismissive or impersonal in the face of heated debate and criticism. She takes responsibility for her side of the equation by being intimately familiar with the mandates her bureau operates under and not taking disagreement or criticism personally.

Maintaining healthy boundaries—knowing when to get involved and when not to; when to take responsibility and when to refuse to; when to push for more information and when not to; when to look deeper and when to look the other way is a critical skill for leaders who have this insight. It is easier to understand what healthy boundaries look like by defining what *un-*healthy ones look like. In my experience, people who don't have very good boundaries in work or life tend to:

- Exhibit symptoms of being overwhelmed or over worked because they cannot set a boundary around what they will and will not do;

- Share inappropriate things about themselves with colleagues or employees;

- Personalize criticism, or do the opposite—act as if criticism doesn't matter;

- Attempt to recruit co-workers into their points of view about issues at work when those co-workers are involved in the issue as well and need to have their own opinion;

- Become involved in things that do not concern them;

- Adopt other people's issues, problems or personal affairs as their own and lose their ability to maintain objectivity about them.

Maintaining good boundaries does not prohibit developing good connections with people; boundaries enable connection—healthy connection. To most of the people with whom she works, Karen Garcia is seen as approachable, friendly, professional, affable and compassionate—even when she is arguing a point or stating an opinion that is diametrically opposed to someone else's. Her ability to set and maintain healthy boundaries helps preserve her own sanity and her relationships with others. In Karen's words: "Knowing when my buttons are being pushed lets me know when I need to step back and take a deep breath before charging forward and making a mistake." Stepping back when we're angry is a great example of setting an appropriate boundary for ourselves and in this example, Karen reveals a piece of her own personal mastery practice. But sometimes when our "buttons are being pushed" it has to do with another skill associated with this insight: understanding *Projection*.

A HOLY, BLESSED OPPORTUNITY

Leaders who have this insight gain another important benefit from their on-going practice of self-awareness and personal mastery. They learn new ways of dealing with feeling frustrated, defensive, afraid or just plain angry when those feelings come up. When they are triggered or emotionally hooked, they have learned to view being hooked as a personal growth opportunity instead of as an opportunity to place blame on others. One of the most cunning impediments to our ability to see people and events as they really are is a phenomenon first labeled by the often quoted, sometimes satirized but frequently accurate Dr. Sigmund Freud. The phenomenon is called projection.

To understand projection you need to do a short reflective exercise:

Resist the urge to read ahead from now through the end of the exercise. You will learn more if you only read the questions when it is time to answer them. After all, the whole point of this exercise is for you to learn something new about yourself, so don't short change the process.

> Take out a piece of paper, it will probably be better if you don't write down the answers to my questions in this book so you can be completely honest with no concern for who else might read this page. Proceed to the next step.

> Think of a person you feel uncomfortable around. Someone you don't like and who you are pretty sure doesn't like you. Write down their name or better yet, draw a little picture of them in the middle of the page. Proceed to the next step.

> What don't you like about them? Write down the terms and adjectives that describe why you don't like them, then proceed to the next step.

> What do you assume they don't like about you? Jot down your assumptions. Once you're finished, go to the next step.

When you think about this person, what feelings come to mind for you? Again, jot down your answers. Take your time answering this question, it takes some of us longer to access feelings than thoughts, now proceed to the next step.

Now that you have a written list of assumptions, thoughts and feelings in front of you, take a look at what you've written. Search your feelings and make one more attempt to write down what comes up for you as you look at what you've written about them. Don't worry if what you've written sounds judgmental, or harsh, or unfair, just let 'er rip!

By now, you should have a fairly complete list. Take one more look at the list. Is there anything missing?

Here's the kicker….
Whatever you wrote down may be about the person you were writing about, but the list is definitely about you.

Want proof?

How many of the adjectives or descriptors that you wrote down are things you really dislike about yourself? Be honest. This is a personal mastery exercise…there is nothing "wrong" with you if you have to admit to flaws about yourself. The only thing that could be considered wrong is thinking that being wrong is, well, wrong.

Of the words you wrote down, how many of them describe things you work hard to not do in your interactions with people?

How many of the words you wrote to describe feelings are feelings you sometimes have about yourself?

Everyone has his or her own version of what is true. "Truth," in this respect, is different than what is commonly known as objective reality, which may or may not exist depending on whom you ask. As far as I'm concerned, the "truth" is whatever we tell ourselves to be true. Unless you have asked the subject of the exercise directly, specifically and clearly about what you believe to be true about them, it is unlikely you know much about what the "truth" is for them. Since you don't really know what is true for them, it is a fair assumption that what you wrote down are those things that you assume the worst about in them, and in you. When we do this exercise in the real world, we tend to assume that what we believe is true, even though we have not checked it out or compared it to actual reality.

> "I refuse to be intimidated by reality anymore. After all, what is reality anyway? Nothin' but a collective hunch. I made some studies: Reality is the leading cause of stress among those in touch with it."
>
> -Trudy the Bag Lady (originally played by Lily Tomlin) in Jane Wagner's
> *The Search for Signs of Intelligent Life in the Universe*

A Wise Quote

When we do this, we are projecting. Projecting allows us to displace those things we don't like about ourselves onto someone else. According to Freud, projection is an unconscious strategy to let ourselves off the hook; we focus on other's negative behavior so we don't have to look at that behavior in ourselves. Projections are denials, denials of what we don't like about ourselves so we don't have to face them or change them. By projecting, we are able to protect our egos; we don't have to look at ourselves and our flaws, we can remain angry at and distrustful of whomever we have decided to project upon.

Nothing interferes with seeing things as they really are like our ability to project our issues onto someone else. Nothing.

If you've followed this line of reasoning this far, you can follow it a bit further:

Everything we think, feel, see or observe is a projection. Everything.

We manage to stay out of hospitals for the mentally ill by not always reacting to our projections. Instinctually, we know that not everything we think is real. We either check out our projections somehow against reality or we refrain from stating what we're feeling. What makes projection cunning is that when we most need to notice that we are projecting is when we are least likely to do so, that is, when our emotions are making decisions without our awareness. Our best decision making occurs when we are aware of how we are thinking and feeling instead of when we are unaware.

When we feel frustrated or triggered by someone, we need to first check out what we are projecting before proceeding. Taking this step—checking out reality—is a practice of personal mastery. Being *able* to take this step is the result of being self-aware.

By challenging our projections, we learn more about ourselves. By not always reacting to what we believe to be true but instead checking out what we are seeing, feeling and thinking, we can learn a lot more about the people on whom we project. By learning about what is real for others, we get a more complete picture of the world as they see it and we increase our ability to connect with them.

Projection is only a problem when we're not aware of it. If we are able to notice when and onto whom we are projecting, understanding our projection is a gift to our self-awareness. My business partner, Betsey Upchurch, notices what she projects onto others as fast as anyone I have ever met. When she becomes aware of her projection, especially if she finds herself becoming irritated or angry, she has a phrase, a code really, that she says to let me know she is in the middle of dealing with someone who is pulling up her projections. She paraphrases part of an ancient Buddhist prayer and says, "Oh Holy, Blessed Opportunity!" The phrase always elicits a chuckle from me, but the point is very serious; it means Betsey has taken a situation she was emotionally hooked by and neutralized it. For example, Betsey remembers having her feelings hurt when she was called an *idiot* as a child. Now, whenever she hears someone say "that's idiotic" or, more directly, "you're an idiot," Betsey has yet another holy blessed learning opportunity. Once she has this awareness (that being called an idiot is a painful memory for her), the way she deals with the person who unwittingly pulled up her projection changes. Instead of reacting to what she is projecting about what the person is saying, she suddenly has options. She can examine what she is *projecting* or, if this would be inappropriate in the moment, she at least is much more able to interact with the person from a place of *understanding* instead of *knowing*. She becomes open, not defensive. She becomes curious instead of needing to express her opinion, and by doing so, the conversation, and Betsey's experience of the interaction, improves.

Managing projection is a personal mastery skill of the highest order. I have seen each of the enduring leaders of this book weed their way through situations in which their projections were pulled up as their buttons were pushed. Each of them has their own unique way of distancing themselves from their pre-conditioned, projection-laden responses to the situation so they can bring their more objective selves to bear on the problem. The methods they use to regain objectivity are important, but even more important is their ability to notice that they are projecting.

BEATING "THE COMMITTEE"

Doug Harper, the Director of Operations of World's Finest Chocolate Company LTD has the same gruff, hard nosed exterior as Tracy Forrest, and he can be equally tough and demanding. When World's Finest was undergoing radical process improvements in manufacturing, Doug was the change champion who helped facilitate the transition. His intuition about how to sequence the radical changes at World's Finest told him to begin systemic change by focusing on the attitudes and morale of the employees and it paid off, which is why I used him as an exemplar of an enduring leader who has the insight of *Perspective*.

According to Doug, some of the perceptions he generated about being tough and demanding came from his own self-doubt. In spite of years of training and professional experience in similar environments in which he was always successful, Doug had to overcome his own lack of confidence. "My 'itty bitty shitty committee' was always on my shoulder telling me I might fail and I had to learn to know that that was just my insecurity talking" Doug said. "Over time, I've become more comfortable in my own skin, which in turn has allowed me to be more comfortable with leading others. Learning more about myself has taught me humility while at the same time giving me the confidence to know what I have to offer others is valid. I've long fought an inner battle in trying to find my value to an organization, but I now believe that being a good leader is a valid role and that there is tremendous value in being just that."

How did Doug beat "the committee"? Doug developed the ability to notice what performance specialists call *negative self-talk* and challenge it. "I'm better when I focus on what's important to others," he says. "This, in turn, has allowed me to become a better coach/mentor. I think more carefully about my responses and treat many situations as opportunities for development. Of course, I find myself trying to enlighten others in areas that I myself am not as skilled as I'd like to be, but I'm learning."

THE IMPORTANCE OF TRANSPARENCY

Karl-Henrik Robèrt, the founder of the international educational organization focusing on sustainability called The Natural Step, developed consensus among scientists about the fundamental issues confronting humankind and its effects on the earth. This process in turn resulted in the systems conditions of the Natural Step, a framework for living and doing business in a sustainable manner. Karl-Henrik is an exemplar of an enduring leader whose mastery in seeing and intervening in systems has had a global impact. Dr. Robèrt is a gifted teacher, facilitator and presenter because of his ability to connect with people transparently with no hidden agendas and no axes to grind. He speaks regularly on contentious issues such as the effects of greenhouse gas emissions on climate, over-consumption of resources by developed nations, the generators of global and civil conflict around the world and increased incidence of cancer in children and he is able to do so without having his discussions and lectures devolve into arguments or shouting matches.

I attended one of the Natural Step's first trainings in 1997. For four days, we listened and learned from Dr. Robèrt and his colleagues as they inculcated us in the science, politics and rationale for sustainability using the Natural Step framework. Well over one half of the focus of the four days was spent learning from Dr. Robèrt how to facilitate discussion and disagreements about the concepts of the Natural Step in a way that promoted learning and inquiry instead of polarization and anger. He implored us to invite and encourage disagreement with our students and to never engage them in a power struggle or metaphorical wrestling match over who was right and who was wrong.

If someone disagreed with a principal or idea we put forth, Dr. Robèrt suggested, find out why. Ask them to elaborate on what, exactly, they disagreed with. If someone challenged a piece of scientific research, invite them to explore the data with you. If someone had a "better way" to explain the value of sustainability, encourage them to share their opinions with the group. In this way, Dr. Robèrt taught us the art of transparency, of being open and of hiding nothing, of coming from a place of understanding, not knowing.

Enduring leaders work to be transparent. They endeavor to tell the truth and share their understanding of what the truth is without pretense or attachment. By doing so, they build strong, resilient connections with people.

By not imposing their view of a situation onto others, they draw out their inquisitiveness and thinking. They promote understanding. Being transparent requires us to suspend our judgments and opinions for a time so that we can be present and listen to the opinions, thinking and judgments of others.

Most surprising of all, no matter what situations we encounter with other people, when we approach the situation genuinely and openly the situation changes. "Transparency" is the act of being ourselves without any pretense or falseness.

THREE
THE PRACTICE

FOR ASPIRING LEADERS

Understand Yourself

We are in a period of unprecedented access to tools, surveys, measurements, coaching techniques, seminars and profiles that can help us develop a self-awareness practice. To paraphrase Doug Acksel, the question isn't *if* our behaviors are having an effect on others, but *how* our behaviors affect others. These tools not only help us get a better fix on how others see us, they also help us understand the origins of our own behavior. Equipped with this awareness, we are better able to control our reactions, feelings and opinions which improve our ability to effectively connect with others.

There are literally thousands of tools at your fingertips, from self-improvement books to web enabled surveys and assessments. All of them have their drawbacks and strengths; and all of them need to be taken with a grain of salt not because they lack effectiveness, but because human beings don't conveniently fit into any one box. A lot of people get turned off to tests and profiles for just this reason. When co-workers come back from a training on, for example, the Myers Briggs Type Indicator, and they walk around work pontificating about someone being an "E" or and "I," they have missed the most important point of the training: a good profile or assessment gives you insight into yourself, not others.

At Bristlecone Learning, we use a variety of instruments and surveys to help our clients assess themselves, their teams and to develop greater self-awareness. Since self-awareness is such a difficult and subjective concept to understand, much less get better at doing, self-assessments and surveys have the advantage of giving participants a statistically valid, tested method of learning to interpret themselves. Surveys, in other words, are harder to argue with than people. To help leaders develop their self-awareness compared to how they are perceived by others, we are partial to the work of the Hay Group and specifically Daniel Goleman's work on "Emotional Intelligence." The purpose in all these surveys is to help leaders take a look at themselves in new ways and to begin to see themselves as others see them, or as they would like to be seen.

What to Do:

Make your pursuit of self-awareness part of your personal mastery practice. Find tools that help you learn more about who you are and use them. Employ a coach who has expertise in self-awareness and emotional intelligence development, attend trainings or personal growth workshops that come highly recommended and have good references. Consider it a lifelong journey where *understanding* is the goal, not expertise. When you are searching for tools to help expand your own self-awareness, use the following as a guideline:

- **Favorable Reports from Others** – If someone whose approach and philosophy you admire has gotten a lot out of a certain school of thought or assessment, start your search here.

- **History and Longevity** – Is the tool proven and effective over the long term, or is it a passing trend? Although we don't use them very often, the Myers-Briggs Type Indicator and the DiSC profile have been around a long time now and are used by a variety of organizations and literally millions of people. Some brand new tools are excellent, but the newer they are, the more research you may want to do about them to assure they are effective and valid.

- Statistical Validation – Is the tool one that has been validated and tested or is it new and untested? The companies who own the rights to tools will usually spend the time and money to insure that what they say the tool measures is actually what it does measure. Statistically valid tools also have the advantage of being less widely misinterpreted by whoever uses them.

- Ease of Use – Can you access the tool on-line? Are there plenty of books that help describe what you're studying, or is it so new and so complex that very few resources on it exist? Again, there are plenty of new tools on the market that are awesome, but do the research. Tools that are easy are not necessarily better. Although the Enneagram self-assessment tool is currently undergoing a rigorous validation process, it is not as thoroughly statistically validated as many other tools *yet*, but we like its depth, which allows the user to drill as deep or stay as shallow as they like.

- Confidentiality and Self Assessment – Make sure the tool you use insures complete anonymity for anyone who is completing a survey (like a 360 survey) on you so you get straight answers. Since part of the purpose of this practice is to enhance your self-awareness, pick tools that have a self-assessment element in them.

- Access to Experts in the Tool – Learning to effectively interpret the results from most instruments is aided through the coaching and input of a skilled practitioner in the tool. When you find one you like, make sure there are people or organizations who are content experts in it who can and will help you interpret your results.

- For deep, personal self-awareness work, our preference by far is the Enneagram system of self-awareness.[11] The Enneagram is based on the premise that people are born perfect and that our "personalities" are the metaphorical armor we add to ourselves as we go through life. Given this, the objective of the Enneagram is to see which of the nine enneatypes we most manifest in the world and, having learned more about the motivations that drive our behaviors, to then learn to make it transparent, revealing as much of our true essence as we can in our day to day life.

- Add a formal or informal "360 Review" to your annual self-evaluation. A "360 Review" is a feedback process that collects information from your supervisor, those who report to you, and colleagues and clients. Done right, it helps you see yourself as others see you. There are formal 360's—usually web enabled—that give you feedback on everything from your level of emotional intelligence to your ability to clearly articulate your values and plans. Make sure you pick people who play many roles in your life, and some who you think may not be your biggest fans. A 360 review should not be used as a popularity contest to confirm how great you are. Anyone can do that. The point is to uncover those elements of your personality you don't see as well or don't understand and begin to understand them.

Be Yourself

Nothing builds *Connection* with others like genuineness, honesty and humility.

What to Do:

Assume that you are no more and no less fallible or flawed than those around you. You are "average" in the positive sense. Assume you are also capable of unlimited brilliance; and that tapping into that brilliance requires a certain amount of self-acceptance of those things in which you are less than brilliant. Spend less energy covering up for those things you don't like about yourself, they are just the trappings of defense and protection. Underneath all of this is your essence. When people see and hear what is close to your essence, they appreciate it.

Make a Shift from Knowing to Understanding

Learning to ask instead of acting like an expert is more of a challenge for aspiring leaders who are just starting off in their careers than for those who have had time to establish a more secure position. The way we have been acculturated through school and society makes this doubly difficult. We are taught that what we *know* is the key to our job security, so we work to develop knowingness. Compounding the problem is the fact that many aspiring managers are being managed by a manager who has the same belief. Knowing gets you a job; learning to come from a place of *understanding* will help you advance past it.

What to Do:

Don't discount your education or experience as important assets to your professional success. You spent a lot of time and probably money learning and experiencing what you have up to this point. However, the quicker you can overcome a constant need to prove what you know and become a student of that which you don't know, the faster you will learn and grow at work.

The trick to doing this is to learn to become egoless. "Egolessness"is not the absence of ego, it is the ability to separate our need to prove ourselves from our desire to learn and serve. Having a healthy ego is critical to being an enduring leader, provided your ego isn't making decisions when your other innate abilities are better qualified to do so. In most enlightened companies nowadays, egolessness is something that managers love to see in employees: people who are eager to learn and secure enough with themselves to be critiqued along the way without taking it personally.

Build on What You Do Best

What to Do:

Do a little four insights assessment on yourself. Which one of the other four insights comes to you most naturally? Check your self-assessment against the opinions of others. Once you have identified your areas of strength in the four other insights, use that knowledge to build connections with others. If you are particularly good at the insight of *Perspective,* your ability to connect will be useful in engaging others in looking for big picture solutions to problems. If you're confident and have built a lot of it through service to others, share your stories of service with others who may be struggling to develop their own courage.

Conversely, which one of the other four insights is the hardest for you to work on and improve? Find people who you think possess that insight and have them coach you. It doesn't matter if they work for you or if you are their supervisor, tap into their knowledge and let them know you're using them as a model and a coach. Build strong connections with those whose capabilities are different than yours.

Have a Plan

Goals, plans and targets are the heart of an effective personal mastery practice. Having a system to organize your plans and targets is what brings your practice to life. Consciously or unconsciously, enduring leaders work on their personal mastery habits regularly and frequently. Here's a partial list of some personal mastery habits:

- Having a system for time and task management
- Practicing impulse and emotional control
- Focusing on wellness—physically, spiritually and emotionally
- Having healthy stress management routines and outlets
- Making time for quiet and personal reflection
- Pursuing personal and non-work interests
- Developing self-awareness
- Defining and updating lifelong priorities
- Updating and tracking short term priorities
- Setting clear and attainable personal and professional goals

Personal productivity coach and consultant David Allen in his book, *Getting Things Done – The Art of Stress Free Productivity* offers a common sense system for sorting tasks and managing information that doesn't require any fancy tools or customized organizational aids.[12] In addition to his simple to use model, the centerpiece of Allen's system, I think, is a weekly review of tasks, projects and goals. By looking at what has been done, what needs to be done, where to sort and store new tasks, objectives and information and how to evaluate new, incoming information for importance every week, we are reminded of what our larger goals are and the steps we need to take in order to achieve them. There are other methods and systems to organize our personal and professional lives; the key is to find one that works for you and then use it.

For Senior Leaders and Coaches

Model, Model, Model

You're being watched. And just as sure as parents who hit their children will create a child who hits, you will create that which you display. If making positive connections with people is an important element of leadership in your company, then it is up to you to model how to do it. If you are coaching others to be more self-aware and to develop more personal mastery, but you have poor relationships with co-workers and you have a hard time restraining your more negative impulses, consider the model you represent.

What to Do:

If this insight isn't one of your strengths, ask for help, and let those you are coaching see you ask for help. If all else fails, find someone else to coach the employee in the development of their self-awareness and personal mastery habits.

Demonstrate your interest in self-improvement by seeking out professional feedback and acting on what you learn. Have some of the aspiring leaders you are working to develop be part of your review team. You have as much to learn from those you manage as from those who manage you, usually more.

Review and Update Your Performance Management System

Far too often, "people skills" are overlooked or only given superficial treatment in an organizations' performance management system. Whether your annual review process is loved or hated by employees, including the elements of this insight in it helps address one of the hardest performance measures to capture and objectively evaluate: how well leaders maintain connections and relationships with their employees.

What to Do:

Make sure your performance management system includes elements of this insight, but including interpersonal performance measures by themselves isn't enough. You also need to clearly articulate why these skills add value to the business in the most concrete terms you can use. By the way, building and maintaining good connections with people doesn't mean your leaders have to win a popularity contest with their employees. Quite the contrary. Leaders who are masters in this insight may be just as tough and demanding on their employees as those who don't have very good connection skills. The difference is, their employees understand why they are demanding and they have confidence that the demands being placed on them are fair, consistent, in the best interest of the organization and take into account their personal and professional development.

It is also important to watch how people who work for a leader respond to him. Be careful here; you have to be able to watch without giving the appearance of watching. No one likes to feel watched when it comes to performance, particularly by a senior leader with a lot of authority. If you are able, try and answer the following questions through your observations:

- Do employees trust the leader's intentions?
- Are they able to speak candidly to the leader?
- What typically happens if the employee disagrees with the leader?
- Do they feel listened to by the leader?
- Are they acknowledged for their accomplishments?
- What you learn will help you determine the leader's effectiveness in this insight and how to be a better coach for them.

Be a Mirror for Those You are Coaching

Becoming self-aware is a process, not a pill. Each of us comes to understand the value of self-awareness on our own time and in our own way. Coaches and mentors can't make someone want to become more self-aware or develop a personal mastery practice, but they can tell the people they are coaching what they see that is working and not working.

Over the years, I have had lots of coaching clients who were specifically referred to me to develop better connection skills with the people with whom they worked. Yet, when I asked them what the central issue was that required coaching, almost no one identified relationships with others as the central problem. Time or job pressures, unrealistic productivity targets, a dysfunctional culture or inadequate office conditions are examples of the presenting problems they felt were the key to improving their personal performance. Even if I had substantive proof that their people skills were lacking in the form of admissions or testimonials from colleagues or employees, they were unlikely to listen to my advice about what they needed to change until they personally experienced and felt the effects of their behaviors on others. When I am faced with this type of situation as a coach, my best course of action is to help the people I am coaching develop an accurate read on the effects their behaviors are having on the environment. I do this by "holding up a mirror" and helping them interpret the cues and signals they are receiving from others.

If they complain that project team members aren't providing frequent enough progress updates, I ask them what it is about their approach that might deter people from wanting to keep them informed. If they complain that their supervisor just doesn't understand the difficulty of a specific situation, I ask them what might be deficient in the way they communicate with their supervisors. In other words, I don't let them off the hook, I make them figure out their contribution to the problem and address that. Time and time again, I have learned through my own life and coaching others that, as much as we like to focus on the need for someone else to change, when we change, so does everything else. This is especially true with the insight of *Connection*.

What to Do:

When you are working with someone who lacks awareness about the effect of their behaviors on others, keep the focus on them by asking them questions that require them to look at what they need to change instead of what everyone else should do. Continually encourage them to look inward, not outward for the solutions to their interpersonal issues. Avoid judging them, sounding punitive or superior. Their resistance to looking in the mirror is normal, and they need to know you'll be there with them when the going gets tough. Taking a deep, hard look in the mirror can be a painful experience, particularly for people who have avoided doing so for any period of time. Be compassionate as you hold up the mirror.

FOR BOTH ASPIRING LEADERS AND MENTORS

Create (and Notice) Your Own Personal Mastery Rituals

John McIntosh, the CEO of NOOD Fashion and CIO of the Dalton Catamounts knew before he was even drafted by Bear Bryant that he was not the fastest or strongest player on the team. Although he had never heard the terms *personal mastery* or *self-awareness* before, he used his realistic assessment of himself and the situation to his advantage by making sure he had trained and prepared harder than whomever he was going to line up across from on game day. When he realized the knee injury he sustained his junior year was never going to return to anything close to the same level of function as before it was injured, he reset his goals in a new (and according to John) much more fulfilling direction. His personal mastery habits helped him prepare for the rest of his career just like he prepared for every game: by out-preparing, outworking and out-hustling the competition.

John, like all of the exemplars used in this book, also has personal mastery habits that help him connect to himself, and therefore enable him to more fully connect with others. John spends a part of every day studying the lessons communicated and taught in the Bible. Tracy Forrest goes to the WPC offices every Sunday night at 5:00 p.m. He uses that time to review his schedule and organize his "to-do" list for the week and to open the weekend mail. Doug Harper plays the guitar and reads. Jon Howard lifts weights, reads and builds in reflective alone time periodically. Doug Acksel coaches volleyball as an outlet and intentionally uses part of his quiet time to re-calibrate his task list and long term goals. Karen Garcia listens to audio books driving to and from work or on road trips on subjects ranging from management practices to history to both decompress and to help her think through complex problems.

What to Do:

Whether you are aware of them or not, you already have personal mastery habits and rituals. Noticing them will help you build on them. Humans are creatures of habit. Notice your habits when it comes to goal setting and planning so you can enhance them, accelerate them and bring more focus to them. By noticing, you may discover you are missing some practices that are important to you. Experiment with how to add them.

Take a Stand for Your Boundaries

Don't let others "trespass" on the boundaries you set up in life and once you have set a boundary, do your best to stick to it. Managing boundaries involves a lot more than managing how we deal with interpersonal relationships. It also involves how much you agree to accept as a workload, how you manage your time and how well you differentiate between what is personal and what is professional in how you deal with employees. When you agree to do more than you know you can do, you are trespassing on your own boundaries, and the result won't be positive. When you allow others to infringe on your personal recharge time, you are allowing them to trespass on your boundaries. In terms of stress, something, somewhere has to give in order for you to get the rest you need. You can set a boundary around your stress load or your body will do it for you in the form of high blood pressure, sickness, heart disease, or worse.

The insight of *Connection* requires you to be present. It requires your presence not just physically, but emotionally and intellectually. You have to show up, and showing up isn't possible if you have no boundaries to inform how you set your schedule, how you take care of yourself, and how you develop and maintain relationships with others.

What to Do:

To quote Malcom X, "If you don't stand for something, you'll fall for any-thing." Take a stand on how you manage your time, your relationships and your emotions.

Learn to balance the personal elements of your working relationships with what is appropriate professionally. "Keeping things professional" doesn't mean you have to avoid developing a human to human connection with the people, it just means you know how to manage that boundary.

Likewise, set boundaries around your time and schedule or on your work-load. There will be times when you have flexibility, but be conscious of when and how.

Notice Your Emotional Discomfort

Your self-awareness can progress in leaps and bounds when you are able to notice and deal honestly with situations that make you uncomfortable emo-tionally. These instances reveal gaps in your self-awareness. Regard them as unturned stones in your quest to know yourself. You may not be ready to turn the stones over and see what is underneath, but note their location and come back to them when you are ready.

What to Do:

Notice when you are uncomfortable to the point of avoiding what would otherwise be healthy conflict. Notice when you rationalize not dealing with emotionally charged issues because "The time isn't right" or "I'm too busy" or you find yourself saying "It won't do any good." Reflect on why you may be trying to avoid the conflict: what is the underlying fear or concern?

Learn from Your Projections

Know that your projections are treasures of learning to be sought after and collected, not feared and ignored. Learn from them. Here's how:

What to Do:

Assume that everything you think about someone or something else is a unique window into what is important to you. It may also be about the person or the situation, but it definitely is about you. In your coaching relationships with aspiring leaders, the things you see in them that you dislike may reveal something in you that you also dislike, or even fear. If you admire a senior leader for their approach or demeanor, what you are seeing is symptomatic of your values and beliefs about what is important in the world.

Notice the judgments you make about others, particularly when those judgments are harsh, or extremely critical, or emotionally charged; they all say something about you if you're willing to look at them.

Pursue Goodness

Throughout this section, the insight of *Connection* has been referred to as a person-to-person insight, and it is. But thousands of companies and organizations around the world are taking the practice of connection and extending it to the way they interact with communities, governments, cultures and the natural environment. How? Most businesses—certainly the ones that value life over death and the ones that consciously try and do less harm—are more likely to be successful if humankind is successful. These businesses invest in humankind in indirect, but profound ways. They refuse to do business with businesses that are harmful or costly to society. They refuse to purchase goods or services from countries with sub-standard human rights practices. When a choice exists, they invest in technologies that are restorative to the environment instead of harmful, or they discontinue a product line if the cost to society or the environment is too high. If your business's purpose is to be successful *and* to help humankind be successful, what are the most direct, influential ways you can do so? Also, what can your business stop doing that violates the rule, "first do no harm"? Pursuing these means is difficult, but it's an investment in the future that everyone needs to make.

As we've learned through this section, heightened self-awareness comes at a cost, and that cost is heightened *understanding* about the state of the world and the people in it.

What to Do:

Use that awareness to make a positive difference with the people, communities, cultures and countries you work with. Develop your personal mastery practices and make sure they include setting goals that help all of us. Make a difference in the world for the better every day.

CONNECTION

Add Value...

- Continually work on your life's most important project, you. By being the best YOU possible, you will add enormous value to your job and to your community.
- Use your personal mastery practice to help you stay in shape, professionally, intellectually, physically and emotionally and know that each one of these elements relies on the other to be complete.
- Take the time to build genuine connections with people who need your help (even if they don't know it) and people whose help you need.

Inspire Others...

- Be yourself. Remove that which is not David, cut the crap.
- Open up to understanding. Drop knowing. Watch how people respond!
- Don't demand goodness from others, work to bring it out...

Change the World...

- Use your awareness of yourself as a tool for change. Be a model. Share your truth.
- Projection is merely a different view of the same event. Be tolerant of people who view the world differently than you do. Don't try to change them, try to understand them.
- Talk about the hard stuff that needs to be talked about without judgment or attachment. The problems facing the world today seem so daunting and difficult, people are afraid to even talk about them. Don't be.

AN INVITATION...

Imagine a world in which there is no need for Outward Bound Discovery because there are no at-risk teenagers. Imagine what the world would be like if businesses and individuals adhered to the systems conditions of The Natural Step. What if the mining industry were as committed to restoring the environment as it is to mining? And finally, what if general contractors and their clients had tangible incentives to construct buildings that used fewer non-renewable resources and less energy?

Is this utopian thinking? Absolutely. Is it possible? You bet, and the leverage point for these and other changes is through businesses and the enduring leaders who guide them. Hundreds, if not thousands, of companies—only a handful of whom were mentioned in this book—are embracing what activist and consultant John Elkington first referred to as the "triple bottom line." The Triple Bottom Line is a balanced scorecard approach—and philosophy—that measures a company's positive impact economically, environmentally, and socially.

Even Wal-Mart appears to be jumping on the social and environmental responsibility band wagon, using their enormous purchasing power to make prescription drugs more affordable, committing to energy efficiency, packaging dematerialization and stocking more organic products. Most investment houses now offer social and environmental "green" investment funds for investors who want to make money but not at the risk of the environment or society. One company, Good Capital, has even linked doing good things like providing job training for at-risk urban youth with financial investing. Good Capital pays a return to investors for meeting performance indicators that are both financial and social, and they provide businesses with hard-to-get expansion capital in the process. What is most important about this trend is that funds with a social or environmental filter tend to outperform their counterparts.[1]

Doing well by doing good thinking happens when people see themselves as part of the larger system of humanity and the environment instead of as a cog in a gargantuan economic machine that is detached from humanity and the environment. And when we see our connection to all things, the organizations for which we work can become a living, positive extension of our values. In this way, doing well by doing good is a growing trend, and the results are paying off.

But there is still a gap between what we need and what we do. What the planet needs, and therefore what we need, is increasingly at odds with what our society emphasizes. Corporate or environmental responsibility takes patience. It doesn't offer the immediate gratification that materialism and sensationalism offer.

Even though it is possible to build a house to "green" standards, for example, and recoup the additional costs of improved, energy efficient materials within five years through reduced energy expenditures, green building is having a hard time establishing a strong foothold in the United States.[2] Why? Many states simply don't provide incentives to do so. Also, the change in building codes to make green building more feasible, practical and possible moves at a glacial pace.

But even more basic, and I think more prevalent, is our willingness to look the other way. We are too eager to avoid unpleasantness and conflict, so we don't take on the hard issues. Whatever we want, we want now and we want it to be convenient. Expedience and gratification appear to have replaced common sense and long term value. Until we think differently, we won't behave differently. The sooner we start thinking differently, the better for everyone. We pay a lot for our convenience and immediate gratification, much more than we are willing to pay to preserve a better future for the next generation of enduring leaders and much, much less than we are willing to pay to reduce human suffering.

Somewhere along the way, for example, we decided it was more convenient to spend hundreds of billions of dollars on jails to put felons away instead of funding programs to find longer-term solutions that reduce crime a generation from now. Felons and juvenile delinquents don't simply "go away," they go to expensive, hard-to-manage penitentiaries and probation programs that eat up money, resources, land and people. Garbage, of course, doesn't go away either. As Paul Hawken wrote, "there is no away."[3] What we find unpleasant or unsightly or dangerous is just removed from sight, but it isn't gone, it's relocated to a place that merely gives us the illusion of being safe from it.

Our take-make-waste society is creating quite a backlog of out-of-sight detritus and the institutions tasked to contain it are straining under the pressure. Everything that goes around truly does come around. Everything. And ignoring the messes our society creates now means only that we'll have to deal with them later.

Still, there is hope, lots of it. It could be argued that the values of capitalism and the values of social responsibility contradict each other. Let's assume they do, but I fervently believe that the contradiction is a benefit to us instead of a problem. Social responsibility without the added requirement of financial success isn't business, it's charity. On the other hand, capitalism without the decision-making filter of social and environmental responsibility can lead to the pursuit of wealth without a crucial awareness of the surrounding political, social, environmental or economic impacts. Commerce is only ethical when we make it so, and making it so only happens when we are awake and alert and willing to deal with that which is inconvenient and not immediate.

Today, companies around the world are doing brilliant work to restore some balance between the ethical principles of so called free market economies and the dire needs facing our society and environment. Smart, competitive, tough minded, enduring leaders guide these companies. The main difference between most of them and their predecessors is that this new generation of leaders sees our societal and environmental woes as part of their responsibility. They are working hard to make money and do what needs to be done to protect and restore the greater good.

As John Foster said in the foreword, get messy with it. Please join the effort.

We need you.

ACKNOWLEDGEMENTS

The colleagues, clients, friends and family who helped me birth The Five Insights are experts in their own right on many of the topics covered in this book. In addition to their editorial and expert assistance, they urged me on when I felt I wasn't up to the task. For that most of all I am grateful.

Telling the story of *The Five Insights of Enduring Leaders* has been a four year process. I am indebted to my family for their gracious understanding, support, patience and love as I learned to tell it. Thank you Jess, Jodi and Dale.

My parents exposed me to the ethos of service and they convinced me from a very early age that if I applied myself, I could make a difference. For that, I am very grateful. My first role model as a leader was my father, James R. Morris, Jr., who taught me to believe in myself as a leader, an educator, a person and a writer. Thank you Dad.

Betsey Upchurch, Managing Partner of Bristlecone Learning, my business partner, friend and collaborator contributed more than anyone else to the content of this book. In many cases, I simply told the story of what Betsey does every day with her clients. Betsey patiently read, re-read and reread again endless revisions to this book offering equal doses of support, critique and perspective. Thanks Bets.

The level of depth with which I discuss the exemplars in this book would not have been possible were it not for their trusting openness with me to discuss themselves and their journeys as leaders. Doug Acksel, Tracy Forrest,

Karen Garcia, Doug Harper, Jon Howard, and John McIntosh—you taught me about the five insights, thank you. Although I did not interview him for this book but rather drew from his teachings during one of the first Natural Step trainings he conducted in the United States, I am deeply indebted to Dr. Karl-Henrik Robèrt for his contribution to the sustainability movement and what he taught me personally about sustainability, systems thinking and transparency.

Cristina Opdahl, editor, teacher and fellow raft guide helped me take incoherent thoughts and turn them into interesting, understandable words. Cristina, you rock!   Based on her experience on this project, Cristina now qualifies to teach advanced reading and writing to anyone who is dyslexic or semi-literate. Our publicist, the multi-talented Lyn Jackson jumped into the editing fray when I was about out of gas and Kathy Isberg nobly and quickly did a supreme job on the final proof. Any errors are mine and mine alone.

I was able to coerce a number of colleagues and friends to read the book as it neared completion. Their loving and sometimes brutal critique saved you from confusion and me from humiliation. Many thanks to Rick North (ret.), Matt Earnest, Dale Morris, Moe Carrick (Moementum), John Foster, Josh Hardwick, Linda Stanley (Think for Results), Mia Logan (LTD Unlimited), Pat Costello (The Prouty Project), Bill Sanford (Team Achievement), Sylvia Dresser, Zeke Zeliff (Outside Perspective), David Kolb (Incite Learning), Doug Bland, David Sides, Mike Wheeler, Congressman Mark Udall, Kevin Cashman (LeaderSource), Linda Condon Logan, Michael Srodes (Crux Move Consulting), Ken Shelton (Executive Excellence Publishing), Rich Lindblad, Julie Cusatis (Breakthrough Learning), Rae Lovenbury, Michelle Morris, and the entire Armbrecht family, including Zeus.

Jan Zimmerman of Watermelon Mountain Marketing offered hours of advice on marketing, agents, publishing and writing. Shan Wells took only words and hand gesticulations and developed a remarkably apt logo and graphic for the Five Insights. Shan also did a superb job on the book's cover and inside layout. Al Lewis's simple graphics tell a story of their own. Literary agents Mike Larsen of Larsen-Poma Literary Agency and Ted Wienstein of Weinstein Literary Management encouraged, critiqued, and gave me the hope and advice so critical for a fledgling author. Thank you one and all.

I owe a huge debt of gratitude to the many leaders, consultants, coaches, educators, trainers, clients, facilitators and mentors who taught me, guided me, coaxed me and encouraged me over the years, only some of whom are recognized as sources in the appendix. Among them are Larry and Hersch Wilson, Richard Schaeff, Linda Brown-Schaeff, Ian Thomson, Dick Krahl and the remarkable folks who were at Pecos River/Aon Consulting from 1994 – 1997; my co-workers and colleagues at one world learning; Duke University's Duke Leadership Training Associates and my colleagues and friends from the ETD Alliance.

Finally, I have to pay homage to the leaders, teachers and managers who taught me as much through what they didn't do or should have done as for what they did do. This book is the result of the lessons you taught me, too.

Thank you.

NOTES

SECTION ONE — THE FIVE INSIGHTS

1   The outplacement and career development consulting group Drake Beam Morin (DBM) examined CEO turnover at 450 of the world's largest corporations. DBM found that approximately half of the CEOs in the study had held their current jobs for less than three years, and that many of the CEOs who left their jobs were either dismissed or forced to resign. Christina & Timbers Quarterly Index of Fortune 1000 replacements shows that, as of June 2001, the rate of replacement of chief executives was 55 percent higher than 2000.

2   "Now, Discover Your Strengths," by Marcus Buckingham, Donald O. Clifton, Free Press, 2001.

3   "State of Food Insecurity in the World 2005"., Food and Agriculture Organization of the United Nations.

4   "World Development Indicators", World Bank Publications, April 2006.

5   "Who Pays for Tort Liability Claims? An Economic Analysis of the U.S. Tort Liability System", Council of Economic Advisers, April 2002.

6   "The Number of Uninsured Americans Continued to Rise in 2004", Center on Budget and Policy Priorities, August 30, 2005, http://www.cbpp.org/8-30-05health.htm

SECTION TWO – FAITH AND AGILITY

1   "Grow or Die: The Unifying Principle of Transformation," George T. Ainsworth-Land, John Wiley & Sons, 1997 (Reissued Edition).

2   Think about it for a minute: Petroleum that is converted to gas and then combusted in vehicles is not gone once it is burned; it has just changed form. The same constituent atoms and most of the molecules still exist. Their configuration has just been altered and dispersed. Using this line of reasoning, we have just as much gas on the planet as we ever had.

3   The concept of positive self-talk goes back a long, long way and the research on the topic is getting more conclusive all the time. A breakthrough book on the subject is "The Power of Positive Thinking" by Norman Vincent Peale which was first published around 1952 (Ballantine Books with arrangement from Prentice Hall). More recently, Deborah Baker-Receniello wrote a wonderful book on the subject of "Manifesting" called "Why It Works!: The Science Behind Manifesting Everything You Desire," Authorhouse, 2004.

4   Whether we believe in evolution or Genesis is not being disputed here. For those readers who believe in a scriptural interpretation of humankind's ascension in the natural order, or for those who firmly believe that Darwinian evolution is how everyone and everything developed, good luck working it out. Whether it happened in a day or over the course of millions of years, or whether it was through divine intervention or a series of coincidences in nature, I hope we can agree that our brains and bodies went through some process of development.

5   "Change or Die, Fast Company Interview with Dr. Miller," Fast Company, May, 2005, Issue 94 by Alan Deutschman.

6   "Further Along the Road Less Traveled: The Unending Journey Towards Spiritual Growth" by M. Scott Peck, Touchstone (Second Edition) 1998.

7   "The Requisite Organization: A Total System For Effective Managerial Organization and Managerial Leadership in the 21st Century," Elliott Jaques, Carson and Hall Publications, 1998 (second edition).

8   "Healing Environments: Mitigating Patient Stress, Improving Medical Outcomes", Surgicenter Online, http://www.surgicenteronline.com/articles/331feat5.html For the purposes of this discussion, these structures include the hypothalamus, the amygdala and the hippocampus.

SECTION THREE - COURAGE THROUGH SERVICE

1   "Mayor of the World...Person of the Year, 2001", by Eric Pooley, Time Magazine, January 7, 2002 Issue.

2   I realize I am on a very slippery slope here. From Darwin on, behaviorists have agreed that we are driven by instinct to do what we do. The point I am making here is about conscious choice and intention, which I am calling "will" or "free will".

3   From the Toastmasters International Website: http://www.toastmasters.org

4   Used by Permission. "Show the Way", Words and Music by David Wilcox, Copyright © 1994 Irving Music Inc. and Midnight Ocean Bonfire Music. All Rights Administered by Irving Music, Inc. All Rights Reserved.

5   "Play to Win (Choosing Growth Over Fear In Work And Life)", Larry and Hersch Wilson, Bard Press, Inc., 1998.

6   "First Break all the Rules: What the World's Greatest Managers Do Differently", Marcus Buckingham, Curt Coffman Simon & Schuster, 1999.
"Now Discover Your Strengths" Marcus Buckingham, Donald O. Clifton, Free Press, 2001.

7   "Toward an Applied Theory of Experiential Learning", Kolb. D. A. and Fry, R. (1975) in C. Cooper (ed.) Theories of Group Process, London: John Wiley.

Section Four – Perspective

1   "Natural Capitalism: Creating the Next Industrial Revolution" Paul Hawken, Amory Lovins, L. Hunter Lovins, Back Bay Books, 1st edition, 2000.

2   "Cancer and the Environment: Gene-Environment Interactions", Samuel Wilson, Lovell Jones, Christine Coussens, and Kathi Hanna, Editors, National Academy Press, 2002.

3   Excerpt from an interview with Karl-Henrik conducted jointly by editor Robert Gilman of the Context Institute and Nikolaus Wyss, a Swiss journalist.

4   "Piercing the Corporate Veil: OE and Army Transformation," Colonel Christopher R. Paparone, Combined Arms Center Military Review, March-April 2001.

5   "Blink: The Power of Thinking without Thinking," Malcom Gladwell, Little Brown and Company, 2005.

6   "Think Like an Entrepreneur – What one quality do all successful business owners share?," Michael Gerber, Entrepreneur.com, 2004.

7   Credit for coining the phrase, I think, goes to Keith Jackson from whom I first heard the term.

8   O.K., some literary license may have been taken here. Psychologists have yet to reach a consensus on when we start sorting and storing information, cognitively, but it is pretty early.

9   Microsoft 2005 Annual Report

10   Fiscal Year Ending, February 2006

11   Publicly published figures for FYE ending 2000 of Patagonia's holding company, Lost Arrow Corporation. Two hundred million is no small company; however, Patagonia competes against giants like Sears and Lands End, both of which are billion + dollar companies.

12   Mr. Chouinard's book, "Let My People Go Surfing" is a refreshing breath of non-conformist anarchy mixed with good story telling wrapped-up in a very good business case study. We have been using it as a case study for a leadership seminar we do with great effect and lots of learning. "Let My People Go Surfing: The Education of a Reluctant Businessman", Yvon Chouinard, Penguin, 2006.

13   Patagonia Company History, from the Patagonia website; http://www.patagonia.com/culture/patagonia_history.shtml#top

14   This is an exercise similar to what has become known as "The Left Hand Column Exercise" designed by Chris Argyris and others in Peter Senge's book *The Fifth Discipline*. While Argyris uses two columns in his exercise, I use three in mine to reveal not only the underlying beliefs that guide our thinking, but the system as it actually exists as well.

15   "Audit the Data - Or Else - Un-audited Data Puts Business at High Risk" A white paper by Baroudi Bloor International, 2005.

16   Before publication of this book, World's Finest sold their Canadian facility in Campbellford, Ontario, to Blommer Chocolate Company of Canada. Doug was named the General Manager of the facility after the sale.

17   Lean thinking is a remarkable system that anyone involved in manufacturing should know about. Check out the Lean Thinking Enterprise Institute at www.lean.org or read "Lean Thinking", James Womack and Daniel Jones, Free Press (2nd Rev.), 2003.

18   Check out the Balanced Scorecard Institute: http://www.balancedscorecard.org/basics/bsc1.html or read The Balanced Score Card by Robert Kaplan and David Norton, Harvard Business School Press, 2000.

SECTION FIVE — PASSION AND TIMING

1   "The Ice Opinion: Who Gives A Fuck?", Ice T and Heidi Siegmund, St. Martins Press, 1994.

2   In the interest of absolute accuracy, WPC did let some employees go in the months following 9/11, but compared to their annual turnover rate, the dismissals were not any higher or lower than the preceding 5 years.

3   "Critical Path", Buckminster Fuller. New York: St. Martin's Press, 1981.

4   Gratitude for the graphic ideas and succinct way of describing precession goes to Stephanie Relfe, www.relfe.com, How to Know Your Life Purpose plus How You Can Make a BIG Difference, http://www.relfe.com/life_purpose.html

5   "The Passion Plan at Work: Building a Passion-Driven Organization", Richard Y. Chang. Jossey-Bass, 2001.

6   "Are You Deciding on Purpose?", Alan Webber, Fast Company #113.

7   Economic Security for a Better World, Socio-Economic Security Programme. International Labour Office, 2004. Website: "http://www.ilo.org/public/english/protection/ses/index.htm" www.ilo.org/ses. and Authentic Happiness: Using The New Positive Psychology To Realize Your Potential For Lasting Fulfillment,Martin E.P. Seligman, Ph.D.

8   I first became aware of this term in Mitch Albom's best selling book, Tuesday's with Morrie., a fabulous book on life, learning, coaching, passion and death.

SECTION SIX — CONNECTION

1   "Pychometric Properties of ECI", Richard Boyatzis and M. Burkle, Hay Group, 1999.

2   "Bush Aide Softened Greenhouse Gas Links to Global Warming", Andrew C. Revkin, New York Times, June 8, 2005.

3   "Former Bush Aide Who Edited Reports Is Hired by Exxon", Andrew C. Revkin, The New York Times, June 15, 2005.

4   "Authentic Leadership – Rediscovering the Secrets to Creating Lasting Value", Bill George, Jossey-Bass, 2003.

5   "Activity Vector Analysis: Some Applications to the Concept of Emotional Intelligence", (White Paper), Walter V. Clarke Associates, Pittsburgh, PA:1996.

6   In organizations, issues of diversity tend to be most apparent when the status quo has been challenged and change is occurring. Therefore, this competency could have easily been included in Section Four – Faith and Agility. However, I think learning to see one's own biases is mostly an exercise in self-awareness, so it was

included in this section.

7   "Molecules Of Emotion: The Science Behind Mind-Body Medicine", Candace B. Pert, Scribner, 1999.

8   "Molecules of Emotion: An Interview with Candace Pert", by Caren Goldman, 2000, Ikosmos Website: http://www.ikosmos.com/wisdomeditions/essays/mw/goldman01.htm

9   Marshall McLuhan, the noted Canadian pop philosopher is credited with the "…who discovered water" saying (1911 – 1980).

10   It is important to note that Jon took immediate and decisive action to address this crisis. I don't want to make it sound like Jon responded by going into a period of intense navel gazing. Nothing could be further from the truth. Jon's invitation for feedback and help from trusted advisors and his willingness to honestly evaluate his capability as a leader is an example of a highly accountable leader.

11   We like "The Wisdom of the Enneagram: The Complete Guide to Psychological and Spiritual Growth for the Nine Personality Types", Don Richard Riso and Russ Hudson, 1999.

12   "Getting Things Done: The Art of Stress-Free Productivity", David Allen, Penguin; Reprint edition, 2002.

AFTERWARD

1   There are multiple sources to choose from that substantiate this assertion, and there are an equal number of dissenters about this topic. On the one hand, in a study conducted by AMP Capital Investors, more socially responsible companies outperformed the less responsible companies by 4.8 per cent over four years and 3 per cent over 10 years. It also showed that high IS-ranked companies outperformed over 10 years by 1.94 per cent. On the other hand,

so-called "sin stocks" in tobacco, alcohol and gambling concerns tend to outperform socially responsible investment funds.

2   Green building actually has a nationally accepted design standard, the Leadership in Energy and Environmental Design (LEED) Green Building Rating System™. For more information on this standard and the remarkable progress being made in green-building design, construction and operation, contact the U.S. Green Building Council.

3   I first read the term "there is no "away" in the Interface Sustainability Report in 1997. Paul Hawken wrote the report so I have credited him here.

Bristlecone Learning is committed to preserving ancient forests and natural resources. We elected to print *The Five Insights Of Enduring Leaders* on 50% post consumer recycled paper, processed chlorine free. As a result, for this printing, we have saved:

15 Trees (40' tall and 6-8" diameter)
6,285 Gallons of Wastewater
2,528 Kilowatt Hours of Electricity
693 Pounds of Solid Waste
1,361 Pounds of Greenhouse Gases

Bristlecone Learning made this paper choice because our printer, Thomson-Shore, Inc., is a member of Green Press Initiative, a nonprofit program dedicated to supporting authors, publishers, and suppliers in their efforts to reduce their use of fiber obtained from endangered forests.

For more information, visit www.greenpressinitiative.org

INDEX

Ordering Information

Make The Five Insights of Enduring Leaders part of your coaching practice, training curriculum or a topic for senior team discussion.

Quantity Purchasing Available.
Retail quantity purchasing rates are as follows:

Order quantity:

5 - 10 books - 23.95
11 - 20 books - 20.95
21 or more books - 17.95

Books must be purchased in one order to receive the discount.
Prices do not include shipping.

Order on-line: www.fiveinsights.com
Order email: info@fiveinsights.com

Postal orders:
135 Country Center Drive,
Suite B5, PMB 225
Pagosa Springs, CO, 81147
USA

(include contact information for ordering, + credit card information)

Find Out More About workshops featuring <u>The Five Insights of Enduring Leaders</u> or Register for an Enduring Leader™ workshop. To subscribe to our mailing list for monthly tips on how to use the five insights, send us a note at info@bristleconelearning.com indicating your interest and we'll add you to the list.*

To register for an Enduring Leader™ workshop, join the mailing list (above) or go to: www.bristleconelearning.com/cgi-bin/shop.pl?schedule=1

For coaching tips on The Five Insights, go to Jim's Blog: www.fiveinsights.com.

To invite Jim or someone from Bristlecone Learning to speak to your group, contact: info@bristleconelearning.com

*It is our policy not to share our lists with anyone. We only use our lists to stay in touch with friends and clients and to keep them informed about what we're up to.